SOUTH ASIAN CULTURES OF THE BOMB

SOUTH ASIAN CULTURES OF THE BOMB

Atomic Publics and the State in India and Pakistan

Edited by Itty Abraham

Indiana University Press

Bloomington & Indianapolis

This book is a publication of

Indiana University Press
601 North Morton Street
Bloomington, IN 47404-3797 USA

http://iupress.indiana.edu

Telephone orders: 800-842-6796
Fax orders: 812-855-7931
Orders by e-mail: iuporder@indiana.edu

The paper used in this publication meets
the minimum requirements of American
National Standard for Information
Sciences—Permanence of Paper for Printed
Library Materials, ANSI Z39.48-1984.

Manufactured in the United States of
America
Library of Congress Cataloging-in-
Publication Data

South Asian cultures of the bomb : atomic
publics and the state in India and Pakistan /
edited by Itty Abraham.
   p. cm.
  Includes index.
  ISBN 978-0-253-35253-8 (cloth : alk.
paper) — ISBN 978-0-253-22032-5
(pbk. : alk. paper) 1. Nuclear weapons—
Government policy—India. 2. Nuclear
weapons—Political aspects—India.
3. Nationalism—India. 4. Civil
society—India. 5. India—Military policy.
6. Nuclear weapons—Government
policy—Pakistan. 7. Nuclear
weapons—Political aspects—Pakistan.
8. Nationalism—Pakistan. 9. Civil
society—Pakistan. 10. Pakistan—Military
policy. I. Abraham, Itty, date
  UA840.S645 2009
  355.02'170954—dc22
                                    2008031607

1 2 3 4 5 14 13 12 11 10 09

Dedicated to the Idea and Reality of South Asia

CONTENTS

ACKNOWLEDGMENTS

This volume owes its institutional origins to the former program on Global Security and Cooperation (GSC) at the Social Science Research Council (SSRC), New York, and its intellectual origins to discussions that have been taking place across two continents between nuclear scholars and activists, especially since May 1998. The project began with a collective discussion regarding the shift in relationships between academic scholarship, social movements, and antinuclear activism in South Asia today. More concretely, participants were asked to reflect on why a mass movement against nuclear weapons—their production and possession—had not gathered momentum in South Asia in spite of the very real dangers associated with nuclear power. From that common starting point, individual contributions went in a variety of immensely productive and unexpected directions, as readers of this volume will see. Support for two workshops that brought project participants together to present draft papers came from the SSRC, aided by grants from the Hewlett Foundation and the John D. and Catherine T. MacArthur Foundation. My thanks, for all their help, to all who participated at those workshops, especially Andrew Lichterman, Akbar Zaidi, Kumkum Sangari, Gaurav Kampani, and S. P. Udayakumar, and to my former colleagues in the GSC program, John Tirman, Veronica Raffo, Petra Ticha, and Munmeeth K. Soni.

SOUTH ASIAN CULTURES OF THE BOMB

I

INTRODUCTION: NUCLEAR POWER AND ATOMIC PUBLICS

Itty Abraham

The Coming of the Nuclear Age

Most observers trace the origins of the nuclear "problem" in South Asia to 1998, the year in which India and Pakistan together conducted eleven nuclear tests and declared themselves nuclear powers. Others, more historically minded, trace the arrival of the nuclear age in South Asia to 1974, when India set off a single underground "peaceful" nuclear explosion. Both views are substantially wrong. The people of India and Pakistan have been subject to nuclear power for more than sixty years. This statement can be read in two ways, both of which reaffirm this important and under-appreciated point. Since 1945, the people of Pakistan and India have been subject to the institutionalized terror represented by the so-called Cold War between the U.S. and the USSR/Russia, a conflict to which the whole globe was held hostage. The legacy of this hostile standoff, though reduced in its current immediacy, remains the most proximate reason why nuclear weapons are desirable objects for states around the world.[1] The continued possession of thousands of nuclear weapons and warheads by Russia and the U.S., a behavior mimicked in smaller proportion by the United Kingdom, China, France, Israel, India, Pakistan, and now possibly also North Korea and Iran, remains a daily reminder of the power of nuclear weapons as an unfortunate guarantee of being taken seriously in the world.

In more local terms, the nuclear age in South Asia began with the end of the Second World War. In spite of the widespread and immediate revulsion at the use of nuclear weapons in Japan,[2] Indian leaders soon decided that the country should develop its own nuclear industry. As a result, nuclear matters became a part of the region's conceptual and industrial landscape from practically the moment of political independence. Nuclear power, enshrined as a state monopoly in the Indian Industrial Policy Resolution of 1948, became the ultimate example of the meeting of universal reason and local ingenuity: an extremely potent symbol and means to industrial development and recognized global importance.[3] The globally appreciated symbolic and practical significance of nuclear power had a similar impact on Pakistan, which would create its own Atomic Energy Commission in 1954. Regardless of whether we take a global or a regional starting point—the nuclear age or the nuclear complex—the apprehensions and exhilaration that come with the presence of nuclear power have shaped and influenced the behavior of both states and their societies since their inauguration as politically sovereign entities.

Even disregarding an institutional history as long as the independent political existence of both countries, given the enormously consequential relationship of nuclear power to questions of death, power, culture, national identity, and fiscal solvency, it is surprising how infrequently nuclear power is considered in the shaping of modern South Asia. For as long as they have been around, nuclear issues have been segregated from studies of contemporary social and cultural life. The work of understanding and interpreting nuclear South Asia has been bestowed upon analysts of security studies and international relations, but not on anthropologists, cultural theorists, sociologists of science and technology, legal scholars, scholars of public policy, labor, or social movements, all of whom have vital things to say about this object and the field of social relations it constitutes.[4] One reason for the relative segregation of nuclear matters from social and cultural analysis is the commonly held assumption that understanding nuclear weapons requires great technical knowledge. This is hardly true for a variety of reasons; perhaps most of all because nuclear technology is not, to borrow a familiar cliché, "rocket science." As is argued below, and developed further in a number of chapters that follow, the seemingly self-evident quality of *expertise*—one aspect of the segregation of nuclear power from social and cultural analysis—should be seen as an expression of dominant power that actively seeks to block public debate over the alleged utility of nuclear power.

This volume is a small first step in redressing that absence. Analyzing nuclear power through its multiple manifestations, including as a material force, site of resistance, techno-political space, symbolic and cultural referent, and state practice (rather than limiting the discussion to nuclear power as either an instrument of diplomacy and national security or a large-scale technological object for the production of electricity), this multidisciplinary collection of essays argues that nuclear power has been an intimate element of India and Pakistan's political, socio-cultural, and technological histories long enough to claim an important place in the shaping of postcolonial South Asian modernity. Hence, the first objective of this volume is collectively to explore the meaning and significance of the nuclear age in South Asia, to domesticate nuclear power as an instrument and outcome of political life, and to offer locally derived insights and concepts that might help shape our understandings of the nuclear age as a global condition.

Security Studies as Ideology

It is now clear that conventional studies of nuclear power, trapped between the constraints of structural realism and nonproliferation policy, cannot find meaning beyond the imperatives of the national security frame.[5] Failing to see national security as itself a discourse of social power with its institutional bases and intellectual exclusions, most studies of the India-Pakistan nuclear complex cannot grasp fully what nuclear power in South Asia means and how it sustains itself. The narrowing of the nuclear frame of reference to military and strategic concerns obscures the intimate and intricate connections between nuclear power, state, and society in South Asia. Politics as a fundamentally social activity, the state as a set of institutions embedded in and inseparable from social forms and cultural meanings, power as the conjoining warp of places, people, events, and meaning—these and other substantial conceptions are lost to conventional understandings of nuclear power that seek to limit this object to instrumental and rational analysis. Hence, it is impossible to see the traditional study of nuclear power as other than itself *ideological,* seeking to justify a vision that consciously separates nuclear power from the political. In other words, the conventional study of nuclear power has become an agent in the constriction of social meaning.

This intellectual aporia marks the point of departure for this volume. To get at the heart of nuclear power in South Asia, at the very least we have to move beyond abstract models of nonproliferation, security studies, and deterrence and begin to ask different questions of this object, and to trace its connections with other forms of power and domination. Neither Pakistan nor India is a stranger to the power of social movements in the shaping of everyday political life. Yet, although nuclear power has the potential of destroying the person, livelihood, habitat, and lived environment of literally millions of innocent people, indifferent to distinctions of class, religion, caste, urbanity or ethnicity, there is no *mass* movement in this region that seeks to end this condition permanently. To make this statement is not in any way to discredit the vitally important work of dedicated antinuclear activists in Pakistan, India, and globally, or to discount remarkable successes achieved in spreading the antinuclear message, raising awareness, and building coalitions between antinuclear and other social movements.[6] It is, however, to acknowledge that South Asian nuclear power is also produced around strong and enduring social relations of consent, pride, and support, as well as tacit acceptance and indifference. Regardless of the many reasons why the exercise of nuclear power may not be compatible with human security, nuclear weapons and nuclear programs in South Asia are not likely to disappear in the near future. Why this is so needs to be understood, but conventional methods offer little insight to these questions. Thus the second objective of this volume is to understand how some South Asian "atomic publics" came to love the bomb, while others grow still further from the meanings, accomplishments, spectacles, and practices of nuclear power.

The contrasting poles of proximity and distance, social consent and political resistance, do not summarize the relations produced by nuclear power; they are only its starting point. More comprehensive and detailed analysis begins by undoing the conceptual and empirical boundaries segregating nuclear power from the everyday exercise of state power, thereby bringing into focus a complex relay between nuclear power, national security, and state legitimacy. Though commonplace, the meanings of these terms—nuclear power, national security, and state legitimacy—and their connections with one another are neither obvious nor consistent across South Asia. The rest of this introduction offers, first, an elaboration of the meanings and practices of nuclear power and national security, and, second, summarizes and integrates the findings of the chapters that follow in relation to these terms and their social relations.

The Postcolonial State in India and Pakistan

The apparent congruence implied by formulations that argue for nuclear symmetry in South Asia—India and Pakistan as nuclear powers—is both correct and misleading. In terms of strategic studies, the equivalence is banal. More important is to recognize that the production of this equivalence, the conjoining of nuclear power, national security, and state power in Pakistan and India, are end points of different historical trajectories, driven by different social actors. That said, striking similarities in the ideological work effected by nuclear power, and the role of middle-class agents, must be noted in both countries.

Since its creation in 1946, the Indian atomic energy complex has had an intimate relationship with state legitimacy. Atomic energy is mentioned in the first industrial policy resolution (1948), identified as a state monopoly along with other "commanding heights" infrastructure industries such as iron and steel. Atomic energy met practical and ideological goals for a new state seeking to establish its national and international legitimacy. As a means of cheap electricity it would overcome a critical infrastructural bottleneck to national development; as a highly advanced indigenously produced technology, it consolidated the advanced standards and modern credentials of a newly formed state emerging from colonial rule. Its progenitors were highly trained middle-class scientists who had arranged for themselves an exceptional degree of autonomy from state control and public accountability. Notwithstanding these advantages, and the enormous resources pumped into the atomic complex from its inception, nuclear power never met these high expectations. By the 1960s, a fundamental shift took place with the decision to develop a covert weapons capability to augment, and eventually supplant, its civilian energy objectives.

The Indian intelligentsia's definition of the national interest had always included indigenous mastery over modern science and technology, an idea usually captured by the trope of self-reliance. From the outset, nuclear power was taken to embody this idea. The aura of nuclear power was strongly reinforced by the relatively small number of countries that had mastered these technologies. As the new definition of nuclear power increasingly began to dominate the idea of the national interest as a means to state legitimacy, driven by both internal and external forces, nuclear power became increasingly associated with national defense and security, rather than its original peaceful civilian mission. When it became clear in the late 1980s that both India and Pakistan had the capacity to build nuclear weapons, nuclear power was increasingly drawn into a new discursive register, namely, that of national security. These developments were taking place in the context of a decline of the founding logic of state power coupled with the rise of new domestic and international political forces. For an increasingly insecure state intelligentsia, the intersection of nuclear power and national security was a powerful resource in the battle for the retention of state power. In brief, the internal historical trajectory of nuclear power in India describes a movement from civilian energy and development to national security.

Pakistan began its nuclear program in 1954. As the following chapter by Zia Mian spells out in new and important detail, this program was a wholly civilian and peaceful program for much of its early history. With technical aid from the U.S. Atoms for Peace program and following extremely successful public exhibitions of nuclear power, the Pakistani nuclear program began to grow slowly over the next decade. The military's interest in nuclear weapons began much later; Mian suggests this may have been an outcome of exposure to U.S. training and cold war military doctrine. Even this greater interest, however, was limited to scientific exploration and had little to do with war-fighting plans. When, in 1972, the Pakistani nuclear program began explicitly to take on a more belligerent cast, it was the result of political decisions taken by the civilian government of Zulfikar Ali Bhutto. From the outset, nuclear power was successfully identified as a civilian national institution, one of the few institutions in Pakistan that could legitimately claim this status.

Only in the late 1970s, with the return of the military to power, did the Pakistani nuclear program become associated with the military. Although it is easy—and not incorrect—to assume that the military saw in nuclear power a military means to counter a growing strategic imbalance with India, Mian argues that the military's desire to control nuclear power was also driven by the high degree of support for this program among the Pakistani elite and public. As Ammara Durrani explains in greater detail in chapter 5, popular affection for Dr. A. Q. Khan, the former head of the Pakistani nuclear program, epitomizes this support and explains why, even in disgrace, he remains a cult figure for many. By extension, even with his personal fall from grace, the nuclear program remains an institution that stands as an emblem of national pride and sovereignty. As a result, no government—elected or authoritarian—can afford to take any action that appears to dilute its potency.

Pakistan is a state born into a condition of physical and existential insecurity. Fears of its dissolution were only exacerbated by the separation of the eastern wing of the country in 1971, following a bloody and bitter civil war. This condition of insecurity, in both its real and imagined forms, has been a driving force in the state's representation of itself and, by the same token, has always offered the military a ready-made rationale for the capture of state power. For the Pakistani military, a middle-class-dominated institution that has directly controlled state power for longer than elected civilian governments, an institutional association with nuclear power had multiple benefits. Not the least of these was the chance to address institutional insecurity through association with a program that had a high degree of popular legitimacy. While never becoming a dominant force with the national political economy, the civilian-led atomic energy project, symbolized by its main power reactor in Karachi, enjoyed, as elsewhere in the world, a high degree of popular approval for its articulation of modernity and scientific progress. Scientists, however, were marginal to state power. By contrast, no one could accuse the Pakistani military, often drawn from the same social base, of marginality. Following the coup led by General Zia, the military-bureaucratic Pakistani state appropriated the civilian project of nuclear power and redefined it as a primary means to resolve national insecurity. There is also little question that the military institution basked in the glow of nuclear power to bolster its own standing as a credible and legitimate institution, especially as news of its covert weapons program became increasingly public. A program that was once directed toward civilians and development transformed, by the late 1970s, into the prime national means to address political and existential insecurities.

The confluence of state power, nuclear power, and national security in contemporary India and Pakistan is often summarized as "nuclear South Asia." At one level, this implicit equivalence of both countries is built around similarities that are real and multiple. Nuclear power acts as both ideological glue and means of state power in both countries. In India, the initial need for state legitimation led to the development of nuclear power, which, following the institutional failure of the atomic agency, eventually turned to national security for justification. In Pakistan, the independent civilian-led project of nuclear power for development was appropriated by an authoritarian state seeking to bolster its political standing, and was transformed into the epitome of national security. Also common in both countries is the structural role of middle-class actors: state institutions once representing the pinnacle of middle-class interests and power, the military in Pakistan and the nuclear scientists in India, have determined the trajectory and outcome of their respective nuclear weapons programs. The final site of equivalence between nuclear India and nuclear Pakistan is the idea of national security.

The term "national security," as used here, is not synonymous with military defense. By historicizing the term, the following section describes the specific characteristics of this practice in general terms. This is followed by a discussion of how the practices of national defense became the performance of national security in Pakistan and India, as nuclear power acquired its present form. Taken together, these two sections offer an interpretation of the particular conjuncture of national security and nuclear power in South Asia and how it came about. These insights form the backdrop for a discussion of the most important difference between these nuclear powers, namely, the form of state power that is produced by nuclear power. Using public opinion data as a first cut into this discussion, what stands out are, first, significant overlaps between popular impressions of nuclear power and corresponding views of state power, and, second, important differences between Indians and Pakistanis in their mutual understanding of nuclear power and state power. A more comprehensive analysis of nuclear power, in other words, offers, as one would expect, insights into the general phenomenon of state power in each country, consistent with its independent historical development.

National Security and the State

Although national security and national defense are often interchangeable terms in everyday parlance, these concepts are actually quite distinct. Their similarity comes from the fact that both national security and national defense are categories of legitimate state violence. If, taken most generally, state violence is legitimized by its provision of internal order and defense against external enemies, national security and national defense are subsets of this larger category, representing a specific conjuncture of ideas, institutions, and practices. By way of illustration, when the army is called out to restore social order after a communal riot, the state does not typically justify this use of state violence as a protection of national security. The restoration of political order is itself a justification of this use of state violence. The provision of order is a constitutive feature of the modern state's legitimacy as a political institution; after all, a permanent breakdown of order is another way of saying that the state has "failed." The state has failed, in other words, to live up to its own self-representation and ideological justification. Similarly, state violence in the furtherance of a public good, when used to remove people forcibly from the path of a cyclone or to inoculate them from an epidemic, might in the process violate individual human rights; such actions, however, are not usually justified in terms of national security.

What we mean by "national security" is a historically specific discourse, and, like all discourses, is produced through an ensemble of discrete institutions and practices, by private and public agents, creating material realities and shaping institutional forms and meanings.[7] Although all forms of state violence are rhetorically justified by their claim to protect the state and its institutions, the territories it claims, and its "ways of life," national security discourse articulates a distinct expression of state violence. Michael Dillon has argued that the making of national security proceeds by the constant identification and delimiting of the sources of "national insecurity."[8] What these are, by definition, can never be specified completely, meaning that national security is a process that can never be complete. Insecurity drives national security; hence, the work of national security institutions is the constant search for and control over sources of social insecurity.

National security enters public discourse most prominently when nuclear weapons become the privileged core of the state's arsenal. Because of the now universal codes surrounding the meaning and deployment of nuclear weapons, common understandings actively promoted by the U.S. since 1945, national security is a mobile sign that replicates its meanings and practices across the globe.[9] For national security to be stable, that is, not lead immediately to interstate conflict, the meanings of these practices must be shared with and common among adversaries. Without a shared template of meaning, national security practices become sources of instability in their own right.[10] Among the most important meanings national security seeks to inculcate is the so-called taboo over the use of nuclear weapons, which transforms nuclear weapons into "political weapons," symbolic possessions for use in international negotiations and military parades but not for battlefield action. Yet, for these weapons to be credible, they must be (at least seen to be) operational in military terms, which, if done successfully, obviously begs the question of whether they are ever really only political. This contradiction is never overcome but stands as a characteristic feature of national security discourse.

Michael Mann, in his all-too-brief discussion of "deterrence-science militarism," points to the following national security practices that further separate it from other meanings and practices of state violence and national defense.[11] First, he notes the importance of "rational" and "instrumental" analysis in the formulation of national security policies and correspondingly new meanings given to what is considered military superiority. With nuclear weapons considered unusable in practical terms, superiority gets redefined as the achievement of a virtual technical edge over the enemy, even if only temporarily. This generates a constant internal pressure to improve, even marginally, the measured performance of weapons systems and their accompanying infrastructure, which then becomes a driving characteristic of organizational behavior within national security institutions.

As a result, the idea of "strategic superiority" is deeply techno-political in its condition and is usually identified in minor increments. It can be measured in terms of increase in nuclear explosive capacities, accuracy of and distance covered by delivery systems—among those criteria easier to measure—but also by the inferred sophistication of early-warning and detection systems and the robustness of command-and-control infrastructure. However, in the absence of use of nuclear weapons, simulations and other computer-generated virtual techniques become necessary and "realistic" means of assessing the relative strength of each country in relation to the adversary.[12] The enormous investment in informational technologies and computers, what Mann calls "high science, computers and mathematical theory," necessary for this enterprise have the additional effect of giving a neutral, technologically mediated aura to the results and findings of war "games."[13]

Another necessary complement of the institutionalization of National Security as a governmental practice, Mann notes, is secrecy. Pointing to the difference with earlier historical periods such as the nineteenth century, the technological imperatives of contemporary national security segregates itself from the private sector and civil society. The arcane, over-robust, and technologically complex hardware required by the national security sector in order to meet postulated conditions of robust deterrence and reliable second-strike capability is beyond the means of most civilian industry, and, equally, offers little to the civilian sector by way of technological spin-off. Technological complexity produces a form of industrial segregation: technological secrecy. "But much else is held secret because it conflicts fundamentally with any principle of legitimation that could be shared with any public. This is true of [weapons of mass destruction] and of many diplomatic activities."[14] In other words, the requirements of national security as a means of defining the security of the state inevitably require actions and policies that a righteous adherence to legally binding norms would most likely suppress. Illicit state activities segregate themselves from civil society through official secrecy. This contradiction is at the heart of all national security discourses, for all states, and is justified ultimately only in reference to itself—*raison d'état.*

This is no abstract or hypothetical charge. In a penetrating analysis of official secrecy surrounding the Indian nuclear program, chapter 3 in this volume, by M. V. Ramana, documents the various ways through which the Department of Atomic Energy (DAE) circumvents statutory requirements of transparency and openness. As he points out, the public's right to information ends where (in the language of the Right to Information Act): "Information, disclosure of which would prejudicially affect the sovereignty and integrity of India, the security, strategic, scientific or economic interests of the State, relation with foreign State or lead to incitement of an offence." Perhaps this is not unreasonable; after all, which state would willingly release strategic information? But the DAE used this loophole to block Ramana and his associates from determining "estimated costs of various steps of the construction and operation of [the fast breeder] reactor, such as that of fabricating fuel and that of waste management." There is nothing remotely strategic about this information, but it does allow the DAE to prevent public scrutiny of cost overruns in their pet project. Worse still, the Indian Supreme Court concurred with the government's position in an important public interest challenge seeking to obtain an internal report critical of safety measures in the nuclear complex. The justices were so cowed by their proximity to nuclear power that they even refused to examine a copy of the report that was submitted to the Court by the DAE. As Ramana dryly comments, "the Bench noted 'we do not think it appropriate to open the seal and read the same.'"

National Security in South Asia

The debate around nuclear weapons in South Asia changed radically to reflect a national security orientation in the 1990s, displacing older concerns and constituencies, and leading to an entirely new "public sphere," if not quite in the sense used by Jurgen Habermas.[15] Prominently marking this change was the extreme narrowing of participation in this public debate. The closing of the debate was not an outcome of national security being "above partisan politics" in the American idiom nor because there was elite consensus about the nature of threats to the state and the appropriate national response to them. After all, South Asian governments of all stripes have faced considerable public pressure when military scandals are exposed and have fallen when it appears that matters of national defense are poorly handled. Rather, a hardy division of labor has emerged that distinguishes between intellectuals and state professionals deemed *competent* to talk about national security, and all others. Greater expertise, in other words, has produced its own boundaries.

This division of labor is synonymous with the rise of an "expert" national security community whose discursive and social boundaries are policed in various ways. According to Achin Vanaik, minimal entry conditions "are a strong commitment to a state-centered official nationalism, and either high-level involvement in security-related official nationalism, or acquisition of a certain level of Realist 'expertise.'" He goes on to identify seven categories of intellectuals and state professionals permitted voice in this debate, and that constitute this atomic public: "active and retired scientocrats, bureaucrats, diplomats, senior armed forces personnel, [select] politicians, policy-oriented journalists [and] academics."[16] This process of expert-formation was catalyzed by the arrival in South Asia of new, especially American, ideas, models, and institutions following the end of the Cold War. This American turn took the form of reports prepared by experts for the Council on Foreign Relations and the Asia Society, and exchanges and meetings held under the auspices of the University of Illinois' program in Arms Control, Disarmament, and International Security (ACDIS). A number of these and other interactions were funded by a relatively small number of U.S. donors, including the John D. and Catherine T. MacArthur Foundation, the Ford Foundation, the W. Alton Jones Foundation, and the U.S. Department of Energy. A good example of the nature of this intervention is the now commonplace idea of confidence-building measures (CBMs), initially promoted by the Washington, D.C.–based Henry A. Stimson Center. Stimson, a think-tank once entirely focused on the Cold War, was reinventing itself in the early 1990s, and sought to contribute insights and experience from the U.S.-USSR experience to other nuclear flashpoints. The details of CBMs and what they promised for the improvement of India-Pakistan relations are not the issue here; more important was the tacit need for a credible and knowledgeable epistemic community with whom foreign experts, think tanks, and governmental agencies concerned with nuclear issues could interact. Although a small number of institutions had always existed to fill this need, most famously the venerable Institute for Defense Studies and Analysis (IDSA) in New Delhi, and its hardy counterpart, the Institute for Strategic Studies in Islamabad, older institutions and university-based experts were soon marginalized by the rapid growth of new institutions and numbers of South Asian nuclear weapons experts, from the 1990s on.

The outcome has been the creation of a new public sphere for the discussion of national security, in the sense defined above. To say this is not in any way to suggest that until the arrival of foreign think tanks there had been either no discussion of defense matters or no strategic experts in South Asia. Such an argument would be empirically untenable. What changed from the 1990s was the formation, as noted above, of a *new* public sphere for the discussion of these issues, which included the creation of a number of new institutions; raising of the threshold of those deemed competent to speak credibly of national security (and, by extension, the dismissal of those who could not); more intensified interaction on a wider scale by members of this community and their counterparts in other countries; and the introduction of new terms and references that nuclear debates in South Asia would internalize.

Karsten Frey, in chapter 10, analyzes the nuclear debate in India to argue first, that "the interaction between elected leaders and the public on nuclear issues is not direct, but occurs through the mediation of a limited number of strategic thinkers." Further, he argues, rather than a response to security concerns or the evil machinations of the Bharatiya Janata Party (BJP), the "strategic community's success in linking the nuclear question to ideology was decisive in paving the way for India's nuclearization." In a careful reading based on content analysis of 705 nuclear-related editorials and opinion pieces published in India's major English-language dailies, he shows that the "strategic community" comprising retired senior military officers, nuclear scientists, and civilian strategists shaped outcomes by personally advising the political elite and were "agents in the creation of public opinion on the nuclear question." Although the nuclear issue appeared to be about matters of high state policy and military strategy, Frey argues that this community achieved its ends by appealing to "dignity, national pride, anticolonialism, and collective defiance," particularly drawing on India's identity as a postcolonial state seeking to alter the prevailing distribution of international power. Most telling is his discussion of this community's fascination with the United States, even as the West was being excoriated in their writings, and the radical shift in discourse following India's nuclear tests, when critical outsider status was rapidly converted into a defense of the (new) status quo.

The counterpoint to this analysis of the proximity of an expert community to state power is Ammara Durrani's chapter 5 on the sociopolitical fallout of the A. Q. Khan controversy and its impact on the nuclear debate in Pakistan. Analyzing a sample of Urdu and English newspapers during the month of February 2004, she shows that the Urdu press, typically considered a jingoistic and parochial voice when compared to the modern and liberal English press, produced far more politically nuanced and complex views of the Khan issue. As she puts it, "contrary to popular perceptions, the 'liberal' English press—in this case, *Dawn*—has shown an increased conformity with the establishment's views on national security and the nuclear program. On the other hand, *Jang,* one of the leading Urdu newspapers and traditionally known for its political conservatism, shows a remarkable intellectual departure by voicing concerns about the fate of world peace in the presence of nuclear weapons and their proliferation." The closer to power one gets, Durrani's chapter implies, the less political dissent is likely. The press becomes a prism of social mores, reproducing within them prevailing fault lines of class and privilege. Durrani insists that an important transformation has taken place as a result of the Khan scandal, namely, to make Pakistani elites and government move away from a relational understanding of their nuclear program, effectively removing India as both cause and reason for nuclearization. The lasting effect of the scandal, she proposes, has been to consolidate the place of Pakistan's nuclear weapons in the national arsenal and to remove from debate any discussion of Pakistan's need for possessing nuclear weapons in the first place.

By conducting an archaeological excavation of national security and tracking its movement to South Asia, the previous section argues that the traditional study of nuclear power is itself deeply ideological. The effect it seeks is to separate the analysis of nuclear power from the larger political frame—state power—and to make the autonomy of nuclear power appear as common sense: a neutral, scientific, and normal set of institutions, practices, and beliefs that are universally adopted and adhered to.

Nuclear Power and Atomic Publics

In general, nuclear power can be understood as a form of power both productive of and embedded within social relations, a cultural object with multiple meanings, and a spectacular techno-political artifact.[17] As such, nuclear power is manifested unevenly across South Asia. In general, distinct social formations are produced through the exercise of nuclear power and act to shape it, though not in equal measure or proportion, depending especially on class and location.[18] The social formations interpellated in and through nuclear power are likewise unevenly distributed. Where and when these constituted social formations enter the public arena in some manner or form, we call them "atomic publics."

Complicating this general formulation is the recognition that nuclear power is, quite uniquely, *ambivalent.*[19] The ambivalence of nuclear power can be understood in the following ways. Most familiar is the condition of nuclear power as simultaneously a means to economic development and an instrument of war. Even as it is represented as a state project of tremendous prestige and a social object of great opportunity, nuclear power is also a source of primitive danger, fear, and threat. Although a technological object built in accordance with universal laws of scientific rationality, the form and sign of nuclear power evokes multiple expressions of religious passion. Nuclear power speaks on multiple registers to proclaim its singularity and importance, but such individuality can only be recognized in relation to other, similar, techno-political projects around the world. In terms of its origins, like nuclear power elsewhere, it is both indigenous and foreign. Nuclear power is a specific mechanism of the state, a technology tying together national and local scales in contradictory ways, while also a legally protected object that is allowed to disregard state laws and norms in its everyday practice.

The ambivalence of nuclear power indicates that it is expressed through and in relation to a *divided* social formation. A similar formulation ("split publics") has been proposed by Arvind Rajagopal as a way of "thinking about an incompletely modern polity, standing for the relationship between the configuration of political society desired by modernizing elites and its actual historical forms."[20] This is a distinction that sets up a politico-cultural fault line within the body politic, a division that starts with language and is effected through the mass media, producing what we might call vernacular and cosmopolitan publics. The ambivalent character of a highly modern nuclear power, however, produces rather different divisions.

Corresponding to the powerful expert community that dominates the representation of nuclear power in the public sphere of (especially English-language) mass media are the great majority of elites in South Asia who find in nuclear power a source of security and strength. The findings of opinion surveys have consistently shown great similarities in the views of Indian and Pakistani elites. One survey showed that 77 percent of elites, on either side of the border, make common assumptions about the nature of state insecurity and agree that nuclear weapons are an appropriate means to reduce that insecurity.[21] This is a community produced and reinforced through relations of social *consent* with nuclear power. Their numerically small counterparts (6–8%) are nuclear abolitionists who disagree entirely about the need for and efficacy of nuclear weapons in maintaining any form of security. This group of elite respondents lie at furthest remove from the majority, and are aligned with the political alliance that altogether rejects nuclear power in all its manifestations: the antinuclear workers and activists who give voice to their rejection of nuclear power through relations of *opposition*. These diametrically opposed points of view are familiar to anyone who has observed the nuclear debates in India and Pakistan, and are usually taken to summarize the parameters of the nuclear debate itself. What this analysis proposes is that the most implacable political rivals are jointly constituted in the region's most visible atomic public. An ambivalent nuclear power has produced, in Pakistan and India, respectively, a *single but divided* atomic public characterized by unequal relations of extreme consent as well as intense opposition.[22]

Put in these terms, the struggle for and against nuclear power seeks to change the balance of forces within the primary atomic public: divided communities that represent opposing views. But once we allow for a complex understanding of ambivalent nuclear power, it is clear that this simplistic dichotomy—for and against—is inadequate to summarize the varieties of communities that may be interpellated by nuclear power, and who may or may not find voice within the public sphere. By analyzing social settings and cultural imaginaries removed from the familiar play of for-or-against nuclear power, ranging from religious festivals to the cultural conceptions of death and devastation, a number of chapters in this volume collectively offer a wide-ranging survey of the nuclear public sphere in South Asia. The net effect is to produce a complex and spatially distributed account of nuclear power and atomic public(s) that is a unique and critical lens through which to observe and understand contemporary topographies of state power in Pakistan and India.

The remarkable correspondence between Indian and Pakistani elites over nuclear power must be set against the results from another set of polls conducted in the two countries. The important difference in the second set of polls is the nature of the population being sampled, which was chosen across social classes. In other words, this second set of surveys, though not directly comparable to the same extent as the elite surveys, offers a view of public opinion that includes non-elite as well as elite views, proportionate to their demographic distribution. In a survey conducted by the Delhi-based Centre for the Study of Developing Societies (CSDS) in 1999, just one year after India declared itself a nuclear weapons state, Yadav, Heath, and Saha found that an extraordinary 54 percent—more than half—of the Indian electorate *had not heard* of the nuclear tests that preceded this announcement.[23] This stunning number compares with 65 percent of the same sample who were aware of the 1999 Kargil conflict, showing that the prior figure cannot be attributed to lack of access to the mass media and other sources of news and information. Twenty-nine percent, or less than one-third of the sampled population, had both heard of the 1998 nuclear tests and approved of them.

This means that while elites are familiar with the Indian nuclear program, and are, by a considerable margin, in favor of its continuance as a weapons program, more than half the electorate did not even know that India had declared itself a nuclear power. Elite and mass opinions in India differed also with respect to the threat posed by Pakistan. More than half the elite population, but only a quarter of the mass sample, felt that Pakistan posed a serious threat to India. Clearly, in India, the contrast between elite and general views of nuclear weapons and their views about the nature of military threats facing the country is both marked and quite significant. This asymmetry in the extent of knowledge about nuclear power is striking and indicates both the narrow public sphere that adjudicated the nuclear debate as well as an important relation of *ignorance* of nuclear power for the majority of India's people.

But what appears to be indifference and ignorance in polling data can, however, also be understood as a "weapon of the weak" in James Scott's apt term: a form of grass-roots bypassing of dominant narratives on the nuclear question. This insight is elaborated in chapter 8 by Raminder Kaur, who explores the various meanings attributed to the May 1998 nuclear tests in vernacular popular culture. As an anthropologist she offers a view that is not purely concerned with statecraft or the public arena of non-state institutions that are described as civil society. Focusing on spectacles and public displays (*pandals*) during Mumbai's enormous Ganapati (Vinayak) festival, she finds a range of popular views that neither merely reproduce state views uncritically nor overtly resist dominant perspectives head on. To some extent, the overt message of the *pandals* can be read off against political identities, for example, chauvinism in the Shiv Sena display and critical engagement in the Dalit one. But that would be offering too deterministic a reading of these polysemic cultural forms. Rather than identifying each display as an already fixed political position, they are more appropriately seen as ongoing engagements with dominant political representations. They embody a private space of public critique and reflection that draw on and subvert elite *and* antinuclear activist discourses, and which cannot be reduced to either one or the other. This, too, is an atomic public, but not one that fits into an easy grid of for-or-against. The engagements with nuclear power that can be seen in chapter 8 are engagements with state power writ large, and reflect contradictory relations of support, opposition, critique, and reflection simultaneously.

The nuclearization of public space is a counterpoint to the production of atomic publics. Through a close visual reading of artifacts, monuments, and media images produced in Pakistan after the May 1998 tests, Iftikhar Dadi in Chapter 9 shows how "practices both by the state and non-state actors in visualizing nuclearization have created an important popular and political arena for a paradoxical, spectral debate on nuclearization." He shows that while, on the one hand, the state's visual repertoire of nuclearization drew heavily on pre-existing and iconic representations of official nationalism, there was, on the other hand, an effort also to appropriate cultural products drawn from the informal sector. The need to represent the nuclear tests at short notice called for a "flexible production" mode of operation, drawing the informal sector into a nuclear public space. That urgency highlighted, in the same instant, the instability of the desired visual representation. The underground test, by its very nature, can only be visualized through the mediation of sophisticated gauges and instruments far removed from the nuclear event. Indexed through historical and spatial proxies—the mushroom cloud and the Chagai Hills monument—nuclear pride soon dissipated and led to a very public reiteration of Pakistan's ongoing political and economic crises. The nuclearization of public space created "new opportunities," Dadi argues, not merely to celebrate, as the state may have hoped, but also "to contest and debate Pakistan's nuclearization program, which includes discursive critiques as well as spectral play between secrecy and visibility."

The social map produced by these engagements help trace a dense web of meanings that underlie and undermine the primary atomic public produced by nuclear power in South Asia. In the survey mentioned above, a high proportion of Indian pronuclear elites made the link between nuclear weapons and international prestige, influence, and bargaining power. Even in the absence of a threat from Pakistan, this finding suggests, nuclear weapons would be a good thing for India to have. Sankaran Krishna, in chapter 4, takes this initial insight much further in a bold analysis of the prevailing mores of the Indian middle class, which is largely supportive of nuclear weapons. Arguing that based on the nature of colonial rule, and the particular conditions under which a modernizing middle class was inserted into the power structure, the self-image of this class is remarkably ahistorical and antipolitical. The middle class tends to see its own rise to power as based purely on individual merit, and understands democratic politics as an illegitimate institutional means by which their just rewards might be taken away. Hence, the effect is to produce a deeply skeptical attitude toward the majority of the country, the poor and underprivileged. It goes so far, Krishna argues, as to consider the desirability of social genocide, a removal of latent "memories of underdevelopment" by the deus ex machina of the nuclear weapon.

The question of correspondence, or the consistency of popular engagements with nuclear power seen against the backdrop of the political economy of state power, is addressed by Haider Nizamani in chapter 7. Nizamani reports on the results of a survey he conducted across Pakistan's four provinces in 2000. His survey, broadly speaking, allows us to assess popular views about two distinct characteristics: confidence in nuclear weapons as a means of deterrence and national prestige, and overall confidence in the national government and military. His findings show, first, considerable divergence from the claims of nationalist and religious leaders who had proclaimed nuclear weapons as the ultimate unifying element in a divided polity. There is a much higher degree of doubt among the Pakistani public about the efficacy of nuclear weapons as instruments of security than we were hitherto aware of. Second, to a remarkable extent, the responses of the surveyed population to questions about nuclear weapons reflect local views of the legitimacy of the national state. On almost every issue, the Northwest Frontier Province (NWFP) and Balochistan were at opposite ends of the scale: the NWFP in support of the government's position, Balochistan opposed. Nizamani points out that respondents in the NWFP responded positively to considerations of national pride and saw themselves as a junior partner in the national ruling alliance. The province of Balochistan is most easily described as economically resource-rich but politically poorly represented. As a result, the province has been increasingly alienated from the national mainstream, a process that has grown worse in recent years, as the national government has increasingly used extreme force to suppress political mobilization and popular resistance to its objectives. In this province, views of nuclear power and the national government were consistent and altogether skeptical. The most powerful and developed provinces of Punjab and Sindh fell in between these extremes, with Punjab generally closer to the government's position, as would be expected. If antinuclear activists were to draw lessons from this data, they would realize that, first, a regional approach might pay greater dividends than a national strategy, and, second, that a form of mobilization that identified nuclear power in relation to the unequal expression of state power might be more fruitful than a strategy that focused solely on opposition to nuclear weapons.

The data from Pakistan suggest that the distance between elite and mass opinions is smaller than in India. India consistently figures as the primary reason for Pakistan's possession of nuclear weapons. Although it was widely felt in Pakistan that nuclear weapons are a reasonable response to its security threat from India, this view does not imply mere belligerence. The fear that nuclear weapons could actually be used was also quite high. Whether by accident or for defense, half the Pakistani sample expressed the fear that nuclear weapons would be used in the region in the near future. Overall, when set against comparable Indian responses, both Pakistani elites and the general population appear to be both more aware and pessimistic about their survival in South Asia's nuclearized environment.

Reading this relation of fear against the grain, Srirupa Roy, in chapter 6, examines the reasons why the discourse of nuclear abolition has failed in its efforts to mobilize the Indian population against nuclear power. By disaggregating the discourses of political mobilization, she explores the cultural worlds and symbolic landscapes of the antinuclear movement in India. Through an interrogation of one of the dominant themes of the antinuclear movement, which draws on what she calls the "apocalyptic imaginary" of mass death, Roy draws attention to the limits of such narratives of fear and the constraints of a "politics of anger" in mobilizing people for political change. Comparing social responses to industrial accidents, natural disasters, and riots, she exposes the complex imaginaries that underlie the representation of mass death in contemporary India. Roy concludes that mobilization against nuclear weapons alone is not sufficient to create a social movement against nuclear power. In order for mobilization to be effective, the principal author of nuclear power—the state—needs to be identified explicitly and the dystopias produced by antinuclear activism supplemented by "positive political imaginaries, desires, and visions."

Conclusion

Maj. Gen. Qureshi said Pakistan and India were responsible states and there was no way anyone could "realistically" think of a nuclear war between the two. Expressing surprise about people "jumping to conclusions" about such a war, he argued that "these [nuclear weapons] are deterrence and not meant to be more than that."

The Hindu (Chennai), 28 December 2001

In closing, let us consider Major General Qureshi's statement. What stands out is its lack of obvious identification: it could just as easily have been the words of an Indian but just happened to be spoken by a Pakistani spokesman. The general's surprise at conclusions drawn about the danger of nuclear weapons in South Asia reflects his own inability to control the "fluid sign" that is nuclear power, as well as his lack of understanding of the larger effects and meanings of nuclear power. Although he thinks nuclear power is for deterrence only, "not more than that," the collective findings in this volume lead to an unambiguous conclusion that nuclear power is *always* "more than that." Once removed from strategy and high politics and returned to social life, nuclear power cannot be seen as anything less than a symptomatic form of the structural distribution of power in South Asia. Nuclear power is no temporary aberration: it holds up a mirror to the power differentials characteristic of national social life even as it reproduces them within its institutions and practices.

These essays mark only the beginning of a critical engagement with the complexities of nuclear power and its atomic publics in South Asia. The addition of a number of other perspectives—for instance, studies of popular mobilization against nuclear power, historical and cultural studies of the popular seductions of nuclear power, epidemiological analyses of indigenous peoples who live on nuclear landscapes, and ethnographic studies of the labor conditions under which this fuel is extracted, transported, and processed—would take the themes addressed in this volume much further.

The ultimate success of this book will be measured by the extent to which it allows nuclear power to be seen in both local and global terms, furthers our understanding of the interrelation of nuclear power and state power, and highlights the value and importance of seeing nuclear power in a context wider than its strategic uses. We invite our readers to join us in this collective and ongoing effort.

Notes

Many thanks to two anonymous reviewers, the contributors to this volume, Kamran Ali, Meredith Weiss, and Dongsun Lee for their valuable comments on earlier versions of this chapter.

1. Traditional academic explanations of nuclear weapons possession are summarized in Scott Sagan, "Why Do States Build Nuclear Weapons? Three Models in Search of a Bomb," *International Security* 21, no. 3 (winter 1996/97): 54–86. For a critique of traditional explanations that include theories that do not explain why countries that could develop nuclear weapons do not, and on the arbitrary separation of nuclear weapons from nuclear programs, see Itty Abraham, "The Ambivalence of Nuclear Histories," *Osiris* 21 (2006): 49–65.

2. Mahatma Gandhi, responding to the suggestion that atomic weapons were so horrific that they would end war, wrote: "This is like a man glutting himself with dainties to the point of nausea and turning away from them only to return after the effect of nausea is well over. Precisely in the same manner will the world return to violence with renewed zeal after the effect of disgust is worn out. ... The atom bomb ... destroy[ed] the soul of Japan. What has happened to the soul of the destroying nation is yet too early to see ... A slaveholder cannot hold a slave without putting himself or his deputy in the cage holding the slave." From "The Atom Bomb, America, and Japan," originally published in *Harijan*, July 7, 1946, and reprinted in *The Gandhi Reader: A Source Book of His Life and Writings,* ed. Homer A. Jack (New York: Grove, 1956), pp. 349–50.

3. Itty Abraham, *The Making of the Indian Atomic Bomb: Science, Secrecy, and the Postcolonial State* (London: Zed Books, 1998).

4. The great exception to this rule, as is often the case, is Ashis Nandy. Especially see his *Science, Hegemony, Violence* (Delhi: Oxford University Press, 1986). Nandy argues that "[The Indian] state had established close, inviolable links with megascience and megatechnology—not only because it must depend on modern science and technology to give teeth to its coercive apparatus, but also because it can use the achievements in these sectors, especially when they are spectacular, to legitimize itself as a repository of scientific knowledge and a negation of native irrationalities" ("The Political Culture of the Indian State," *Daedalus* 118, no. 4 (fall 1989): 10). Although a number of prominent social scientists have written about nuclear politics, they have typically written as activists not scholars. For an important exception to this rule, see *Prisoners of the Nuclear Dream,* ed. M.V. Ramana and C. Rammanohar Reddy (Delhi: Orient Longman, 2003).

5. R. B. J. Walker, *Inside/Outside: International Relations as Political Theory* (Cambridge: Cambridge University Press, 1993); Michael Dillon, *Politics as Security: Towards a Political Philosophy of Continental Thought* (London: Routledge, 1996).

6. For the most comprehensive collection of writing by South Asian critics of regional nuclear programs, see the South Asians Against Nukes Web site www.s_asians_against_nukes.org.

7. Bob Jessop, *The Capitalist State: Marxist Theories and Methods* (New York: New York University Press, 1982).

8. Dillon, *Politics as Security.*

9. For a discussion of how national security "travels," see my "National Security/ Segurança Nacional," in *Words in Motion*, ed. Carol Gluck and Anna Tsing (Durham, N.C.: Duke University Press, 2009).

10. One of the functions of international military training by the United States and other major powers is precisely to introduce common frames of reference and meaning to national security professionals the world over. See Michael Mann, "Roots and Contradictions of Modern Militarism," in *States, War and Capitalism* (Oxford: Blackwell, 1988).

11. Ibid.

12. James Der Derian, *Virtuous War: Mapping the Military-Industrial-Media-Entertainment Network* (Boulder, Colo.: Westview, 2001).

13. The effect of this shift can be seen among the personnel who work in this sector. "Officers, especially higher commands, are introduced to complex techniques of the behavioral and natural sciences. They play war games in which computer simulation of the complex chains of interaction between levels of decision-making and weapons capacity require clear, logical thought. As [the purpose of these games] is to 'think the unthinkable' it develops a distinctive form of *esprit de corps:* 'tough-mindedness,' the clear-sighted 'hawk,' with a capacity to keep going while the bombs fall" (Mann, "State, War and Capitalism," p. 179).

14. Ibid., p. 180.

15. Jurgen Habermas, *The Structural Transformation of the Public Sphere* (Cambridge, Mass.: MIT Press, 1989).

16. Achin Vanaik, "Unraveling the Self-Image of the Indian Bomb Lobby," *Economic and Political Weekly,* November 20, 2004.

17. Michel Foucault, *Power/Knowledge: Selected Interviews and Other Writings, 1972–1977* (New York: Pantheon Books, 1980 [1972]).

18. Jessop, *Capitalist State*, p. 131.

19. This argument is more fully developed in Abraham, "The Ambivalence of Nuclear Histories," *Osiris* 21 (2006).

20. Arvind Rajagopal, *Politics after Television: Hindu Nationalism and the Reshaping of the Public in India* (Cambridge: Cambridge University Press, 2001), p. 152.

21. The results presented here come from the surveys conducted by the University of Notre Dame's Kroc Institute in 1994 (India) and 1996 (Pakistan), a few years before India and Pakistan declared themselves nuclear weapons states. Each survey included between nine hundred and one thousand persons, all living in major urban areas, the majority of whom were "middle and upper class men," reflecting "elite society in the two countries" (David Cortright and Amitabh Mattoo, eds., *India and the Bomb: Public Opinion and Nuclear Options* (Notre Dame, Ind.: University of Notre Dame Press, 1996). Also see David Cortright and Samina Ahmed, eds., *Pakistan and the Bomb: Public Opinion and Nuclear Options* (Notre Dame, Ind.: University of Notre Dame Press, 1997).

22. The apparent anomaly represented by the Communist Party of India (Marxist) (CPM), a party that is against nuclear weapons but in favor of nuclear power (for electricity), becomes easier to understand in this light. The CPM represents the middle ground in this atomic public, between consent and opposition, and, most important, does not lie outside it.

23. The poll was conducted in 108 Indian parliamentary constituencies, sampling 9,069 persons. Reported in *Frontline* 16, no. 24, November 13–26, 1999.

2

FEVERED WITH DREAMS OF THE FUTURE: THE COMING OF THE ATOMIC AGE TO PAKISTAN

Zia Mian

*Too little attention has been paid to the part which an early exposure
to American goods, skills, and American ways of doing things can
play in forming the tastes and desires of newly emerging countries.*

President John F. Kennedy, 1963

On October 19, 1954, Pakistan's prime minister met the president of the United States at the White House, in Washington. In Pakistan, this news was carried alongside the report that the Minister for Industries, Khan Abdul Qayyum Khan, had announced the establishment of an Atomic Energy Research Organization. These developments came a few months after Pakistan and the United States had signed an agreement on military cooperation and launched a new program to bring American economic advisers to Pakistan. Each of these initiatives expressed a particular relationship between Pakistan and the United States, a key moment in the coming into play of ways of thinking, the rise of institutions, and preparation of people, all of which have profoundly shaped contemporary Pakistan.

This essay examines the period before and immediately after this critical year in which Pakistan's leaders tied their national future to the United States. It focuses, in particular, on how elite aspirations and ideas of being modern, especially the role played by the prospect of an imminent "atomic age," shaped Pakistan's search for U.S. military, economic, and technical support to strengthen the new state. The essay begins by looking briefly at how the possibility of an atomic age as an approaching, desirable global future took shape in the early decades of the twentieth century. It then sketches the way that this vision was expressed in the American elite imagination after World War II, and how, with the coming of the Cold War, it became a central element of U.S. foreign and security policy. The essay goes on to examine how, against this background, those of the emergent elite of newly independent Pakistan sought to end their sense of national insecurity, poverty, and backwardness, and secure their position and that of the state, both within their own society and internationally, by developing military allies and capabilities, planning economic development, and establishing a scientific community and public sensibility that would be appropriate to the atomic age. Their aspirations and decisions exemplify a broader pattern that Eqbal Ahmad identified as characteristic of Third World societies, where people find themselves "living on the frontier of two worlds—in the middle of the ford—haunted by the past, fevered with dreams of the future."[1]

Pakistan's elite has succeeded, at great cost and with help from the United States, in making its dreams come true. They have created a Pakistan that has nuclear weapons, nuclear power plants, and a nuclear complex that dwarfs all other areas of science and technology. But in this fifty-year-long effort, Pakistan's elite has failed to meet many of the basic political, social, and economic needs of its citizens. The essay concludes by looking at the aftermath of the 1998 nuclear tests and the state's promotion of nuclear nationalism as the basis for a shared sense of identity and achievement. My argument is that the peace movement in Pakistan, if it is to prevail, needs to look beyond a simple opposition to nuclear weapons. It must also offer a vision of an alternative future.

Atomic Futures and American Dreams

The idea of an atomic age is as old as atomic science. In 1901 Fredrick Soddy and Ernest Rutherford discovered that radioactivity was part of the process by which atoms changed from one kind to another and involved the release of energy. Soon Soddy was writing in popular magazines that radioactivity was a potentially "inexhaustible" source of energy, that atomic science meant that "the future would bear . . . little relation to the past," and offering a vision of an atomic future where it would be possible to "transform a desert continent, thaw the frozen poles, and make the whole earth one smiling Garden of Eden."[2] Soddy, along with other scientists and commentators, also talked of how atomic energy could possibly be used in weapons to wage war, and this soon became the stuff of science fiction in the hands of writers such as H. G.

Wells, whose novel, *The World Set Free*, was dedicated to Soddy and described "atomic bombs," the idea of a "chain reaction," and the effects of an atomic war.[3]

The future hurtled closer with the 1939 discovery of atomic fission, the process that underlay radioactivity; as one historian of the nuclear age observed: "journalists and scientists everywhere were caught up in the excitement," and there were countless "awestruck stories" of what might be possible. Part of this future became all too real when in 1945 the United States built the first atomic bombs and used them to destroy the Japanese cities of Hiroshima and Nagasaki. The U.S. soon deployed its new weapons to confront the Soviet Union in a divided Europe, and in 1949 the Soviet Union tested its first atomic bomb. The Korean War broke out in June 1950, and on the first day of that war U.S. leaders privately discussed the use of nuclear weapons; in subsequent months the question was raised repeatedly in the press, with President Truman inciting an international uproar by announcing in November that "there has always been active consideration of its use."[4]

The development of nuclear weapons proceeded at a furious pace. Britain became the third nuclear armed state when it conducted its first nuclear test in 1952. That same year the United States developed and tested the hydrogen bomb, with a yield many hundreds of times that of the bombs that had destroyed Hiroshima and Nagasaki, and the Soviets tested theirs a year later. By 1953 the United States had more than a thousand nuclear weapons, roughly ten times as many as the Soviet Union, and by 1955 both had twice that number.[5] As ever larger bombs were tested year after year, one was hard-pressed to ignore the importance of nuclear weapons and the threat of nuclear war.

In these years the United States also led the way in shaping the ideas and hopes for an atomic-powered utopia. The day after the bombing of Hiroshima, the *New York Times* wrote: "We face the prospect either of destruction on a scale that dwarfs anything thus far reported or of a golden era of social change which could satisfy the most romantic utopian."[6] Three days after Nagasaki was destroyed, the *New York Times* editorialized that atomic technology "can bring to this earth not death but life, not tyranny and cruelty, but a divine freedom," and could bring "dazzling gifts" to the "millions of China and India, bound for so many ages in sweat and hunger to the wheel of material existence."[7] Books soon began to appear about the wondrous prospects made possible by atomic technology; a 1947 book, *Atomic Energy in the Coming Era*, claimed that the future would be "as different from the present as the present is from ancient Egypt," and captured some of the practical qualities of the atomic dream:

> No baseball game will be called off on account of rain in the Era of Atomic Energy. No airplane will bypass an airport because of fog. No city will experience a winter traffic jam because of heavy snow. Summer resorts will be able to guarantee the weather, and artificial suns will make it as easy to grow corn and potatoes indoors as on the farm.... For the first time in the history of the world, man will have at his disposal energy in amounts sufficient to cope with the forces of Mother Nature.[8]

The possibilities seemed both limitless and immediate. The *New York Times* told its readers in 1947 that Africa "could be transformed into another Europe," and the *Woman's Home Companion* explained in 1948 that it would be possible to "make the dream of the earth as the Promised Land come true in time for many of us already born to see and enjoy it."[9] Contemporary surveys suggested that these ideas were championed by nuclear scientists, parts of the media, some in government and some industrialists, with support largely limited to affluent and well-educated Americans, while the general public focused more on the threat of nuclear weapons.[10] It was these groups, however, with their shared vision of saving the world through atomic science, that quickly came to dominate the debate in the United States.

The idea of the atomic future soon came to play an important role in U.S. foreign policy. America's determination to save the world—from the Soviet Union, from Communism, and from poverty and suffering through the application of its military strength and its technology—had been laid out by President Truman in his inaugural address in January 1949. He declared:

> The American people desire, and are determined to work for, a world in which all nations and all peoples are free to govern themselves as they see fit, and to achieve a decent and satisfying life.... In the pursuit of these aims, the United States and other like-minded nations find themselves directly opposed by a regime with contrary aims and a totally different concept of life.... We will provide military advice and equipment to free nations which will cooperate with us in the maintenance of peace and security.... [And] we must embark on a bold new program for making the benefits of our scientific advances and industrial progress available for the improvement and growth of underdeveloped areas.[11]

It was left to Truman's successor, Dwight Eisenhower, to bring the peaceful atom into the Cold War and onto the global stage. In a speech to the UN General Assembly in December 1953, President Eisenhower detailed the destructive power America could now wield with its atomic weapons, and announced that America wished all to share in the bounty of the atomic future that had now arrived.[12] He declared:

> Today, the United States' stockpile of atomic weapons, which, of course, increases daily, exceeds by many times the explosive equivalent of the total of all bombs and all shells that came from every plane and every gun in every theatre of war in all of the years of World War II. . . . But the dread secret, and the fearful engines of atomic might, are not ours alone. The United States knows that if the fearful trend of atomic military build up can be reversed, this greatest of destructive forces can be developed into a great boon, for the benefit of all mankind. The United States knows that peaceful power from atomic energy is no dream of the future. That capability, already proved, is here—now—today.[13]

The speech was broadcast around the world, and the U.S. government used it as part of an intense international effort in the years that followed to show that, unlike the Soviet Union, it believed in developing and sharing the peaceful uses of atomic energy. The atomic dream was an American dream, and America would ensure that every nation could have a share in it.

It must be said, however, that there was little evidence to support Eisenhower's grand claim that the atomic future was "here—now—today." In late 1951 the Argonne National Laboratory had generated a token amount of electricity from a small experimental reactor, which had been widely publicized and led to suggestions that nuclear power was "imminent."[14] In June 1953 the U.S. Atomic Energy Commission, under pressure to speed up the development of nuclear power, had decided that the quickest way to build a full-scale nuclear power plant was to allow Admiral Hyman Rickover to modify the pressurized water reactor that had been under development for use in aircraft carrier propulsion.[15] It only began operation in 1957. The imagined peaceful and prosperous atomic future was still just a vision. Nuclear weapons, the "fearful engines of atomic might," were all too real.

Securing the State

While the atomic age was taking shape, Pakistan, too, was no more than an idea and a hope. The Muslim League, founded in 1906 and led by Mohammad Ali Jinnah, eventually succeeded in establishing the state of Pakistan.[16] The history and geography of India's Muslims, their encounter with British colonialism and their relationship with India's struggle for independence, combined with the nature of the Muslim League movement, left important legacies that shaped Pakistan's early years and to some degree continue to have an influence. These included what has been called a "low level of political culture" in the feudal and tribal leaderships that dominated much of the Muslim majority areas that became Pakistan, the "poor institutionalisation" of the Muslim League as a mass-based political movement in these areas, the conflict between diverse local and regional identities and the new national identity, and the simple fact that to create a large constituency the League had been "deliberately vague about the nature of a future Pakistani state."[17]

On this basis the new leadership set about to achieve what it considered its primary task, to create a nation-state.[18] The leadership's ability to exercise power at the national level was limited, and a sense of direction was in short supply. As one historian observed:

> The chaos that overwhelmed Pakistan independence was a consequence of little planning and virtually no conceptualization . . . neither Jinnah nor any of his immediate circle was moved to lay out on paper the blueprint for the state they intended to create. There is nothing in the archives to even hint that someone was responsible for defining the nature and structure of the state, its purposes and functions, its powers and limitations.[19]

A measure of the chaos may be seen in the effort to create a new constitution through a constituent assembly. Established in August 1947, the assembly never managed to gather all its sixty-nine members—some chose to go to India and were never replaced and others simply did not show up at meetings. It met for only 4 days the rest of that year, a mere 11 the subsequent year, and eventually was dissolved in 1954, having met for a total of 116 days.[20]

There were other problems. The thoughtless and hurried partition of British India into the new states of West and East Pakistan and India created millions of refugees who trekked in opposite directions across the new borders, seeking new identities and the promise of justice and security. Within months, a war erupted over Kashmir. It ended in a stalemate, with India and Pakistan each controlling parts of Kashmir. Crisis followed crisis. Mohammad Ali Jinnah, who had centralized political and bureaucratic power by making himself the governor-general of Pakistan, died in 1949, leaving a leadership vacuum. Then, in 1951, it was revealed that Maj. Gen. Akbar Khan had been working with a group of left-wing officers and a handful of activists of the Pakistan Communist Party since 1949 in an effort to seize power.[21] The first prime minister, Liaquat Ali Khan, was killed in October 1951 as he was about to address a public meeting in Rawalpindi. There were to be three governor-generals and six prime ministers before a coup in 1958 led to more than a decade of military government.

As the new national elite in Pakistan struggled to establish itself and create institutions it could call its own, it is easy to see why it sought access to resources and support from powerful international allies. In the immediate aftermath of partition, Pakistan sought to develop a strategic relationship with Britain. Morris James, the British Deputy High Commissioner noted that the Pakistanis "in those early years were willing to range themselves at the side of Britain, then still a major world power, if in return we would help them to redress the strategic balance between themselves and the Indians. They sought a powerful outside friend and patron."[22] The search for a "friend and patron" to help counter India can be understood in large measure as a "continuation of the political struggle before partition" that Pakistan's eventual leaders had waged against the Congress Party, and for whom "the habit of criticism could not be effaced by the drawing of a new boundary."[23] It was this sensibility that led them to interpret and respond to disputes over Kashmir, the division of rivers, the distribution of financial and military resources, refugees, and so on, as proof of Indian hostility.[24] This sensibility has crystallized in the educational system and is present in the national curriculum and school textbooks in Pakistan even today.[25]

Although Britain was not able to play a role as patron, the Cold War eventually offered both Pakistan and the United States an opportunity for such a relationship. Whereas British India had been vital to the British Empire, the United States saw Pakistan as "the hastily created by-product of Britain's retreat from empire, a nation plagued by such immense internal and security problems that it offered little promise for future international prominence."[26] As the Cold War set in, however, the U.S.

military planners began to see Pakistan as important because of its "proximity to the Soviet Union; its proximity to the oil fields of the Middle East; its potential role in the defense of both the Indian Ocean area and the Indian subcontinent; its position as the largest Muslim nation in the world; and its army."[27] Despite this, nothing substantial happened. The U.S. did not want to undermine the possibility of a good relationship with India and so left Pakistan on the margins of the Cold War.

Pakistan's representatives for their part tried to incite the U.S. to reach out. They "carefully couched all appeals to the United States in a virulently anti-Soviet rhetoric that they hoped would strike a chord with the Truman administration's Cold War planners."[28] Success came not because of their entreaties but with the outbreak of the Korean War in 1950. By late 1951 the U.S. had decided to sell military equipment to Pakistan, and in early 1952 Pakistan and the U.S. signed the first of a number of supplementary agreements on security, which Pakistan soon tested by asking for $200 million in military aid.

U.S. concerns and interests in Pakistan were summed up in an August 1953 Memorandum to the National Security Council from the Acting Secretary of State. The memorandum observed:

> There was a noticeable increase in the activities of the mullahs (orthodox religious leaders) in Pakistan. There was reason to believe that in face of growing doubts as to whether Pakistan had any real friends, more and more Pakistanis were turning to the mullahs for guidance. Were this trend to continue the present government of enlightened and Western-oriented leaders might well be threatened, and members of a successive government would probably be far less cooperative with the West than the present incumbents.[29]

In February 1954 the U.S. announced that it would be giving military aid to Pakistan. This was followed, in May 1954, by Pakistan formally signing the Mutual Defense Assistance Agreement with the United States. A U.S. Military Assistance and Advisory Group was created, and these military advisers moved into the General Headquarters of Pakistan's armed forces.

The consequences for Pakistan of this new relationship with the U.S. were enormous. Since independence, Pakistan's political and military leaders had been spending an extraordinary share of available government resources on the military and it was unsustainable. In both 1948 and 1949, over 70 percent of government expenditure went to the military. This fraction did not fall to 50 percent in any year in the first decade of independence, and the military only consumed less than half of government spending for two years in the early 1960s before the 1965 war caused the military share to rise again.[30]

The new strategic relationship with the U.S. had a strong impact on Pakistan's military. U.S. training and techniques flowed in along with military aid: "The United States connection led to the complete revision of tables of Organization [of the

Pakistan Army], the addition of several entirely American-equipped divisions ... and the adoption of American techniques (in gunnery for example)."[31] Along with this went training for the Pakistani military, with hundreds of Pakistani officers attending U.S. military schools between 1955 and 1958. Some of these officers who trained in the U.S. became very prominent. General Zia ul-Haq, who became chief of the Army Staff in 1976, and in 1977 staged a coup and ruled until his death in 1988, was an early gradu-ate of the Command and Staff College and trained at Fort Leavenworth (where he took the Associate Command and General Staff Officer Course). General K. M. Arif, who trained at the U.S. Armor School at Fort Knox, Kentucky, went on to become chief of staff to General Zia in 1977 and in 1984 became vice-chief of army staff.[32]

The American support for Pakistan apparently "made a deep impression on thou-sands of Pakistani officers."[33] Eqbal Ahmad suggested that this training left a legacy of officers who "have come to respect American technology, crave for contemporary weapons systems, and favor alliances which promise hardware."[34] Not surprisingly, the Pakistani military began to turn its attention to the role of nuclear weapons. By the time of the Korean War, the U.S. had started to incorporate nuclear weapons into its military strategy and tactics, from bombs, short- and intermediate-range missiles, to an early nuclear howitzer.[35]

In 1954 Maj. Gen. M. A. Latif Khan became the first Pakistani Commandant of the military Command and Staff College, Quetta. In the official history of the college, he recalled that,

> On taking over as Commandant I found that the study of the various operations of war under nuclear warfare conditions was carried out in an elementary form and a few enquiries made by me soon revealed the fact that this subject had not received the attention it deserved. The time had come for us to start making a serious study of fighting the next war which would, whether we liked it or not, be fought with nuclear weapons.[36]

Gen. Latif Khan appointed a senior officer to deal with "future warfare," and thus began the practice whereby, "during the study of each operation of war, the same problem was considered under nuclear conditions."[37] These exercises included tactical war games without the use of troops, in which hypothetical scenarios were tested out on actual terrain and existing military doctrines rehearsed.

The United States played a direct role in this training. In the years that followed, Pakistan's Staff College was visited from time to time by a special U.S. Nuclear Warfare Team. The history of the college notes approvingly that "this visit proved most useful and resulted in modification and revision of the old syllabus to bring it into line with the fresh data given by the team."[38] This was to be part of a more enduring program, as the his-tory notes that there were "periodic visits by American nuclear experts."[39] General Khan remarked that "it was generally agreed that this subject required serious study, even if we ourselves were not going to be likely to possess nuclear weapons for many years."[40]

These military exercises were among the first nuclear practices in Pakistan. It is difficult to fathom these rehearsals for nuclear war, in which Pakistanis planned and imagined the use of a weapon that no Pakistani had actually seen or experienced. The psychological and institutional implications of several generations of young Pakistani military officers playing these fantasy nuclear war games merit further study.

How the Pakistani military thought they would eventually acquire nuclear weapons is not clear. Perhaps they believed that these weapons would come to Pakistan as part of the alliance with the United States. In 1956 the U.S. Joint Chiefs of Staff compiled a list of states which they wanted to serve as bases for intermediate-range ballistic missiles, armed with nuclear weapons. The "most desirable" states for such deployments were Turkey, Norway, Britain, Japan, Okinawa, and France, and the states considered merely "desirable" were Pakistan, Greece, Iran, Taiwan, Denmark, West Germany, the Philippines, Spain, Italy, and Libya.[41] The U.S. went on to base its nuclear weapons in Turkey, Britain, Okinawa, Greece, Taiwan, Denmark (actually Greenland, which was part of Denmark until 1979), West Germany, the Philippines, and Italy; other nuclear weapons were stored in Spain.[42]

Apparently, for reasons that are not clear, Pakistan, Iran, and Libya were the only states from the original list where no U.S. nuclear weapons were placed. There may have been concern about these countries' stability. As suggested in the 1953 National Security Council memorandum cited earlier, U.S. policy makers feared that the pro-Western government in Pakistan might not last.

What is clear is that after the 1958 coup by General Ayub Khan, which put in place a military government that lasted until 1971, the armed forces apparently did not pursue a focused nuclear weapons program. They seemed to have been content with their strong relationship with the U.S. and access to American military aid and high-tech conventional weapons. The political decision to pursue nuclear weapons had to wait until the end of military rule, and ultimately was taken only in early 1972 by Zulfikar Ali Bhutto, a civilian leader. Also curious is that even though Pakistan had completed its development of nuclear weapons by the early 1980s, the military government of General Zia ul Haq resisted calls for testing these weapons. Instead, he preferred keeping them under wraps and maintaining ties with the United States, receiving military aid and modern American weapons such as F-16 fighters. Only in 1998 did Prime Minister Nawaz Sharif decide to test nuclear weapons. Pakistan's last military ruler, Gen. Pervez Musharraf, also emphasized the need to maintain a relationship with the U.S. and obtain American military aid and weapons.

Planning the Future

The challenge and pattern of economic development has been of central concern for Pakistan's decision makers since independence. They recognized the weak economic foundations of the new state carved out of the western and eastern peripheries of

British India. Indeed, Pakistan's economic prospects were uncertain even before its independence in 1947.[43] In March 1946, at a meeting in Calcutta, Jinnah was asked about the relative backwardness of the country he envisioned: "What of the economic situation in Pakistan? There is no iron, no coal, no hydro-electric power, no industries." Jinnah replied, "I am fully aware of these things. Our people have had no opportunity to develop these things. I have every faith . . . that, given the opportunity, they will achieve all this."[44] At other times, Jinnah was less optimistic: "If the worse comes to the worst, like a sensible man we will cut our coat according to our cloth."[45]

Pakistan's first efforts at planning its economic development were launched in 1948, when the government set up two official bodies, a Development Board and a Planning Advisory Board.[46] The former began its task by asking government ministries to "re-examine and update" projects that had been planned for the area that was now Pakistan by the Department of Planning and Development of the Government of British India. The Board dealt with one project at a time and "made no attempt to prepare a plan or even to relate projects to one another."[47] In 1950, however, as part of the agreement to create coordinated six-year development plans for the members of the Colombo Plan for Co-operative Economic Development in South and Southeast Asia, the Board did put together a larger plan. Still, the plan was little more than a set of "projects which had been selected on an ad hoc basis without reference to available resources and the requirements of the economy."[48]

In 1951 the Development Board and the Planning Advisory Board were combined to form a new Planning Commission, but this, too, quickly failed to find its feet. This led, in 1952, to the creation of an Economic Appraisal Committee that believed no harm had been done so far by the failure to plan properly but advised that "an adequate and efficient planning organization is essential."[49] The government responded, in July 1953, by establishing a Planning Board that was to come up with a five-year development plan to begin in April 1954.

The evidence that Pakistan's economic planners and managers were failing was abundant. Economic growth had been poor; from 1949 to 1954 GNP per capita had risen barely 1 percent, and per capita rural incomes (reflecting the livelihoods of a great majority of the population) had fallen by 3 percent.[50] The arbitrary character of the plans suggested a lack of coherent goals in the planning process. Economists were also in short supply; in fact, a history of the discipline notes that, "at independence, there were hardly any economists in Pakistan."[51] The first chief economist of the Planning Commission had actually been a chemistry teacher at Delhi University before 1947, and, out of his own interest, had obtained an MA in economics.[52]

The chairman of the Planning Board looked for help outside the country and found it in the United States. In February 1954 the Ford Foundation agreed to fund a program whereby Harvard University's Graduate School of Public Administration would "recruit and guide a group of experts who would assist Pakistan's Planning Commission."[53] It should be noted here that Pakistan was not alone in turning to

American economists for help with planning; India did the same.[54] The first economic advisers for Pakistan arrived in April 1954 (around the same time as the military advisers); their work was expected to be mostly completed in about eighteen months. The program grew with time, however, and lasted much longer than anticipated. The last adviser left Pakistan in the mid-1970s.[55]

The planners saw their task as guiding the transformative movement of the economy, society, and culture of Pakistan along a technological axis. The opening page of the first five-year plan declared:

> Planning in the present stage of our society means the formulation of programs and policies designed to lead it by a consciously directed and accelerated movement from a largely technologically backward and feudalistic stage into the modern era of advanced technology now on the threshold of atomic age.[56]

The idea of a planned "accelerated movement" from a "stage" that is "backward" to one that is "modern" is premised on a notion that the difference between societies and economies is not one of history, geography, and culture but rather of different points along a single trajectory. Development meant catching up with the United States.

For the planners, speed was essential in this endeavor. Their passion to achieve their goal quickly seemed to overwhelm any reasonable sense of how to accomplish the complex and unprecedented task of economic, social, and cultural transformation. The planners insisted that,

> A country which has a leeway of centuries to make up cannot think of rest periods ... Consolidation and development must proceed simultaneously; the very idea of a breathing time to look back, take stock, settle down comfortably, and then think of the next stage is inconsistent with the speed and tempo of the atomic age.[57]

In addition to its role in planning the economy and advising the government, the Harvard Advisory Group (HAG) was also charged with training Pakistani economic planners. To this end, HAG members worked closely with their Pakistani counterparts to set up a graduate training program for Pakistani economists at leading U.S. universities, including Harvard, Yale, and Princeton. The result was a group of Pakistani economists who shared the values of the HAG as well as an understanding of planning priorities. These economists became dominant figures in Pakistan's economic decision making for the next several decades. One of the most prominent among them, Mahbub-ul Haq, served as Chief Economist of the Planning Commission during 1957–70 and went on to become Minister of Finance, Planning, and Commerce from 1982 to 1988.

The new economists shared with their mentors a clear perception of the state's role in the economy, the need for a "modernizing elite" to manage it, and the role nuclear energy would play. Indeed, the latter seems to have overwhelmed their economic rationality. The first study on the economic viability of nuclear power in Pakistan was undertaken in 1955 by Maurice Kilbridge, a HAG member, with input from other members. Kilbridge concluded not only that "there does not seem to be much of an economic case for the use of large-plant nuclear power in either East or West Pakistan" but that the pursuit of such a goal was unrealistic for the foreseeable future, noting that "probably not more than 10 persons in all Pakistan ... have any extensive training in nuclear technology, and ... not many more [have] the basic education necessary to absorb such training."[58]

The Kilbridge study should have dampened the enthusiasm to develop nuclear power in Pakistan, but it did not. The determination to hasten Pakistan over the threshold into the atomic age remained strong. Even a decade later, in 1966, at meetings of the Planning Commission, "those in charge argued vehemently that nuclear energy was the wave of the future, that we could develop many peaceful uses of nuclear energy, and that we would be left behind in the race of modern science and technology unless nuclear research was given adequate funds."[59] Forty years later this vision continues to drive the allocation of large funds into nuclear energy projects that provide electricity at much higher costs than other available energy sources, and are located at unsafe sites that add to the risk of catastrophic accidents.[60] It is ironic that Pakistan's decision makers remain intent on the nuclear dream when in the home of that dream, the United States, no new nuclear reactor has been built in three decades.

Science and the Nation-State

Kilbridge had pointed out in his study that perhaps fewer than a dozen scientists in Pakistan were trained in the nuclear sciences, and few among these had the ability to take advantage of this training. This assessment reflected the general state of science in the areas that became Pakistan. Before partition, India had a Directorate of Scientific and Industrial Research modeled on the British structure for integrating research with the needs of industry. All its laboratories, however, were in cities that remained part of India.

After independence, Pakistan established its own Directorate of Scientific and Industrial Research, and in April 1953 this body, headed by Salimuzzaman Siddiqi, set up a Council of Scientific and Industrial Research (CSIR). This council then set up a Planning Committee, headed by Nazir Ahmad (who had trained as a physicist in Britain in the 1920s), to determine where and what kinds of government research laboratories should be built to aid in national development. Ahmad's task was soon made easier, at least in part. U.S. president Dwight Eisenhower, in his December 1953 "Atoms for Peace" speech, declared that "experts would be mobilized to apply atomic energy to the needs of agriculture, medicine, and other peaceful activities. A special purpose would be to provide abundant electrical energy in the power-starved areas of the world."[61]

Pakistan's media welcomed the speech and the promise of the wondrous prospects of atomic energy. In the days following the speech, *Dawn,* Pakistan's leading English-language newspaper (which was read by the national elite) carried many reports on current and future possibilities. These were illustrated with photographs and elaborate graphics obviously produced by U.S. and British atomic establishments. The stories included U.S. proposals for the use of radioactive waste,[62] British ideas on using nuclear materials in industry,[63] the economics of nuclear power,[64] surveys of how the U.S. Atomic Energy Commission was assisting countries worldwide,[65] Britain's plans to produce nuclear electricity within a few years,[66] an introduction to Britain's atomic establishment,[67] the announcement by the American company RCA that it had invented an "atomic battery" that converted atomic energy into electricity,[68] and an introduction to the physical principles underlying atomic energy.[69]

Pakistan, however, could hardly take advantage of these technological prospects. As Vice Chancellor of Peshawar University Raziuddin Siddiqui explained in his presidential address to the Sixth Pakistan Science Conference in Karachi in January 1954, even though Pakistan's scientific community was in poor shape, it wanted to play its role in building the nation.[70] Siddiqui claimed that science was being neglected, with scholars "at the mercy of petty officials and clerks"—this despite the fact that science and education were a "defense against ignorance and the consequent poverty and disease." But, Siddiqui argued, science and education were more than that : "scientific research education and research is the real and only defense of a country in these days, as modern defense is mainly a technical affair requiring scientific skill and knowledge of a fairly advanced type." With the Manhattan Project barely a decade old and the Cold War arms race raging, not to mention the struggle for independence from colonialism still fresh in people's minds, it is clear that Siddiqui was making the case for the role of science in Pakistan's national security. He went on:

> It cannot be denied that in this age of power politics not only the security but even the free existence of the eastern countries is at stake, because of their backwardness in scientific and technical knowledge. . . . Hence we must have a vast army of those trained in all the fundamental and important scientific and technical subjects.

The first evidence that Pakistan's government was thinking of taking a scientific interest in the "Atoms for Peace" program came in late September 1954. The U.S. National Planning Association announced that it was to conduct a series of country studies to look at the "economic problems and policy issues raised by the rapid increase in technological knowledge of atomic energy and its potential contribution to industrial and agricultural development and improved standards of living."[71] Pakistan was chosen to be one of the countries in the study, along with Japan, Korea, Brazil and Israel, because the Planning Association claimed that "all these countries [have] 'special institutions' which might make nuclear development interesting."[72] Oddly, however, Pakistan had no "special institution" at that time working on nuclear research. The report becomes understandable if a decision had been made in principle to start work on atomic energy in Pakistan at this time but had not yet been made public.

The announcement that Pakistan was looking toward atomic energy came some weeks later, at the second meeting of the Pakistan Council for Scientific and Industrial Research in Karachi on 19 October 1954. Khan Abdul Qayyum Khan, Pakistan's Minister of Industries announced:

> The government is conscious that with the enormous progress the world is making towards the utilization of atomic energy for civil uses, adequate steps have to be taken without delay in Pakistan to work out a phased program of survey, research and ultimate developments in this field.[73]

Apparently, at least at this stage, atomic science was to fall within the purview of scientific and industrial research, suggesting that starting an atomic science program may have been driven partly by the desire of the Pakistani scientific community to gain access to what looked like major new sources of funding, overseas training, and so on, in order to gain more advanced ideas about science, technology, and development. In this they were using the same strategy as their peers in the areas of economic planning and the military, completing the triumvirate of the state-modernizing elite.

It was left to Salimuzzaman Siddiqi, the dean of CSIR, to establish a committee that would draw up a "detailed, phased Atomic Energy Program." According to Siddiqi, the first task "was to survey and assess the country's resources in radioactive minerals." However, any effective program, he pointed out, would require a large nuclear science community and that meant sending "young scientists abroad for specialized training."[74]

The extreme need for scientists of all kinds was clear, but Pakistan's educational system was not equipped to produce them domestically.[75] In 1953 Pakistan had only six universities—two in East Pakistan and four in West Pakistan—and not until 1961 would four new universities be created. In these six universities and associated colleges, 57,654 students were enrolled in arts and sciences courses and 2,138 in engineering.[76] A total of 680 students graduated in 1953–54 with a Bachelor of Science degree, and 107 students graduated with a Master of Science degree. In contrast, 2,122 Bachelor of Arts degrees were awarded that year, and 241 Master of Arts degrees. Not one Ph.D. was awarded—two had been awarded in science in 1949 and 1950 by the University of Dhaka, and another in 1954–55, but no others were awarded until 1965.

The first opportunity to take advantage of the Atoms for Peace program came a month or so later. The Raw Materials Sub-Committee of the U.S. Congress Joint Committee on Atomic Energy visited Pakistan as part of a whistle-stop tour that included New Zealand, the Philippines, Formosa, Thailand, India, Iran, Turkey, Greece, Spain, and Australia. The U.S. delegation described their visit to Pakistan in effusive terms:

In Karachi we had the very real pleasure of meeting first with Prime Minister Mohammed Ali, and later with the Council of Scientific and Industrial Research for Pakistan. Long and hard though the road ahead is for the people of Pakistan, they see and are attempting to grasp the opportunities to make their passage along that road faster and better through the use of atomic energy.[77]

Their Pakistani hosts did not lose an obvious opportunity to make a case for the importance of U.S. help in their endeavor to set up atomic energy. The committee wrote, "scientists and government administrators alike made it clear to us while we were there conferring with them that they must have assistance and would welcome it particularly from the United States."[78] They praised the effort of Pakistan's would-be nuclear scientists, "men of scientific and technical stature who are trying . . . with their limited means to bring their country the benefits of this most revolutionary science."

The major public announcement of Pakistan's nuclear plans came on 1 January 1955, in Prime Minister Mohammad Ali's "first of the month" broadcast to the nation. After laying out a number of decisions taken by the government on constitutional and economic issues, he declared:

> While concentrating our attention on matters of vital interests to your daily life we have not been unmindful of the need for the country's progress and development in other spheres. A step forward in the scientific field was the formulation of a scheme to set up a Nuclear Research Centre for exploring the possibility of obtaining uranium from the mountainous regions of our country with a view to production of atomic energy for the country's economic development.[79]

The visit of the Congressional Joint Committee was viewed as a certificate of approval for Pakistan's plans. The prime minister announced that "four members of the United States Joint Committee on Atomic Energy visited us . . . I am happy to state that the U.S. delegation has not only given us encouragement but has expressed their appreciation of our efforts in this direction."[80]

The public also soon provided opportunities to glimpse the dawn of the nuclear age. In January 1955 the U.S. ambassador opened a traveling public exhibition on the Atoms for Peace program, created by the U.S. Information Agency.[81] The exhibition, occupying 3,000 square feet, used pictures, films, and models to show the development and possibilities of nuclear science and technology. The show opened in Bahawalpur and was reported to be a "smash hit," with more than twenty-five hundred people viewing it within the first two hours of its opening and as many as six thousand visitors two days later.[82] Eventually fifty thousand people were reported to have seen it.[83]

After Bahawalpur the exhibition, now jointly sponsored by the Pakistan Atomic Energy Committee and the U.S. Embassy, moved to Karachi, the capital, where it was opened by Finance Minister Chaudri Mohammad Ali.[84] During the two weeks of the exhibition some three hundred thousand people came.[85] It then went on to Lahore and Peshawar, and toured most of the other major cities, drawing large enthusiastic crowds.

The atom was now firmly part of the public consciousness of a significant number of urban, middle-class Pakistanis.

On 11 August 1955 Pakistan and the U.S. signed a five-year Agreement for Co-operation on the Civil Uses of Atomic Energy. The U.S. provided funding for a small research reactor, fissile material to fuel it, an archive of technical reports and papers on many aspects of nuclear science and engineering, and a training program for scientists and engineers. By 1961 the newly created Pakistan Atomic Energy Commission (PAEC) had 144 scientists and engineers, who either had already received training abroad or were currently being trained abroad. Among those trained in the U.S. was Munir Ahmed Khan, who would return to Pakistan and in 1972 become chairman of PAEC, with the responsibility for launching Pakistan's nuclear weapons program. The program took on more urgency after India's May 1974 nuclear weapons test, and continued despite U.S. sanctions and pressure in the late 1970s. This pressure was eased after Pakistan joined the U.S. in a proxy war against the Soviet Union after its invasion of Afghanistan. The program succeeded in the early 1980s and, following additional nuclear tests by India, Pakistan tested its nuclear weapons in May 1998.

Conclusion

This essay argues that the ideas of an atomic future that were developing in the United States became a central element in its relationship with Pakistan as soon as the U.S. began to engage with that country. The relationships between Pakistan's military, economic planning, and scientific institutions and the United States were all informed at some level by the idea of this imminent atomic future. For Pakistan's new national elite, embracing this future offered a way to affirm a shared perspective on what it meant to be a modern state and society in the contemporary world and what the future would be like. The pursuit of this future also privileged those who could operate at the national level and with the United States.

The embrace of an atomic future essentially distinguished those who saw a way for the country to become modern at home and part of the modern world from those who were rooted in the past and locality, clung to tradition, and did not believe in rapid social change. In this respect, the idea and ideal of an atomic future may be read as representing both the future and the universal as opposed to the local and the present. Based on this radical vision of a future world, these new bureaucracies of economy, violence, and technology, exposed at a formative stage to American goods, skills, and ways of doing things, imbued with certain American tastes and desires, and all privileging "technical superiority," set about creating the necessary conditions for the exercise of their power.

For those Pakistani elites able to create and take advantage of them, ties to the United States offered preferential access to power, resources, and privilege. Pakistan's army saw in the U.S. a source of money, weapons, training, strategic support, and the future of warfare. Its economic planners saw development as stemming from access to U.S. aid and knowledge, and aimed at creating a society modeled after a United States that was entering the nuclear age. For the scientists, a path was opened by President Eisenhower's Atoms for Peace plan with its vision of a shortcut to a nuclear future, with scientists as the indispensable guides.

These ideas of past, present, and future, of change, progress, and possibility, and the institutions that claimed to embody them were to have an impact comparable in some respects to the much earlier experience of some nominally independent countries importing European ideas and institutions during the colonial period.[86] Pakistan was to see the emergence of a military that dominates national politics and the allocation of national resources, one that has seized power three times and ruled directly for over half of Pakistan's history so far. It has had a process of economic planning and management that has failed to provide basic needs to a large proportion of citizens, and remains dependent on international aid to meet its most basic developmental needs. Pakistan has witnessed the creation of a nuclear estate of nuclear power plants, nuclear weapons, and nuclear science and technology research and development. But Pakistan's nuclear estate can offer only a nuclear nationalism, evident in the models of the nuclear weapons test site and ballistic missiles that were put up in major cities, as well as the annual celebration of the anniversary of the May 1998 nuclear tests.

The narratives and displays that made up the first May 28 celebration, in 1999, are revealing. The plans for what the government called a celebration of "self-reliance," and of an "impregnable defence" included "a competition of ten best Milli songs, seminars, fairs, festive public gatherings, candle processions, sports competitions, bicycle races, flag hoisting ceremonies etc. People will offer Namaz-e-Shukrana as well. Apart from this special programmes for children would be arranged. Debates would be held among schoolchildren."[87]

To make sure that no one missed out on this new common sense about the meaning of Pakistan's nuclear weapons, and those who made them, there were to be programs "broadcast on national network as well as locally by all 24 stations of the radio. In addition to the national language Urdu, programmes in regional languages, including Punjabi, Sindhi, Pushto, Balochi, Brahvi, Saraiki, Potohari, Hindko, Balti and Shina will also be broadcast. The external service and world service will air special programmes in 15 foreign languages for listeners in Europe, Middle East, Africa and South East Asia. The Azad Kashmir Radio will also broadcast special programmes on the occasion in Kashmiri, Gojri, Pahari and English languages."[88] This would ensure that everyone heard and understood the new national story of nuclear Pakistan. The audience was also meant to be global; as Information and Culture Minister Musha-hid Hussain proudly put it, the nuclear test site at Chagai "has become a symbol of Pakistan's identity all over the world."[89]

Absent from this celebration of nuclear weapons, apart from the recognition that these are weapons of mass destruction that the world has struggled to eliminate since they were first created, is the acknowledgment that Pakistan's nuclear achievements were anything but proof of national self-reliance. The nuclear project from its inception relied on outside support. Pakistan's nuclear scientists were trained abroad, at the expense of others, its nuclear research and nuclear power reactors were imported, the key technology for producing the fissile material for its nuclear weapons was bought abroad covertly by A. Q. Khan, and even the design of its bomb may have come from China.

Rather than proving national strength and self-reliance, the coming of the bomb exposed Pakistan's fundamental weaknesses. Indeed, the events after the May tests provided clear evidence of just how weak Pakistan actually is. The sanctions imposed by the international community in response to the nuclear tests were quickly lifted not because the world was awed by Pakistan's new nuclear might but because they saw its fragility. It appeared that the country was about to fall apart and no one wanted to see that happen.

Pakistan's claims to national technological and military prowess through mastery of the bomb, the reactor, and the missile provide a flimsy veil over its many basic failures as a state and society. It is this recognition that shapes the efforts of the small, emerging antinuclear movement in Pakistan to embed its prudential and moral critique of nuclear weapons and nuclear power in a broader challenge to prevailing ideas and practices of national security, development, and the politics of knowledge.[90] To repeat the call made in *Out of the Nuclear Shadow:*

> The tasks that confront the peace movements in India and Pakistan are unprecedented. Not only must they educate their fellow citizens in what it means to live with nuclear weapons in their midst, they must do so without creating such fear that people are immobilised. They must organise to abolish nuclear weapons but cannot concentrate simply on the technology, politics, economics and culture of nuclear weapons because nuclear weapons cannot be abolished from South Asia or globally while leaving everything else unchanged.[91]

This means imagining and building a future that goes beyond emulating the states, economies, societies, and knowledge systems of the "developed" world. It requires new dreams.

Notes

This paper was written as part of a project on *Nuclear Cultures in South Asia,* organized by Itty Abraham. I am grateful for comments and encouragement from my fellow participants in the workshops.

Epigraph quote from H. Magdoff, *The Age of Imperialism, Monthly Review,* 1969, p. 133.

1. Eqbal Ahmad, "From Potato Sack to Potato Mash," in *Between Past and Future (Selected Essays on South Asia by Eqbal Ahmad),* ed. Dohra Ahmad, Iftikhar Ahmad, and Zia Mian (Oxford University Press, 2004), p. 11.

2. Spencer R. Weart, *Nuclear Fear: A History of Images* (Cambridge, Mass.: Harvard University Press, 1988), p. 6.

3. Ibid., pp. 25–26.

4. Richard K. Betts, *Nuclear Blackmail and Nuclear Balance* (Washington, D.C.: Brookings Institution, 1987), pp. 32–33.

5. "Global Nuclear Stockpiles 1945–2000," *Bulletin of Atomic Scientists,* March/April 2000, p. 79.

6. "Science and the Bomb," *New York Times,* 7 August 1945, cited in Paul Boyer, *By the Bomb's Early Light: American Thought and Culture at the Dawn of the Atomic Age* (Chapel Hill, N.C.: University of North Carolina Press, 1994), p. 125.

7. "One Victory Not Yet Won," *New York Times,* 12 August 1945, cited in Boyer, *By the Bomb's Early Light* (Chapel Hill, N.C.: University of North Carolina Press, 1994), p. 122.

8. Cited in Boyer, *By the Bomb's Early Light,* p. 112.

9. Weart, *Nuclear Fear,* p. 159.

10. Ibid., p. 162.

11. Available at http://www.trumanlibrary.org/whistlestop/50yr_archive/inagura120jan1949. htm.

12. For a history of this speech, see Richard G. Hewlett and Jack M. Holl, *Atoms for Peace and War, 1953–1961: Eisenhower and the Atomic Energy Commission* (Berkeley: University of California Press, 1989).

13. "President Dwight D. Eisenhower's 'Atoms for Peace' Address to the United Nations General Assembly, December 8, 1953," in *The American Atom: A Documentary History of Nuclear Policies from the Discovery of Fission to the Present, 1939–1984,* ed. Robert C. Williams and Philip L. Cantelon (Philadelphia: University of Pennsylvania Press, 1984), pp. 104–111.

14. R. G. Hewlett and J. M. Holl, *Atoms for Peace and War, 1953–1961: Eisenhower and the Atomic Energy Commission* (Berkeley: University of California Press, 1989), p. 190.

15. Ibid., p. 192.

16. Ayesha Jalal, *The Sole Spokesman: Jinnah, The Muslim League, and The Demand for Pakistan* (Cambridge: Cambridge University Press, 1985).

17. Ian Talbot, *Pakistan: A Modern History* (Karachi: Oxford University Press, 1998), pp. 94–95.

18. For a history of the early efforts at creating a national, central authority, see, e.g., Ayesha Jalal, *The State of Martial Rule: The Origins of Pakistan's Political Economy of Defence* (Lahore: Vanguard Books, 1991).

19. Lawrence Ziring, *Pakistan in the Twentieth Century: A Political History* (Karachi: Oxford University Press, 1997), p. 98.

20. Keith Callard, *Pakistan: A Political Study* (London: Allen and Unwin, 1957), p. 80.

21. Hasan Zaheer, *The Times and Trial of the Rawalpindi Conspiracy 1951, The First Coup Attempt in Pakistan* (Karachi: Oxford University Press, 1998).

22. Morris James, *Pakistan Chronicle* (New York: St. Martin's, 1993), p. 5.

23. Callard, *Pakistan,* p. 15.

24. Pervaiz Iqbal Cheema, *Pakistan's Defence Policy, 1947–1958* (London: Macmillan, 1990); and, more broadly, Hasan Askari Rizvi, *Military, State, and Society in Pakistan* (London: Macmillan, 2000).

25. A. H. Nayyar and Ahmed Salim, eds., *The Subtle Subversion: The State of Curricula and Textbooks in Pakistan* (Islamabad: SDPI, 2004).

26. R. J. McMahon, *The Cold War on the Periphery: The United States, India, and Pakistan* (New York: Columbia University Press, 1994), p. 36.

27. Ibid., p. 69.

28. Ibid.

29. "Memorandum by the Acting Secretary of State to the Executive Secretary of the National Security Council," 19 August 1952, *FRUS, 1952–1954*, Vol. ii, Pt. 2 (USGPO, Washington, D.C., 1983), p. 1059.

30. *Years of Pakistan in Statistics,* Federal Bureau of Statistics, Government of Pakistan, 1997.

31. S. P. Cohen, *The Pakistan Army* (Berkeley: University of California Press, 1984), p. 64.

32. K. M. Arif, *Khaki Shadows: Pakistan 1947–1997* (Karachi: Oxford University Press, 2001), pp. 140–145.

33. Cohen, *The Pakistan Army,* p. 66.

34. Eqbal Ahmad, "Signposts to a Police State," in D. Ahmad, I. Ahmad, and Mian, *Between Past and Future,* p. 54.

35. Thomas B. Cochran, William M. Arkin, Milton M. Hoenig, *U.S. Nuclear Forces and Capabilities* (Cambridge, Mass.: Ballinger, 1984).

36. Maj. Gen. M. A. Latif Khan, "The Staff College as I Saw It," in *Command and Staff College Quetta, 1905–1980,* ed. and comp. Command and Staff College, Quetta (Command and Staff College, Quetta, 1982), pp. 139–140.

37. Ibid.

38. Ibid., p. 88.

39. Cohen, *The Pakistan Army,* p. 65.

40. Khan, "The Staff College as I Saw It," pp. 139–140.

41. K. W. Condit, *History of the Joint Chiefs of Staff,* Vol. 6: *The Joint Chiefs of Staff and National Policy, 1955–1956* (Historical Division, Joint Chiefs of Staff, Washington, D.C., 1992), p. 146.

42. Robert S. Norris, William M. Arkin, and William Burr, "Where They Were," *Bulletin of the Atomic Scientists* 55, no. 6 (November/December 1999): 26–35.

43. For the debates prior to independence on the economic viability of Pakistan, see Naureen Talha, *Economic Factors in The Making of Pakistan, 1921–1947* (Karachi: Oxford University Press, 2000), see, esp., pp. 145–157.

44. Hector Bolitho, *Jinnah: Creator of Pakistan* (Karachi: Oxford University Press, 1954), pp. 158–159.

45. Cited in Talha, *Economic Factors in The Making of Pakistan,* p. 152.

46. Albert Waterston, *Planning in Pakistan: Organization and Implementation* (Baltimore: Johns Hopkins University Press, 1963), p. 13.

47. Ibid., p. 15.

48. Ibid.

49. Ibid., p. 21.

50. Omar Noman, *The Political Economy of Pakistan, 1947–1985* (London: Kegan, Paul, 1988), p. 10.

51. Nadeem ul Haque and Mahmood Hasan Khan, "The Economics Profession in Pakistan: A Historical Analysis" in *50 Years of Pakistan's Economy—Traditional Topics and Contemporary Concerns,* ed. Shahrukh Rafi Khan (Karachi: Oxford University Press, 1999), p. 471.

52. Ibid.

53. *Design for Pakistan: A Report on the Assistance to the Pakistan Planning Commission by the Ford Foundation and Harvard University,* Ford Foundation, New York, 1965, p. 2.

54. For a comparative history, see George Rosen, *Western Economists and Eastern Societies: Agents of Change in South Asia, 1950–1970* (Baltimore: Johns Hopkins University Press, 1985).

55. Dickson Keith Smith, *Foreign Aid and Economic Development in Pakistan—The Ayub Years (1958–1969),* Ph.D. dissertation, University of Utah, 1974, p. 106.

56. *The First Five-Year Plan, 1955–1960*, National Planning Board, Government of Pakistan, Karachi, 1957, pp. 1–2.

57. Ibid., p. 395.

58. Maurice D. Kilbridge, *The Prospect for Nuclear Power in Pakistan*, National Planning Association, Washington, D.C., 1958, p. 55.

59. Mahbub ul Haq, "Wasted Investment in Scientific Research," in *Science and the Human Condition in India and Pakistan*, ed. Ward Morehouse (New York: Rockefeller University Press, 1968), p. 128.

60. Zia Mian and A. H. Nayyar, "Another Nuclear White Elephant," *Dawn*, 25 July 2004.

61. "President Dwight D. Eisenhower's 'Atoms for Peace' Address to the United Nations General Assembly, December 8, 1953."

62. R. C. Cowen, "Radioactive Wastes Now Marketable," *Dawn*, 13 December 1953.

63. H. Seligman, "Atoms for Peace," *Dawn*, 17 December 1953.

64. G. Hutton, "Economics of the Atom," *Dawn*, 15 January 1954.

65. "Atoms for Prosperity," *Dawn*, 17 January 1954.

66. "A-Energy to Generate Electricity: British Plan," *Dawn*, 19 January 1954.

67. K. E. B. Jay, "We Are on the Brink of a Profound Change," *Dawn*, 24 January 1954.

68. "Atoms for Peace," *Dawn*, 2 February 1954.

69. L. Amour, "Backdrop to the Atom," *Dawn*, 2 February 1954.

70. "Dr. Raziuddin's Address," *Dawn*, 19 January 1954.

71. "A-Energy for Peaceful Ends: 2-Year Probe Opens in USA: Pakistan Likely to Be among 'Selected Areas,'" *Dawn*, 28 September 1954.

72. Ibid.

73. *Dawn*, 20 October 1954.

74. Ibid.

75. *Years of Pakistan in Statistics, Volume II, 1947–1972*, Federal Bureau of Statistics, Government of Pakistan, Karachi, 1997.

76. Ibid., Table 13.17, p. 240.

77. *Report of the Raw Materials Subcommittee on Its Visit to Australia*, Joint Committee on Atomic Energy, 9 February 1955.

78. Ibid.

79. "Immediate Steps for Popular Rule in E Wing, Atomic Schemes to Be Pursued," *Dawn*, 2 January 1955.

80. Ibid.

81. "Atoms for Peace Exhibit Opens," *Dawn*, 22 January 1955.

82. "Atoms for Peace Exhibition—Great Success at Bahawalpur," *Dawn*, 25 January 1955.

83. "Atoms for Peace Exhibit Popular at Bahawalpur," *Dawn*, 1 February 1955.

84. "Finance Minister Opens Atom Exhibition," *Dawn*, 6 February 1955.

85. "Over 2 Lakhs People Visited Atomic Show in Karachi," *Dawn*, 21 February 1955.

86. David B. Ralston, *Importing the European Army: The Introduction of European Military Techniques and Institutions into the Extra-European World, 1600–1914* (Chicago: University of Chicago Press, 1990).

87. "PM Says May 28 Reminds of Objectives of National Agenda," APP, 8 May 1999.

88. PBC to Broadcast Special Programmes on 28th," *The News*, 22 April 1999.

89. "May 28 to Go Down in History as Symbol of National Pride," *The News*, 22 April 1999.

90. See, for instance, *Out of the Nuclear Shadow*, ed. Smitu Kothari and Zia Mian (Delhi: Oxford University Press, 2003).

91. Ibid., pp. 9–10.

3

INDIA'S NUCLEAR ENCLAVE AND THE PRACTICE OF SECRECY

M. V. Ramana

A secret is an invaluable adjunct of power.

Robertson Davies

Secrecy itself, especially the power of a few "designated" experts to declare some topic off limits, contributes to a political climate in which the nuclear establishment can conduct business as usual, protecting and perpetuating the production of these horror weapons.

Howard Morland

If I may say so, this secrecy is intended to screen the inefficiency, waste and perhaps the shady transactions of the AEC.

N. Sreekantan Nair, Indian Parliament, May 10, 1954

That the nuclear program in India operates secretively should not be a surprise to anyone. It has long been recognized that nuclear weapons pose structural necessities that contradict the spirit of democratic government, largely through the promotion of secrecy in decision making regarding their production and use. Nuclear weapons complexes around the world have functioned largely in secret. To a lesser extent, the same charge has also been leveled at nuclear energy establishments. All of these factors would therefore suggest that the same is true in India.

In India, however, two additional factors have influenced the scope and practice of secrecy. The first has to do with the inception of the program as one ostensibly devoted only to developing atomic energy for peaceful purposes. The use of nuclear energy for peaceful purposes, however, is strongly linked to its use for defense. Those in charge of the nuclear establishment recognized this connection even as the program was being initiated; indeed, the internal view within the Atomic Energy Commission (AEC) was that its aims were to develop "atomic energy for *all purposes.*" In the face of this inextricable link, the supposed restriction of the applications of atomic energy to peaceful uses while also pursuing weapons capabilities necessarily meant that some aspects of the program had to be closed off from public gaze. This situation has changed slightly with the 1998 nuclear tests and, more recently, the U.S.-India nuclear deal that is being discussed; now some facilities within the nuclear complex have been explicitly marked off as military or strategic. Still, this has not meant that the nuclear establishment has become very open with respect to information about the other "civilian" facilities.

The second factor is the adoption, deliberately or through the vicissitudes of history and circumstance, of "opacity" as the basis of nuclear strategy.[1] In his authoritative study of the nuclear weapons program of Israel, a country that also follows a somewhat similar strategy and is widely believed to possess nuclear weapons though it has never officially declared so, Avner Cohen defines opacity as a "situation in which the existence of a state's nuclear weapons has not been acknowledged by the state's leaders, but in which the evidence for the weapons' existence is strong enough to influence other nations' perceptions and actions."[2]

A natural outcome of an opacity strategy is uncertainty about the qualitative and quantitative extent of nuclear weapons capabilities. If the size, potential or real, of the nuclear arsenal was to be kept secret, then various details about the operations and sizes of many nuclear facilities could not be revealed publicly. This is in contrast to the United States, France, and the United Kingdom, where quite a lot of information is available about the nuclear arsenal and the production complex. Even the Soviet Union, which was otherwise considered quite secretive, was *relatively* open about its nuclear weapons capabilities.

At the same time, many find the notion of a highly secretive enterprise in India counterintuitive. Cultural stereotypes of the country would have us believe that it is hard to keep anything really secret. I remember a conversation in 1997 with an academic and high-ranking member of the Communist Party (Marxist) who assured me that there was no weapons program within the Department of Atomic Energy (DAE), because in no way could such an activity be held secret. Although this might be seen as an instance of ignorance—after all, there was a burgeoning literature at that time about the Indian nuclear weapons program, especially within the U.S. nonproliferation community—many members of the elite shared this view.

Those who do realize that nuclear matters are held secret also often make it a point to stress that this is an exception. An example is Raj Chengappa, a journalist with close access to various officials, who states in the prologue to his book on the Indian nuclear bomb that "for a garrulous nation the nuclear weapons programme is one secret that India, surprisingly, keeps well."[3]

Within the DAE, there is a sense of having to be careful to avoid public knowledge of the department's activities. Anand Patwardhan's prize-winning documentary, *Jang aur Aman,* for example, records former Atomic Energy Commission (AEC) chairman Raja Ramanna elaborating on how the planners of the 1974 nuclear test took care not to put any decisions on paper so as to avoid leaks. Similar measures were apparently adopted during the 1998 tests as well, and on both occasions only a few select individuals were informed of the decision to test. Despite this concern about maintaining a cover over its activities, the practice of secrecy by the nuclear establishment has been somewhat selective and irregular.

This paper, which looks not only at secrecy in the context of nuclear weapons but also in the arena of nuclear energy, presents in some detail the ways in which the nuclear enclave in India has practiced secrecy and documents instances of this practice in three thematic areas. The first is the intent of the program and its infrastructural components, namely, whether it is intended for making weapons or limited to electricity production. The second is the broad area of the program's safety and impacts on public and occupational health and the environment. The third is the costs associated with different aspects of the program. In each of these areas I detail several cases where the nuclear establishment has tried to conceal its activities, refused to reveal information that should be openly available in the public interest, or indulged in obfuscations of various kinds. The result has been the absence of an open and well-informed debate about the state's nuclear pursuits.

Nuclear Weapons, Nuclear Energy, and the Varieties of Secrecy

As mentioned earlier, one motivation for imposing secrecy on the nuclear program involved its supposed restriction to peaceful applications. The lack of transparency then enabled the quiet effort to cultivate and broaden a nuclear weapons capability. There is also substantial overlap in the facilities and personnel involved in the two pursuits, and the weapons and energy components of the Indian nuclear program can be said to be fungible.[4] For these two reasons alone, confining this paper to just the weapons program would be methodologically indefensible. But even if one were to be able to carve out a program solely aimed at developing nuclear energy, secrecy in such a project is an even greater affront to democratic values and so should be of inherent interest.

This is not to say that no differences exist in the levels of secrecy practiced within the energy and weapons sectors (to the extent that they can be differentiated). Even officials belonging to the nuclear establishment would admit that they do not want to be transparent about activities related to weapons (or "national security," as it is euphemistically termed). Indeed, they often pride themselves on their ability to maintain secrets. For example, the inability of U.S. satellites to detect preparations at the Pokharan test site for the 1998 explosions has been touted as a great success. High-ranking nuclear establishment officials such as R. Chidambaram and Anil Kakodkar, former and current heads of the AEC, take pride in wearing military fatigues to keep up the deception. Of course, the element of seeming resistance to U.S. imperialism also makes such concealment attractive in postcolonial India.[5] Given this backdrop and the opacity strategy described earlier, finding any official information on various aspects of the nuclear weapons program, for example, the extent of India's weapons grade plutonium stockpile, is highly unlikely. This is in contrast to the United States and the United Kingdom, both of which have published official declarations of their weapons plutonium holdings.

While discussing the atomic energy program, on the other hand, the nuclear establishment has maintained that it is open. For example, V. K. Chaturvedi, the former head of the Nuclear Power Corporation (NPC), declared: "There is no secrecy in our nuclear power programme. . . . We are transparent. You go to our site on the Internet and you find all the details about our projects and specification."[6]

There is some truth to this assertion—the NPC website does indeed offer plentiful information about various projects and some operational details, for example, the amounts of electricity produced by different reactors. This information could, inter alia, be used to calculate the approximate amount of plutonium that would be in the spent (irradiated) fuel produced by the reactor.[7] In contrast, the DAE's Web sites and annual reports give no information on the operational levels of the CIRUS or Dhruva plutonium production reactors. However, Chaturvedi is incorrect in claiming that one can find "all the details." The fact is that neither the NPC Web site nor any publications put out by the nuclear establishment provide the numerous pieces of information that are critical to making informed assessments of the economics of nuclear facilities, their environmental and public health impacts, or their potential for serious accidents.

The differences in secrecy practices between the energy and weapons sectors point up the multiple meanings that the term "secrecy" encompasses and the assorted methods that could be classified as secretive.[8] Secrecy about the nuclear weapons arsenal, for example, refers to denial of information. As we shall see later on, such denial also occurs in the case of ostensibly civilian nuclear facilities.[9] When civilian facilities are used to further the nuclear weapons program, however, "concealment" or "camouflage" better describe what is practiced than denial of information. Finally, a range of actions are practiced that are tantamount to secrecy, including publishing information in obscure documents and making them inaccessible to the public, resorting to technical jargon in answering direct questions, and utilizing poor or confusing accounting practices.

Enabling Factors

Before turning to the actual practice of secrecy, I first describe some, though perhaps not all, of the factors that enable its practice and effectiveness. These include typical bureaucratic habits, structural characteristics peculiar to the nuclear establishment, the relatively esoteric nature of the subject and paucity of independent expertise, the prestigious status of the nuclear enterprise among the public at large, and the failure of the media to play a sufficiently critical role.

The first enabling factor is that Indian bureaucracies and institutions generally lack accountability. Despite the adoption of a Right to Information (RTI) bill in 2005, it is difficult to obtain information on a range of projects and programs, whether road construction, defense procurement, or the public distribution system for foodstuffs. The nuclear establishment also suffers from (or enjoys, depending on one's perspective) a similar lack of accountability, but it goes further. While one can resort to the use of "influence" to get, say, one's birth certificate, even relatively senior politicians often cannot obtain information about nuclear matters.

As the well-known politician Jayanthi Natarajan despaired publicly:

> I have been a Member of the Parliamentary Consultative Committee for Defence and Atomic Energy, and have tried time and again to raise issues relating to public safety, both at Parliamentary Committee hearings, and in the Rajya Sabha, and have achieved precious little for my pains. Since I was an MP [Member of Parliament] at the time, and a pretty aggressive one, I had to be dealt with. But they simply drowned me with totally obscure and incomprehensible scientific terms and explanations, which sounded impressive, and meant nothing. The rest was simply not forthcoming because they claimed it was "classified." I have repeatedly raised the issue of the hazards of radiation leaks, safety procedures, and environmental contamination that might flow from the atomic power station at Kalpakkam, but have always received the bland and meaningless reply that the radiation was "within acceptable limits."[10]

The second factor is the structure of the atomic establishment and the constraints this structure poses on external oversight. Unlike most policy matters where the cabinet has the ultimate authority, the agency in charge of nuclear affairs is the AEC, which was constituted under a special act of parliament. The AEC is composed primarily of scientists and dominated by the top leaders of the DAE. The DAE was set up in 1954 under the direct charge of the prime minister, a decision that is largely the result of the close relationship between Homi Bhabha, the architect of the nuclear program, and Jawaharlal Nehru, who offered almost unstinting support for the nuclear program and allowed strong secrecy clauses in the Atomic Energy Act.

When the bill enabling the creation of the AEC was introduced at the Constituent Assembly in early 1948, Nehru gave two reasons for the imposition of secrecy, both
somewhat disingenuous: "The advantage of our research would go to others before we
even reaped it, and secondly it would become impossible for us to cooperate with any
country which is prepared to cooperate with us in this matter, because it will not be
prepared for the results of researches to become public."[11] In response to one member
of the assembly pointing out how, in the British act, secrecy is restricted only to defense
purposes and demanding to know if in the Indian case secrecy was insisted upon even
for research for peaceful purposes, Nehru publicly admitted: "I do not know how to
distinguish the two [peaceful and defense purposes]." Nevertheless, Nehru allowed
the nuclear establishment to operate without oversight and to decide by itself on the
contours of its program.

Nehru's complicity did not stop with just setting up the atomic establishment
in this fashion. He continued to support the AEC's secretive functioning even after
several politicians and policy makers were troubled by it. In a revealing 1952 letter to
his minister of finance, who had expressed concern about the high costs of the AEC,
particularly when it provided so little information to justify its need for money, Nehru
said explicitly, though disingenuously, "The work of the AEC is shrouded in secrecy. I
try to keep in touch with it and get reports from time to time. . . . I do not know how
else we can proceed in this matter."[12]

This structure makes it difficult for most politicians or bureaucrats, let alone
commoners, to challenge the DAE's policies or practices. The DAE thus exempli-
fies Max Weber's observations about bureaucracies: "Bureaucratic administration
always tends to be an administration of 'secret sessions': in so far as it can, it hides its
knowledge and action from criticism. . . . In facing a parliament, the bureaucracy, out
of a sure power instinct, fights every attempt of the parliament to gain knowledge."[13]
The esoteric nature of nuclear science and technology, coupled with the connection
to national security, has permitted the DAE to be more successful at this pursuit of
secrecy than most bureaucracies.

An example of the DAE fighting an attempt by parliament to regulate the department is its struggle with the parliamentary Committee on Public Accounts, as well as
the Comptroller and Auditor General (CAG), whose function is to enhance accountability of various public-sector organizations and departments to the parliament and
state legislatures. The dispute stemmed from the CAG trying to estimate the cost of
heavy water production at the DAE's facilities and producing a figure about three times
the cost estimated by the DAE. When questioned about this discrepancy, the DAE
was unable to provide any calculations to substantiate its figure. The parliamentary
committee considered this "another instance of lack of proper accounting procedure
which in turn is due to their disregard of accountability on their part. The Committee
strongly deprecate such attitude." In its response, the DAE stated: "Heavy Water being
strategic material, it is not advisable to divulge information relating to its production

and cost to functionaries at all levels." The committee did not agree and maintained that "as already recommended proforma accounts will have to be compiled. . . . [T]he Committee do not understand how preparation thereof will result in release of any sensitive data. The Committee consider such claim as a way of evading accountability by escaping scrutiny of audit and this Committee under the guise of sensitivity, public interest etc." More than a year after the Public Accounts Committee tabled its report at parliament, the CAG complained: "The proforma accounts of Heavy Water Pool Management for the years 1982–83 onwards have not been sent for audit so far despite this fact being mentioned in successive Reports of the Comptroller and Auditor General of India: Union Government (Scientific Departments) since 1987."[14]

In August 1998, finally, the Heavy Water Board "made available the pro-forma accounts for the period 1993–94 to 1996–97 . . . for audit certification." But what the CAG found, perhaps not surprisingly, was "that the cost of production of heavy water had been reckoned at a rate lower than the actual cost . . . As a result, the pool prices of heavy water notified by DAE during 1993–98 on provisional basis were less by Rs. 409 to Rs. 2168 per kg than the actual pool charges derived from the certified pro-forma accounts, except for the year 1993–94, where it was slightly higher."[15]

A third factor supporting secrecy is the legal structure. Two acts are particularly relevant: the 1962 Atomic Energy Act and the Official Secrets Act. The first act has been widely written about in the literature on the Indian nuclear program; essentially it empowers the DAE to restrict practically any information related to atomic energy. The latter posits strong prohibitions against the "misuse" of official information regarding facilities relating to the military establishment or electricity "works," especially with "foreign agents."[16] Both acts have been used only rarely, but this is largely because few occasions have occurred where the DAE was put in a position where it could have been forced to reveal information that it would have preferred not to. On those occasions the DAE invoked the Atomic Energy Act to refuse to divulge potentially embarrassing information. The judiciary has also often interpreted these laws in favor of secrecy rather than the people's right to know. More on this below.

The DAE has also used the legal structure on occasion to subject those who have exposed its technical and safety failures to harsh punishment. A tragic example involved B. K. Subbarao, a naval officer who was appointed to work on the secret nuclear submarine program. Subbarao challenged the designs produced by DAE scientists for the submarine's nuclear reactor on technical grounds, leading to the rejection of these designs.[17] In 1988 he was arrested in the Bombay airport en route to the U.S. and charged under the Official Secrets Act and the Atomic Energy Act with trying to smuggle secret documents out of the country.[18] All he was carrying with him was his Ph.D. thesis and related papers. Subbarao was imprisoned for five years and denied bail. After a prolonged legal battle, he was acquitted by the Supreme Court and awarded Rs. 25,000 as "costs for his mental suffering and financial loss." Those behind his prosecution went unpunished.

Not only has the DAE used existing laws to shield itself from adverse criticism, it has also tried to further strengthen some of the provisions to allow for harsher punishments. In 1992 journalist Rupa Chinai disclosed in an article in the Bombay newspaper *The Sunday Observer* that there had been a major radioactive leak at the Bhabha Atomic Research Centre.[19] The DAE's reaction to the article was to try to "amend the 1962 act to increase punishment for unauthorized disclosure to 5 years rigorous imprisonment instead of 3 earlier and to allow them to prosecute without first seeking the solicitor general's approval."[20]

Another enabling factor is the near absence of independent sources of expertise on nuclear matters outside the DAE. This paucity of knowledge outside the nuclear establishment about various aspects of science and technology involved acts that are, in effect, a source of secrecy in two ways: certain facts do not come out in public because no one has asked the right questions, and the establishment can escape responsibility for scientific and technical obfuscations, whether deliberate or inadvertent.

A notable instance where the DAE's assertions were challenged on technical grounds was the 1998 nuclear tests, though the challenge came from experts outside India. The DAE claimed that the total explosive yield from the tests of May 11, 1998, was about 60 kilotons. However, based on seismic signals detected around the world, international seismologists suggested that the total yield was only 16–30 kilotons. Similarly, the DAE's claims about the tests of May 13 were also disputed. Faced with such technical criticism, the DAE had to enter the debate and write a number of papers arguing for its version of the yields. Many of these papers suffered from serious scientific flaws.[21] For example, one paper about the yield of the May 13 nuclear test contained graphs with no units or markings on the axes.[22]

Even if one were to reject the yield estimates of the international seismologists, the DAE's estimates were based on inconsistencies. In particular, the DAE's estimate of about 60 kilotons assumed that the yield of the 1974 test, conducted at the same location, was 13 kilotons. Ever since 1975, the DAE had maintained that the yield of that test was 12 kilotons.[23] Without that difference of 1 kiloton, the 1998 yield estimates would be lower by about 5 kilotons, even by the DAE's own methodology.

Despite numerous scientific papers on the subject, no one in the media or even the antinuclear movement (barring a few exceptions) caught on to the debate or its implications. Some in the antinuclear movement were concerned that questioning the success of the 1998 tests might lead to renewed pressure from bomb designers to conduct further tests. However, this resulted in a wasted opportunity to question the basic technical competence of the nuclear establishment and its habit of making unscientific and wrong claims.

Incompetence in the nuclear establishment has also been displayed on matters concerning the environment and health. Two papers, for example, state how much gaseous Argon-41 was released from the Madras Atomic Power Station in 1990; however, the numbers in the papers are not the same and differ by 37.5 percent. What makes this inexplicable is that both papers were co-authored by the same scientist, M. A. R. Iyengar.[24] Nuclear establishments elsewhere—in the United States, for example—have also been incompetent when it comes to environmental and health concerns.

The general lack of expertise in nuclear matters among laypersons has reinforced the effectiveness of DAE's secrecy practices. Many, even those who may have an anti-nuclear bent, have assumed that they are incapable of analyzing nuclear policy issues. By and large, therefore, the implications of even the limited amount of information available on economics, safety, environmental impacts, or occupational and public health effects have not been analyzed thoroughly. This also reflects on the inability of the antinuclear movement in India to attract technically trained people into its ranks and have them *use their technical expertise* to critique the nuclear program.[25] This is quite unlike the United States, where one criticism of the antinuclear movement has been its excessive focus on technical critique.

If and when anyone challenges the DAE's expertise or competence, the typical response has been to brand that person or persons as anti-national and desiring to undermine India's capabilities in a highly technical field. In 1984, the journalist Praful Bidwai, one of the few journalists with some knowledge of nuclear technology, wrote a series of five articles in the *Times of India* pointing out how poorly the DAE's heavy water production facilities were functioning. In response Raja Ramanna, chairman of the AEC at the time, protested to the prime minister and convened a press conference where he publicly branded Bidwai as unpatriotic and said that the publication of the articles was a waste of newsprint.[26]

Such accusations equating criticism of the nuclear program to anti-national attitudes resonate powerfully among India's postcolonial middle classes and elite. These classes have long had a high regard for the nuclear program, thanks in part to systematic propaganda by the DAE and the Indian state extolling the virtues of atomic energy. With the 1974 test at Pokharan, these sentiments became even more pronounced and criticism even more undesirable. As the Indian Institute of Public Opinion pointed out in 1978, "Ever since Pokharan, nuclear energy has become an issue of national prestige . . . [and] a symbol of the technology and scientific advance we are seeking and which we believe are capable of achieving."[27]

The effectiveness of secrecy is enhanced by the practical difficulties even in obtaining information that is in principle available to the public. I once participated in a collaborative study of the economics of the DAE's heavy water reactors using the Discounted Cash Flow method of accounting which required not just the total cost of the reactor, information widely available, including on the NPC Web site, but also the year-by-year breakdown of this cost.[28] Despite numerous e-mails and a personal visit, the NPC did not give us this information. At least when I visited the NPC office, the NPC's spokesperson did not refuse to give me the information but said instead that he did not have the information on him but he would get back to me soon with the details. That never happened. Ultimately I managed to obtain a copy of the DAE's

Performance Budget that had the required information. Thus, it was not that the information we were seeking was not available in the public domain but that the agency responsible refused to supply it. Such practices allow the DAE (or those who support it) to assert that the organization is not secretive and yet know that there is little chance anyone will obtain information that potentially could embarrass the DAE.

Still another factor supporting the secrecy regime is that the media generally supports the nuclear establishment and has largely avoided offering critical perspectives on nuclear issues.[29] Most articles about nuclear programs are based either on press releases issued by the DAE or on interviews with officials in the nuclear establishment. Some journalists, and the newspapers or magazines they write for, act as mouthpieces for the nuclear establishment. They are rewarded in various ways. One such journalist reportedly was given a contract by the NPC to "educate" other journalists about the many advantages of the Koodankulam project and to allay the safety concerns expressed by many. The DAE and the different organizations affiliated with it also publish their own propaganda magazines, for example, *Nuclear India* and *Nu-Power,* and a host of glossy pamphlets extolling their many achievements.

The media has been criticized often for reporting failures of the nuclear establishment. When journalists reported a leak at the Tarapur nuclear reactor on March 14, 1980, for example, the DAE secretary Homi Sethna went into "a tirade against the press" describing "reporters as 'irresponsible,' 'self-styled experts' writing about things on which they lack even 'elementary knowledge.'"[30] Often journalists who ask uncomfortable questions are ostracized by the DAE. Gopi Rethinaraj, who had a masters degree in physics and could understand relatively technical material, read a report on heavy water and found a passing reference to the extraction of tritium from irradiated heavy water in Indian reactors. He rightly recognized the importance of tritium for thermonuclear weapons and wrote about it in an international defense journal.[31] Soon after, Rethinaraj was no longer allowed into the DAE's press conferences,[32] which effectively banned him from the "nuclear beat." He ultimately quit journalism and pursued a Ph.D. in the U.S.

Barring such exceptions, the media lacks the expertise to evaluate the claims of the establishment; few newspapers and magazines seek counter views. At the same time the relative freedom of the media in India and the media's desire for newsworthiness has led on occasion to investigative journalism and exposés. However, this is often owing to a proclivity for sensationalism rather than principled commitment to transparency and democracy.

Even scientific journals are uncritical of the DAE. For example, *Current Science,* which publicized estimates of the yields by DAE scientists, refused to publish a paper by this author calculating the number of casualties that would result from the explosion of an atomic bomb over Bombay.[33] Probably the best sources of reliable information about the DAE are international nuclear trade magazines such as *Nuclear Fuel* and

Nucleonics Week. Correspondents who write for these magazines are more conversant with the technicalities of nuclear reactors and other facilities, and seem to have easier access to DAE officials as representatives of international media.

For all these reasons, the nuclear establishment has successfully managed to control the information available about the nuclear program and thereby stifle, if not altogether eliminate, criticism of its activities. The following sections elaborate the ways in which this has been done.

Secrecy and the Intent of the Program

A substantial literature now exists which demonstrates that, although India's nuclear program was ostensibly for peaceful purposes, the weapons option was consciously kept open.[34] Nevertheless, the facade of only pursuing peaceful uses of nuclear energy pervaded for decades. One way of maintaining this pretence was by not revealing the true nature of many of the activities being carried out.

An early aim of the DAE program was to acquire the capability to chemically process ("reprocess") irradiated nuclear fuel to extract plutonium, which could be used to make nuclear weapons. However, the only reason publicly acknowledged was its use in breeder reactors, which produce more fissile material than they consume.[35] Although this was technically true, for the DAE to produce plutonium in the quantities required for breeder reactors, the department would first have to set up several uranium-based reactors.[36] At the time when the reprocessing plant was established, there was no such reactor in the country; not had a single unit of nuclear electricity been produced. The true nature of the DAE's priorities for plutonium may be inferred from the fact that the first nuclear explosion conducted by the DAE was in 1974, whereas the first breeder reactor reached criticality only in 1985.

Nevertheless, with the breeder reactor program officially endorsed, the DAE could comfortably proceed and publicly announce the construction of the Trombay reprocessing plant along with the inevitable listing: "only four other countries [have] operating plutonium plants—France, the UK, the USA, the USSR." In contrast, Israel, which at that time was also acquiring the technology to reprocess spent fuel from France but had no interest in breeder reactors, was completely silent about this. As Avner Cohen observes, "the most sensitive and secret aspect of the agreement [with France] was the reprocessing plant, to which there was no reference in the official documents."[37]

The DAE's effort to create the wherewithal to produce nuclear weapons required that the plutonium obtained through reprocessing at Trombay be free of international safeguards, that is, measures to ensure that material was not diverted from nuclear energy production to weapons. This meant not only that the indigenously constructed (though based on blueprints obtained from the U.S.) Trombay plant had to be un-safeguarded, but so, too, did the reactor where the fuel was irradiated prior to reprocessing. This reactor was CIRUS, a gift by Canada under the Colombo plan that was based on the same design as the NRX reactor at Chalk River in Canada.

Some Canadian diplomats and scientists realized that CIRUS could lead to India acquiring weapons-useable plutonium. The NRX reactor was an efficient producer of plutonium because of its high neutron economy. Nevertheless, the initiative went through because it was assumed that India would be able to acquire a reactor from some other source. Despite consistent efforts on the Canadians' part, the DAE adamantly refused to accept any kind of voluntary controls or safeguards on the spent fuel produced that would have precluded the use of plutonium produced in CIRUS for nuclear weapons.[38]

Publicly the refusal was justified by a leap of logic, namely, that the imposition of safeguards would disallow plutonium acquisition, essential for the breeder program. This was simply wrong. There is no a priori reason why the imposition of safeguards would prevent the development of a breeder program. For example, the Japanese breeder program runs fully under international safeguards. But with practically no one in the country outside of the nuclear establishment familiar with technology, questions about the proffered excuse were never raised.

Unlike reprocessing, no such publicity accompanied the establishment of groups studying various aspects of nuclear explosions and acquiring the technology needed to conduct such explosions. For example, in 1960 Bhabha sent Vasudev Iya, a young chemist, to French laboratories to absorb as much as possible about polonium, a chemical element used to trigger a nuclear explosion.[39] Two years later Bhabha set up a small group to study the physics of the materials under the high pressures experienced during a nuclear explosion. With Prime Minister Lal Bahadur Shastri endorsing the idea of studying peaceful nuclear explosions (PNEs), this group grew in strength.[40] But none of this was known publicly. Once set up, the group then acquired momentum and continued working even after Vikram Sarabhai took over after Bhabha's death and called off the PNE program. (The pro-weapons group was, in effect, engaged in an act of revolt within the nuclear establishment.)

The existence of groups working on various aspects of nuclear weapons design and manufacture was revealed at the time of the 1974 test. In an impressive demonstration of the DAE's abilities to maintain secrets, these groups continued to remain active and develop new nuclear weapons designs with no public knowledge of these activities. Many seemed to assume that these groups were quiescent. The conversation mentioned earlier with the senior CPM member is an example.

This is all the more remarkable because of the DAE's and the government's intense effort to reassure international and domestic audiences that the 1974 test was indeed a PNE and that the nuclear program remained peaceful in character. In fact, one prime minister, Morarji Desai, in office between 1977 and 1979, was strongly opposed to nuclear weapons. Still, the DAE managed to keep its weapons program going.

Secrecy in Safety and Health

The possibility of catastrophic accidents and radiation-related damage to health has always been an important consideration in the public's acceptance of nuclear power. This consideration has become even more salient after Chernobyl.[41] Not surprisingly, therefore, nuclear establishments have played down the possibility of such accidents. Similarly, they have also been anxious to persuade the public that radioactive materials from nuclear fuel-cycle facilities have not damaged anyone's health.

Indian officials are no exception to these tendencies. For example, following the Tokaimura accident in Japan, India's AEC chairman claimed that there was no possibility of any nuclear accident in India because the DAE had a track record of "150 reactor years of safe operation."[42] Likewise, A. N. Mullick, who served as UCIL's chief medical officer for twenty-five years reportedly said: "I have not come across any radiation-related ailments during my entire career."[43]

Yet practically all nuclear reactors in India have had accidents of varying severity. As a result of several such accidents, in 1995 the Atomic Energy Regulatory Board (AERB), which oversees the safe running of all civilian nuclear facilities in the country, initiated an evaluation of the safety status of all nuclear installations. The resulting report identified 134 safety issues, of which about 95 were considered "top priority." That many of these problems had been identified in earlier DAE evaluations in 1979 and 1987 as items requiring "urgent action" but had not been addressed reveals the low priority that the DAE placed on safety. Not surprisingly, the DAE kept the AERB report a secret.

When news of the report came out, the People's Union for Civil Liberties (PUCL) filed a public interest petition in the Bombay High Court calling for the AERB report to be made public. The Sarvodaya Mandal, a Gandhian organization in Mumbai, also filed a supporting petition. Their primary argument was that safety dangers in nuclear plants constituted a challenge to people's "right to life" and that the people also had the "right to know."

In response, R. Chidambaram, then head of the DAE, filed an affidavit which said:

> I say that the aforesaid document, prepared by the Atomic Energy Regulatory Board in November 1995 which, among others, is a subject matter of this petition, is a document classified as Secret as it pertains to the nuclear installations in the country which include several sensitive facilities, carrying out activities of a highly classified nature, under the enabling provisions of the Atomic Energy Act, 1962.[44]

Chidambaram also invoked the provisions of Section 5 of the Official Secrets Act, 1923, and Section 18 of the Atomic Energy Act and stated, "I am the appropriate authority empowered to act on behalf of the Central government for the purpose of Section 18 of the Atomic Energy Act."[45]

Chidambaram's affidavit went much further:

> In the event of this hon'ble court holding that the plea of privilege is required to be taken even in a case of a document in respect of which an order has been issued under Section 18 of the Atomic Energy Act, I hereby claim privilege in respect of this particular document, viz. "Safety Issues in DAE Installations," in view of the fact that the government of India is apprehensive of the possible repercussions of the public disclosure of the said document on matters concerning national security. Privilege over the said official document is, therefore, claimed under the enabling provisions of Sections 123 and 124 of the Indian Evidence Act, 1872. I say that I have gone through the document personally and have given my careful attention to the said aspects before claiming privilege. I respectfully say and submit to this Hon'ble Court that if this document (which was submitted to the Atomic Energy Commission and is classified as SECRET) is required to be published, then it will cause irreparable injury to the interests of the State and will be prejudicial to national security.[46]

Chidambaram's affidavit was accompanied by six other massive affidavits and two sur-rejoinders from the senior officials of the nuclear establishment. Every affidavit, in effect, assured the Bombay High Court that all was well in the DAE's nuclear reactors. As B. K. Subbarao, the lawyer who represented PUCL and, as mentioned earlier, a trained nuclear engineer himself, noted: "To assure nuclear safety through affidavits is a unique invention of our nuclear establishment."[47]

On the basis of the affidavits submitted by the nuclear establishment, the Bombay High Court dismissed the petition from PUCL and the Sarvodaya Mandal. The two citizens groups then appealed to the Supreme Court. A. Gopalakrishnan, who headed the AERB when the 1995 report was prepared, was also a petitioner. He contended that "serious nuclear accidents" could take place at some facilities.

In January 2004 the Supreme Court rejected the appeal and ruled that information relating to nuclear installations could not be made public. Rather than view the case as "an opportunity to decide what was required for [the] protection of human health and environment," the Court restricted itself "only to the issue of confidentiality vis-à-vis right to information."[48] As justification for its decision, the Court said that the citizen's fundamental right to information was subject to restrictions in the interest of national security and the only test was "how reasonable" the restriction imposed by *the government of the day*.[49]

The Court took the extreme view that, although the government had supplied the court with sealed copies of the 1995 AERB Report and Attorney-General Soli Sorabjee, who represented the government and the DAE, had offered to read the report, the Bench noted, "We do not think it appropriate to open the seal and read the same."[50] Sorabjee claimed that the AERB report would reveal to "enemies" data containing "inventories, spent fuel, waste, etc., facilitating the calculation of the country's nuclear programme potential." Its contents, therefore, should not be revealed even in the name of "fundamental right to information."[51] The Court appears to have essentially accepted this line of reasoning without scrutinizing these contentions.

Two ironies underlie this decision. First, knowledge of the deficiencies listed in the 1995 report would not reveal the "nuclear programme potential"; the nuclear program *potential* depends essentially on just the broad design features of the reactors discussed in the AERB report. These details are publicly available at a number of places including the Internet sites of the DAE and the Nuclear Power Corporation (NPC) or assorted publicity material published by the nuclear establishment. Thus, if the Court were to be truly concerned about enemies spying on the country's nuclear potential, it would have to order these agencies to censor themselves.

More to the point, there is little technical basis for classifying the potential problems listed in the AERB report. Examples of problems identified by the AERB as likely to lead to serious accidents appear in Gopalakrishnan's various articles in magazines and journals. These include serious deficiencies in the emergency core cooling systems in some of the operating power reactors, and cracking or structural weakening of certain system components or internals needing repairs or replacement. Other problems involved the reactor instrumentation and protection systems, which had degraded the reliability and safety of the reactors. None of these is related in any way to the nuclear weapons potential of these facilities. Knowledge of these foreseeable problems, however, is likely to cause greater public concern about these facilities; hence the DAE's reluctance to make the information public.

The second irony is that many of the problems listed in the 1995 report appear to have been remedied in subsequent years. In 2002 Gopalakrishnan himself attested that "according to a recent communication from AERB Secretary K. S. Parthasarathy ... 119 out of the 134 safety issues are reported to have been completely resolved. The AERB communication does not, however, state which of the high-priority issues are still among the unattended ones, nor does it clarify any details of the already resolved issues."[52] The DAE did not, however, use the Supreme Court case to publicize its efforts to address safety problems.

Though the DAE has argued that nuclear accidents are not possible in India, it has also prepared emergency plans for dealing with such accidents. Such plans are typically justified as "a measure of abundant caution" by DAE personnel.[53] But again, typically, the DAE has made these emergency plans inaccessible to the public, who should be the real audience for these plans. Apart from the culture of secrecy and arrogance characteristic of the nuclear establishment, there are two other plausible reasons for this: first, publicizing such plans would make people realize that nuclear reactors and other fuel-cycle facilities are hazardous; and, second, examination of these plans by those outside the bureaucracy would reveal that they would not work.[54]

Consider, for example, what occurred when the emergency plan for the Kakrapar reactors in Gujarat was accidentally revealed. The Kakrapar reactor is located on the banks of a river that has only one bridge across it in the vicinity of the reactor. The plan, which required all evacuees in the event of an accident to cross this single bridge, was a sure recipe for a major traffic bottleneck. The plan also absurdly required people in villages and towns farther up the river to come *toward* the reactor first, cross the bridge, and then move away from the reactor. Finally, several of the facilities such as schools that were assigned as temporary shelters were grossly inadequate for the likely number of people to be housed there.

The DAE has also made efforts to curb public discussion of safety in its nuclear reactors. In 1985, for example, Max Mueller Bhavan of Bombay had organized a seminar on nuclear safety in Germany and India. Five days before the event, the seminar was cancelled at the instruction of the External Affairs Ministry, acting on the behest of the DAE.[55]

A widespread concern about nuclear power and weapons facilities is that these produce high-level waste that remains radioactive for tens of thousands of years. While the public has generally been concerned about these wastes and their impact on the environment and health, nuclear establishments have portrayed the problem of waste disposal as nonexistent or at most a minor, largely solved, concern. The DAE has even expressed the view that highly radioactive spent fuel should not be considered waste, that "it is a resource to extract plutonium."[56]

Once having decided that radioactive waste is not a problem, it is not surprising that the DAE has neither announced how much waste has been or is being produced and where it will eventually be disposed. Further, when discussing waste quantities, many DAE papers typically use figures from the Western literature, which are derived for Light Water Reactors (LWRs) rather than the heavy water reactors the DAE uses—yet another display of scientific and technical incompetence.

The DAE's efforts at trying to identify a site for geological waste disposal are also shrouded in secrecy. In March 1997 the inhabitants of Sanawada village near Pokhran were told that the Minerals Exploration Corporation Ltd. (MECL) was digging for precious stones. It was later discovered, accidentally, that the drilling was being done by the BARC and that Sanawada was being considered as storage location for nuclear waste. Apparently even the chief minister of Rajasthan did not know of these plans. Thanks to a campaign by antinuclear activists, the BARC stopped drilling. Shortly afterward, BARC director Anil Kakodkar maintained that a final decision had not been taken and that India was still "several decades away from the necessity of having such a site."[57] The DAE's plans for disposing of high-level waste are still secret.

Secrecy and Costs

The costs associated with the nuclear program are important for two reasons. First, unlike many other countries, the elite debate in India over the acquisition of nuclear weapons has focused at great length on the costs it would impose on the economy.[58] Opponents of the bomb typically claimed that these costs would be significant, perhaps prohibitive, for a developing country like India. In return, nuclear weapons advocates argued that they were cheap and affordable. Prominent among the latter was Homi Bhabha. On October 24, 1964, for example, in a broadcast on the state-run All India Radio (AIR), Bhabha quoted a paper published by the Lawrence Radiation Laboratory in Livermore, California, to assert that a 10 kiloton (kT) bomb would cost only U.S.$350,000 or Rs.17.5 lakhs. Based on these figures, he claimed that "a stockpile of fifty atomic bombs would cost under Rs.10 crores and a stockpile of fifty-two-megaton hydrogen bombs something of the order of Rs.15 crores" and argued that this was "small compared with the military budgets of many countries."[59] This pattern of debating the cost of a nuclear arsenal and its economical significance has persisted. Secrecy about the economic costs associated with the different components of the nuclear program has made this debate baseless.

Second, as generally understood at the time it was set up, the DAE's primary task was to provide cheap nuclear electricity. As early as 1958, barely a few years after the DAE was established, Homi Bhabha, the chief architect of the program, projected "the contribution of atomic energy to the power production in India during the *next 10 to 15 years*" and concluded that "the costs of [nuclear] power [would] compare *very favourably* with the cost of power from conventional sources in many areas."[60] The "many areas" referred to regions that were remote from coalfields. This projection was not fulfilled. In the 1980s the DAE stated that the cost of nuclear power "compares quite favourably with coal fired stations located 800 km away from the pithead and in the 1990s would be even cheaper than coal fired stations at pithead."[61] This projection, too, was not fulfilled.

A Nuclear Power Corporation (NPC) internal study from the late 1990s came to the less optimistic conclusion that the "cost of nuclear electricity generation in India remains competitive with thermal [electricity] for plants located about 1,200 km away from coal pit head, when full credit is given to long term operating cost especially in respect of fuel prices." This seems to be the DAE's most comprehensive study so far, at least on the basis of the summary of this study that is available on the Nuclear Power Corporation's Internet site.[62] However, when asked for a copy of the full study, the Nuclear Power Corporation's spokesperson maintained that it was not available to the public. Thus, we cannot know the methodology used or the assumptions made in any great detail. Many of the assumptions listed in the publicly available summary—for example, about the capital cost of reactors—do not hold up to scrutiny. Our independent comparison of the costs of electricity from nuclear reactors and thermal plants showed that nuclear electricity would be cheaper only under unrealistic circumstances.[63]

Despite the importance of the economics in the nuclear weapons debate, it is difficult if not impossible to examine the costs of the weapons program for a number of reasons. First, even government bureaucracies like the Comptroller and Auditor General (CAG) and the Ministry of Statistics and Programme Implementation, whose function is to monitor expenditures and criticize cost overruns, do not seem to have access to expenses relating to weapons facilities. Second, the overlap between the two programs and the use of the same facilities for both purposes means that expenditures on the weapons program can be passed off as part of the energy program. Finally, in the case of most nuclear fuel-cycle facilities (with the exception of reactors, whose electricity generation is publicly known), the level of performance is never revealed. The DAE Annual Performance Budgets list, for example, the annual electricity production at various reactors; conspicuously absent, however, are any numbers for heavy water production or the throughputs of reprocessing plants. The DAE has claimed that because of its strategic value, it would not disclose production levels of heavy water.

Technically there is nothing more strategic about heavy water than, say, coal. The only way that heavy water could be seen as having a strategic implication is if the reactors in the country involved in plutonium production were facing a shortage of heavy water and therefore could either not be commissioned or function efficiently. In such a circumstance, if people know that there is a shortage of heavy water, they could conclude that the country's stockpile of weapons-usable plutonium is smaller than estimates based purely on reactor size. In other words, the strategic value of heavy water is generated only by the DAE's difficulties at producing adequate quantities of it.

The same excuse of having strategic value has also allowed the DAE to explain away cost overruns. For example, in the case of the Manuguru Heavy Water Plant, the CAG found that the cost of the facility had increased by 133 percent; when questioned about the cost escalation, the DAE stated that "the grounds for sanction of this project was strategic and not commercial."[64]

Finally, referring back to the earlier discussion about different forms of secrecy, the DAE is not being secretive by refusing to reveal the cost of making, say, a single bomb. In all likelihood, the DAE has never engaged in a rigorous calculation of this cost and so does not even know the true answer to that question. Secrecy in this context is an effect of the DAE not revealing the costs of specific facilities, for example, the one involved in plutonium metallurgy, or the performance figures for many more facilities, for example, reprocessing plants. This has made it impossible for anyone to calculate the costs of weapons production with any confidence.

Secrecy: Selectiveness and Irrelevance

Nuclear reactors, according to Langdon Winner, "require authoritarian management and extremely tight security. It is one of those structures, increasingly common in modern society, whose hazards and vulnerability require them to be well policed. What that means, of course, is that insofar as we have to live with nuclear power, we ourselves become increasingly well policed."[65] In some ways the nuclear establishment fits this description.

In other ways, however, the practice of secrecy by the nuclear establishment has been quite uneven. In a stereotypically Indian fashion, the DAE has not followed or implemented the rules it has itself set. An illustration is the rule that nuclear reactors must have an exclusion zone, a circle of radius 1.6 km around the facility where the public is not allowed.[66] But if one were to look closely at the fence that cordons off this area around one of DAE's reactors, one might well discover a hole that some enterprising local inhabitant has cut. Through this hole, goatherds routinely take their animals into the exclusion zone to graze. Others may go in to collect biomass for burning. DAE personnel discovering such activities are quite likely to look the other way.

In addition to such security breakdowns, lapses in secrecy have occurred that embarrassed the DAE. Some of these lapses have involved information leaks from the nuclear establishment, which have come in at least two forms. The first are public revelations typically made by workers and their unions of radioactive leaks or safety violations. At the Kalpakkam Reprocessing plant in January 2003, for example, six workers were exposed to high radiation doses following a valve failure.[67] This accident came after repeated warnings by the Workers Association of safety problems. Following the accident, the association reiterated these problems in a letter to the authorities demanding that the problems be addressed immediately. When the authorities did not act on their demands, the workers went on strike. The authorities retaliated by transferring one of the key leaders of the strike, and others who participated were served warnings. The Association then leaked information about the safety violations to the media, and the accident became public news, but about six months after the event. Another instance of the worker's union using press publicity to negotiate with the authorities occurred in 1999, when a major heavy water leak occurred at the Madras Atomic Power Plant.[68]

The second form of information leak involves passing on information in order to achieve some strategic goal or settle internal differences. For example, in a recent article referring to the May 11, 1998, weapon test, nuclear strategist Bharat Karnad talked about the "40 kiloton dud" and pointed out that evidence for the failure of the test included "crater morphology [and] large traces of lithium at the site indicating that the lithium deuteride fusion fuel did not fully burn, whence the small, insignificant, yield."[69] Clearly the DAE would have liked to keep this information secret. It is also apparent that Karnad had been fed this information by insiders who are presumably interested in a resumption of explosive testing. Another form of lapse in secrecy has been information about the DAE's activities or blunders gathered by investigative journalists or antinuclear activists. Some instances have been described earlier.

The DAE has responded to this kind of activity in an uneven manner. We have already discussed the cases of people such as Gopi Rethinaraj and B. K. Subbarao. In contrast, the DAE dealt with Surendra Gadekar, a well-known antinuclear activist, largely by ignoring his activities. In July 2000 Gadekar was measuring radiation levels near the tailings pond at Jaduguda (where the radioactive waste from the uranium mill is dumped). "While I was taking the readings a guard came but I just ignored him and continued to take the readings as if I was an official of the department and if he wondered about the strange officer who wore pyjama kurta that was his problem."[70]

Gadekar has also been publishing *Anumukti,* India's only dedicated antinuclear journal for two decades, without the authorities trying seriously to prevent it.

There are three reasons for this uneven approach. One is the need for the DAE to maintain the appearance of legitimacy or openness and avoid overreaction. Historically the important period was the 1980s and 1990s, when the DAE and its allied organizations suffered some loss of legitimacy because it failed to generate the promised quantities of electricity and so it attempted to reinvent itself publicly as a more transparent organization. The push for greater openness in some measure was owing to the personality of M. R. Srinivasan, head of the Atomic Energy Commission in the late 1980s, who has always advocated greater transparency.[71] This pressure for relative transparency has been accentuated by recent efforts to involve the private sector in generating nuclear energy.

The second reason is that the effort involved in purging those responsible for security breaches, and the possible negative publicity that would result, are not deemed worth the gain in maintaining secrecy about, say, radiation levels. Activist researchers who do collect such classified information would be faced with a number of hurdles. It would be difficult to get such material published in a media outlet given the incomprehensibility of the subject to the wider public. Even if the media were interested, they almost certainly would ask the DAE for comments, and the DAE would cast doubt on the researchers' competence, accuse them of undermining the nuclear program and challenge their patriotism. Finally, the DAE would subject the media outlet to a litany of technical balderdash: exposures are ALARA (As Low As Reasonably Achievable); what we had was not an accident but an incident; or the risk of dying of cancer from this dose is much smaller that the probability of dying from a road accident.

Even if a media outlet published a sympathetic account of an activist researcher's findings, the matter would generally end there, as the available structures of governance and decision making do not offer any avenues to challenge the DAE or hold it accountable. This is the third and possibly most important reason for the DAE not being as draconian as it could and for remaining relative lax in dealing with lapses in secrecy. Time and again we have had revelations of radiation leaks, safety errors, cost overruns, and workers subjected to high levels of radiation, but none has forced the DAE to undertake major policy changes. The lack of accountability begins at the highest levels; seldom have any meaningful debates on these issues been held in parliament or in legislative assemblies. Courts have generally favored the DAE in their interpretation. Thus, even lapses in secrecy do not substantially affect the DAE's ability to carry on as it pleases.

Public debates, even if they do influence popular opinion, have not resulted in changes in the DAE's mode of functioning. A rare public debate occurred in the late 1980s over the construction of a nuclear power plant in Kaiga, Karnataka. As part of the debate, a National Workshop on Nuclear Power that was organized in Bangalore in December 1988, involved both officials from the DAE and others from civil society.

An important component of that debate was economics. It turned out that those who argued that nuclear power was uneconomical had done more careful analysis and used better methodology and more reliable data compared to DAE officials.[72] But construction of the Kaiga nuclear power plant continued unaffected.

One of the more amusing reasons given for the DAE's refusal to part with information emerged at the Bangalore workshop when the AEC chairman M. R. Srinivasan said, "We have no objections to giving information. But giving all the information needs a lot of paper which we cannot afford."[73]

The lack of forums for challenging the DAE also means that it is more difficult for potentially embarrassing information to be forced out. In the United States, for example, various flaws in reactor design have come to light during the course of public hearings. A good example is the case of the hearings on the Emergency Core Cooling System (ECCS). The ECCS is designed to inject large amounts of water into the reactor core in the event of an accident that drains out some of the coolant so that the core threatens to overheat and melt. In July 1971 the Union of Concerned Scientists (UCS), a nongovernmental organization, "published a report critical of the ECCS, saying that there was little evidence other than abstract computer simulations that these vital systems would work when needed."[74] The report resulted in the U.S. Atomic Energy Commission (AEC) holding hearings on the ECCS beginning in January 1972.[75] Originally intended to last six weeks, the hearings lasted more than a year and became a forum for the UCS to bring to light intense disagreement within the nuclear establishment about ECCS technology. Much of the disagreement came from engineers within the establishment who supported nuclear power in general but believed that safety was being compromised in the effort to build more reactors quickly. Although, in the end, the hearings did not produce dramatic changes in the U.S. AEC's approach to safety, it did prompt reorganization to provide for greater emphasis on safety research.[76]

Contrast this with the case in India, where again reactors rely on the ECCS as a safety measure.[77] Yet, the Kakrapar-I (KAPS-I) reactor was commissioned without "integrated testing of the ECCS."[78] As in the U.S., the information was leaked by someone within the nuclear establishment, possibly someone involved in the workers' union.[79] The revelation prompted some antinuclear activists, particularly the well-known Gandhian Narayan Desai, to fast and resort to other means of protest. Despite these efforts, the reactor was commissioned without adequate testing.[80] This is one more example of how the DAE was under no pressure to respond to public concerns.

One more question can be asked in this context: Why have there not been many whistle blowers, or truth tellers, as some others have named them. As mentioned earlier, there have been instances of such actions, but that alone cannot suffice to induce more. Rather, what might inspire or discourage others from being whistle blowers is knowledge of what happened to the people who did speak up about hazardous practices. An example concerns Gopalakrishnan, who headed the Atomic Energy

Regulatory Board in the 1990s and produced the report listing 134 safety problems with the DAE's reactors. After some years of criticizing the DAE publicly, in his recent articles Gopalakrishnan has taken a more conciliatory attitude toward the DAE.[81] Even without knowing the reasons for his apparent change of attitude, this shift by a well-known personality like Gopalakrishnan would likely only demoralize anyone within the establishment who might be contemplating taking on the DAE. More demoralizing would be the case of Subbarao discussed earlier. There are also those who have challenged the DAE and, in the process, came to be regarded as cranks.

Conclusions

Pronuclear advocates in India often claim that the May 1998 tests proceeded after a quarter-century of democratic debate on whether to "go nuclear."[82] The extent of democracy in the debate is itself highly debatable. An exit poll conducted during the 1999 national elections found that, despite the massive official propaganda effort extolling the tests, 54 percent of those polled had not even heard of the nuclear tests conducted the previous year.[83] Even among those cognizant of nuclear issues, few feel they have adequate information about the nuclear program. A 1996 poll among elites found that only 13 percent thought that information on nuclear issues was easily available.[84]

It is only partly true that information is unavailable. As we have seen above, the Indian nuclear establishment does not employ secrecy in the all-encompassing totalitarian way that some suggest. The pressures of legitimizing the establishment within a democratic society, the demands posed by other organs of the state such as accounting bureaucracies, as well as jockeying for a place in the partly competitive business of electricity generation does lead to some openness.

At the same time, the information available is very limited and significant pieces of information are denied. This state of affairs has not changed even with the adoption of a Right to Information (RTI) Act. The DAE and its attendant organizations all have prominent pages on their Web sites about how they have been implementing this right. Yet, when we recently sent an RTI petition to IGCAR and BHAVINI—the organizations involved in designing and building the PFBR—asking for data on the estimated costs of various steps of the construction and operation of the reactor, such as the cost of fabricating fuel and of waste management, concerned authorities refused to provide most of the requested information. Their excuse was that Section 8(1)(a) of the RTI Act stipulated that there shall be no obligation to give information, among other things, pertaining to "information, disclosure of which would prejudicially affect the sovereignty and integrity of India, the security, strategic, scientific or economic interests of the State, relation with foreign State or lead to incitement of an offence." Their reply stated: "It is felt that the information you have requested falls within the above definition and, therefore there is no obligation to give the information requested to anyone."[85] How, for example, annual waste management costs would fit the description above is anybody's guess. An appeal under the RTI Act resulted only in a few more numbers and a continued denial of most of the sought-after information.

By and large the information kept secret typically relates to the major, publicly perceived problems with nuclear energy: its connection to nuclear weapons; the possibility of catastrophic accidents with the release of radioactivity into the environment and the consequent effects on public health; the as yet unsolved problem of dealing with nuclear waste that remains radioactive for tens of thousands of years; and the poor economics of nuclear power generation. With the 1998 nuclear tests, the connection with nuclear weapons became a moot point, and the nuclear establishment has begun taking pride in something that was always privately or unofficially acknowledged—the use of facilities that supposedly were intended only for nuclear energy production to aid in the development of nuclear weapons. Ever since those tests, national security has been increasingly invoked as the necessity for imposing secrecy on practically all aspects of the nuclear program.[86]

The virtually impenetrable secrecy of the Department of Atomic Energy and its power to function without any forum where it can be held accountable has resulted in a stunted debate on an issue that can literally be termed a life and death matter. Even without prejudging the results of such a debate, the best interests of democratic decision making will be served by curbing this secrecy and increasing transparency in the Department of Atomic Energy.

Notes

I thank all the people who attended the two intense workshops on Culture, Society, and Nuclear Weapons in South Asia in Amsterdam and Washington, D.C., and offered comments, criticism, and suggestions to improve this paper. In particular, I thank Itty Abraham for pushing me to closely examine the notion of a secret itself and to point out the nuances in the practice of secrecy. I am also grateful to Surendra Gadekar, Sharad Lele, J. Y. Suchitra, and the anonymous reviewer for useful comments and suggestions. I alone am responsible for any remaining deficiencies.

Epigraphs from, respectively, Robertson Davies, *The Manticore* (New York: Penguin Books, 1972), p. 114; Howard Morland, "The H-Bomb Secret," *The Progressive*, November, 3–12, 1979; and Santimoy Chatterjee and Jyotirmoy Gupta, eds., *Meghnad Saha in Parliament* (Calcutta: Asiatic Society, 1993), p. 201; cited in Ravi Shukla, "Technology and Democracy: Exploring the Nuclear Energy Debate in India," M.Phil. diss., Jawaharlal Nehru University, 2006.

1. In India's case, it has been argued that this opacity was the outcome of "indecision at the highest levels of political decision-making" (Itty Abraham, "The Ambivalence of Nuclear Histories," *Osiris* 21 [2006]: 49–65). Others, like former national security adviser Satish Chandra, have argued that as "a new Nuclear Weapons State, [India needs] to have opacity." See Sheela Bhatt, "World doesn't know how many bombs India has": Interview with former deputy national security adviser Satish Chandra, Rediff, August 11, 2005.

2. Avner Cohen, *Israel and the Bomb* (New York: Columbia University Press, 1998), p. ix.

3. Raj Chengappa, *Weapons of Peace: The Secret Story of India's Quest to Be a Nuclear Power* (New Delhi: Harper Collins, 2000), p. xv (my emphasis).

4. If the commitments India made as part of the Indo-U.S. agreement of July 2005 to separate its civilian and military nuclear program were implemented strictly and comprehensively, then this situation may change, though not completely. There seems, however, to be substantial resistance to this separation, or at least efforts to minimize it, from many within the DAE.

5. One of the double standards in Indian, and even global, discourse about nuclear activities in South Asia is that any secrecy on the part of Pakistan regarding its nuclear activities is portrayed as a sign of the weakness of its democracy and institutions, as well as a general lack of accountability, but, in the view of Sankaran Krishna, the author of chapter 4 in this volume, such questions are seldom raised about India (personal e-mail to this author, 2005).

6. Interview with V. K. Chaturvedi, November 25, 2000.

7. Such calculations were presented by Zia Mian, A. H. Nayyar, R. Rajaraman, and M.V. Ramana in their report "Fissile Materials in South Asia: The Implications of the U.S.-India Nuclear Deal," International Panel on Fissile Materials, 2006.

8. I thank Itty Abraham for emphasizing this.

9. The denial of information is justified usually on the grounds of national security. But although national security is the stated reason, a multiplicity of reasons could cause such denial of information, for example, the arrogance of people on the inside, who believe "they know best," and the resistance to opening up nuclear policy making to public debate or questioning. At an arms control meeting in 2004, a former head of the Indian Air Force said, quite bluntly, that he would not answer any questions relating to the nuclear arsenal because he felt that what he said could lead to a public debate about the characteristics of the arsenal. This was, in his opinion, undesirable because the subject should only be debated by "knowledgeable people" within the establishment. At the same time he revealed, indeed boasted, that he had recommended air attacks on Pakistani supply lines and other facilities across the border during the Kargil War.

10. Jayanthi Natarajan, "Classified Dangerous," *New Sunday Express,* July 29, 2003.

11. Shyam Bhatia, *India's Nuclear Bomb* (New Delhi: Vikas, 1979).

12. Jawaharlal Nehru, Letter to C. D. Deshmukh, June 23, 1952, in *Selected Works of Jawaharlal Nehru,* ed. S. Gopal, 2nd series, Vol. 18 (Delhi: Jawaharlal Nehru Memorial Fund, 1996); cited in Robert Anderson, "Why Lord Buddha Smiled," *Times Literary Supplement,* January 8, 1999, 26.

13. Max Weber, "Bureaucracy," in *Essays in Sociology,* ed. H. Gerth and C. Wright Mills (New York: Oxford University Press, 1975).

14. CAG, "Report by the Comptroller and Auditor General of India" (New Delhi: Comptroller and Auditor General of India, 1994).

15. CAG, "Report by the Comptroller and Auditor General of India" (New Delhi, Comptroller and Auditor General of India, 2005), p. 21.

16. The Official Secrets Act has been used extensively to indict many people on charges of spying. See, for example, Iftikhar Gilani, "Inside Tihar Jail: 'Nothing Official or Secret,'" Confederation of Human Rights Organizations. Available at http://www.humanrightskerala.com/modules.php?op=modload&name=News&file=article&sid=604 (accessed September 20 2005).

17. T. S. Gopi Rethinaraj, "ATV: All at Sea before It Hits the Water," *Jane's Intelligence Review* (1998): 31–35.

18. M. S. Siddhu, "Victimised by the Official Secrets Act: The story of Dr. B. K. Subbarao," *Manushi* 108 (1998).

19. Rupa Chinai, "Radioactive Leakage at the Bhabha Atomic Research Centre," *Sunday Observer*, September 6, 1992.

20. Surendra Gadekar, personal e-mail to this author.

21. M. V. Ramana, "The Question of Nuclear Yield," *Frontline,* January 21, 2000, pp. 94–96.

22. R. B. Attarde, V. K. Shukla, D. A. R. Babu, V. V. Kulkarni, and Anil Kakodkar, "Fission Signatures of Tests on Sub-kiloton Devices," *BARC Newsletter*, September 1999.

23. R. Chidambaram and Raja Ramanna, "Some Studies on India's Peaceful Nuclear Explosion Experiment," in *Peaceful Nuclear Explosions IV: Proceedings of a Technical Committee on the Peaceful Uses of Nuclear Energy* (International Atomic Energy Agency, 1975), pp. 421–436.

24. I. S. Bhat, M. A. R. Iyengar, R. P. Gurg, S. Krishnamony, and K. C. Pillai, "Environmental Impact of PHWR Type Power Stations—India Experience," In *Conference Proceedings on Small and Medium Scale Nuclear Reactors*, ed. M. A. R. Iyengar (New Delhi, 1991), pp. 532–539; and E. Chandrasekharan, V. Rajagopal, M. A. R. Iyengar, and S. Venkatraman, "Dose Estimates Due to Argon-41 in the Kalpakkam Environment," *Bulletin of Radiation Protection* 15, no. 1 (1992): 18–19.

25. M. V. Ramana, "Scientists, Nuclear Weapons, and the Peace Movement," *Economic and Political Weekly* 39, no. 46–47 (2004): 5013–5016.

26. Praful Bidwai, "The Ethics of the Right to Information," in *Nuclear Energy and Public Safety*, ed. Vinod Gaur, pp. 96–101 (New Delhi: INTACH, 1996).

27. Cited in George Perkovich, *India's Nuclear Bomb: The Impact on Global Proliferation* (Berkeley: University of California Press, 1999), p. 216.

28. M. V. Ramana, Antonette D'Sa, and Amulya K. N. Reddy, "Economics of Nuclear Power from Heavy Water Reactors," *Economic and Political Weekly* 40, no. 17 (2005): 1763–1773.

29. On the media coverage of the 1998 nuclear tests, see J. Sri Raman, "The Climber's Case," in *The Media Bomb* (Chennai: Journalists Against Nuclear Weapons); reprinted in Smitu Kothari and Zia Mian, *Out of the Nuclear Shadow* (Delhi, London, and New York: Lokayan; Rainbow Publishers, Zed Books, 1998).

30. K. S. Jayaraman, "The 'Leak' That Leaked to the Press," *Science Today,* May 1980.

31. S. Gopi and T. Rethinaraj, "Tritium Breakthrough Brings India Closer to an H-Bomb Arsenal," *Jane's Intelligence Review* (1998): 29–31.

32. Buddhi Kota Subbarao, "India's Nuclear Prowess: False Claims and Tragic Truths," *Manushi* (1998): 109.

33. Amulya Reddy, "Designing Nuclear Weapons: The Moral Question," in *Prisoners of the Nuclear Dream*, ed. M. V. Ramana and C. Rammanohar Reddy, pp. 189–205 (New Delhi: Orient Longman, 2003).

34. Itty Abraham, *The Making of the Indian Atomic Bomb: Science, Secrecy, and the Postcolonial State*. New York: Zed Books, 1998; Perkovich, *India's Nuclear Bomb*.

35. H. J. Bhabha and N. B. Prasad, "A Study of the Contribution of Atomic Energy to a Power Programme in India," in *Second United Nations International Conference on the Peaceful Uses of Atomic Energy* 1:89–101, Geneva.

36. A single 220-MW reactor working at 100 percent efficiency (capacity factor) would take more than twenty-five years to produce sufficient plutonium for the initial core and the first couple of reloads needed for the Prototype Fast Breeder Reactor (PFBR) being constructed at Kalpakkam. After that, the breeder reactor would, in principle, become self-sufficient in plutonium.

37. Cohen, *Israel and the Bomb,* p. 59.

38. Ruth Fawcett, *Nuclear Pursuits: The Scientific Biography of Wilfrid Bennett Lewis* (Montreal: McGill-Queen's University Press, 1994), pp. 110–114.

39. Chengappa, *Weapons of Peace*, p. 85.

40. In South Africa, too, the effort to build nuclear weapons had its origins in the 1960s under the auspices of a PNE program (David Albright, "South Africa and the Affordable Bomb," *Bulletin of the Atomic Scientists* (1994): 37–47.

41. The first reaction to the accident by Soviet authorities was to impose enormous secrecy on the event itself and its fallout (Grigoriæi Medvedev and Andreæi Sakharov, *The Truth about Chernobyl* [New York: Basic Books, 1991]). Decree U-2617 C of the Soviet Health Ministry, issued June 27, 1986, states: "Secrecy is imposed upon any data concerning the accident. Secrecy is imposed upon the results of treatments for sicknesses. Secrecy is imposed upon the data about the extent of radioactive contamination of personnel who took part in the liquidation of the accident at the Chernobyl atomic power plant" (Ute Watermann, "The Consequences of Chernobyl: Truth's Uphill Battle," in *Chernobyl Years After—Myth and Truth,* ed. A. Yablokov, R. Braun, and U. Watermann [Muenster: Agenda Verlag, 2006]).

42. Pradip Datta, "Safety in Indian Nuclear Plants: Assurance Is Not Enough," *Ananda Bazar Patrika,* November 2, 1999.

43. Manish Tiwari, "A Deformed Existence," *Down to Earth,* June 15, 1999.

44. Subbarao, "India's Nuclear Prowess."

45. Ibid.

46. Ibid.

47. Ibid.

48. Sanjay Parikh, "Nuclear Options: Is Secrecy Safe for Environment and Human Health," *Lawyers Collective,* August 5–10, 2004.

49. R. Venkatraman, "Nuclear Veil in Place with Rights Rider," *The Telegraph,* January 7, 2004.

50. J. Venkatesan, "Information on Nuclear Installations Cannot Be Made Public: Supreme Court," *The Hindu,* January 7, 2004.

51. Venkatraman, "Nuclear Veil in Place with Rights Rider."

52. A. Gopalakrishnan, "Evolution of the Indian Nuclear Power Program," *Annual Review of Energy and Environment* 27 (2002): 369–395.

53. A. R. Sundararajan, "Emergency Preparedness in the Indian Nuclear Power Stations," *Risk Analysis* 11, no. 3 (1991): 389–391.

54. The sociologist Lee Clarke has coined the term "Fantasy Documents" for such pieces of work. These, according to Clarke, "are rhetorical instruments that have political utility in reducing uncertainty for organizations and experts" (*Mission Improbable: Using Fantasy Documents to Tame Disaster* (Chicago: University of Chicago Press, 1999).

55. "The Seminar That Never Was," *Indian Express,* December 15, 1985.

56. R. Chidambaram, "India Is Not Isolated," interview with AEC Chief R. Chidambaram, *Frontline,* November 29, 1996, pp. 86–89.

57. "Bhabha Atomic Research Centre Yet to Decide on Nuclear Waste Dump," *The Hindu,* August 27, 1999.

58. On the debate in 1964, see, for example, Perkovich, *India's Nuclear Bomb,* pp. 60–85.

59. J. P. Jain, ed., *Nuclear India* (New Delhi: Radiant, 1974).

60. Bhabha and Prasad, "A Study of the Contribution of Atomic Energy to a Power Programme in India," in *First United Nations International Conference on the Peaceful Uses of Atomic Energy* 1:89–101 (emphases added).

61. M. R. Srinivasan, "The Indian Nuclear Power Programme," in *Indo-French Seminar on Nuclear Energy,* pp. 9–21. Bombay: Department of Atomic Energy, 1985.

62. A. K. Nema, "Nuclear Generation Cost in India," *Nu-Power* 13, no. 1 (1999).

63. Ramana, D'Sa, and Reddy, "Economics of Nuclear Power from Heavy Water Reactors," pp. 1763–1773.

64. "Report by the Comptroller and Auditor General of India," Comptroller and Auditor General, Government of India, 1994.

65. Langdon Winner, *The Whale and the Reactor: A Search for Limits in an Age of High Technology* (Chicago: University of Chicago Press, 1986), p. 175.

66. U. C. Mishra and S. Krishnamony, "Radiation Protection and Environmental Impact from Nuclear Power Plants," *Indian Journal of Power and River Valley Development: Development in Nuclear Power Generation* 44 (1994): 332–346.

67. S. Anand, "India's Worst Radiation Accident," *Outlook*, July 28, 2003, pp. 18–20.

68. T. S. Gopi Rethinaraj, "In the Comfort of Secrecy," *Bulletin of the Atomic Scientists* 55, no. 6 (1999): 52–57.

69. Bharat Karnad, "Remember the Tritium," *Deccan Chronicle*, August 7, 2005.

70. Surendra Gadekar, personal e-mail to this author.

71. In a recent newspaper article, for example, Srinivasan argues that "the DAE must adopt an enlightened policy of keeping the public informed at all times about safety aspects of its installations" (M. R. Srinivasan, "The Fast Breeder Reactor," *The Hindu*, September 17, 2003.

72. This was later published as Amulya K. N. Reddy, "Is Power from Nuclear Plants Necessary? Is It Economical?" in *National Workshop on Nuclear Power Plants with Specific Reference to Kaiga* (Bangalore: DST, 1988); and elaborated in *Seminar*, no. 370 (1988): 18–26.

73. Vinod Gaur, ed., *Nuclear Power and Public Safety* (New Delhi: INTACH, 1996), p. 93.

74. James M. Jasper. "Nuclear Politics: Energy and the State in the United States, Sweden and France" (Princeton, N.J.: Princeton University Press, 1990), p. 11.

75. The AEC held such centralized hearings primarily to avoid multiple repetitions of the arguments regarding the safety of the ECCS that utilities around the country would have to make as part of their licensing procedures.

76. Joel Primack and Frank von Hippel, *Advice and Dissent: Scientists in the Political Arena* (New York: Basic Books, 1974), pp. 230–231.

77. However, four of the older reactors, RAPS-I and II at Rajasthan and MAPS-I and II at Kalpakkam, operate with an inadequate, obsolete, and unsafe ECCS (A. Gopalakrishnan, "Issues of Nuclear Safety," *Frontline*, March 13–26, 1999.

78. Rupa Chinai, "Critical Safety Checks Not Being Observed in KAPP-1," *Sunday Observer*, July 26, 1992.

79. On many occasions unions have been the source of information about safety- and health-related violations in nuclear facilities.

80. It is not clear whether the reactor was commissioned without any testing or that tests were conducted but the ECCS did not function as designed. A likely reason for the haste in commissioning was that P. K. Iyengar, then head of the DAE, was due to retire and thought that bringing KAPS online might help him get an extension of his term. His hope did not materialize (Surendra Gadekar, telephone interview by author, March 15, 2005).

81. For example, see Gopalakrishnan, "Evolution of the Indian Nuclear Power Program," pp. 369–395.

82. Brahma Chellaney, "Gatecrashing the Nuclear Club," *Nature*, September 9, 1999.

83. Yogendra Yadav, Oliver Heath, and Anindya Saha, "Issues and the Verdict," *Frontline*, November 13, 1999.

84. David Cortright and Amitabh Mattoo, eds., *India and the Bomb: Public Opinion and Nuclear Options* (Notre Dame, Ind.: University of Notre Dame Press, 1996).

85. Letter dated August 4, 2006, from A. Ananth, BHAVINI, to J. Y. Suchitra.

86. National security has been the justification for secrecy even earlier. Its invocation, however, especially even by people and institutions not necessarily connected with the nuclear establishment—the Supreme Court, for example (see section on Secrecy in Safety and Health), certainly seems to have increased.

4

THE SOCIAL LIFE OF A BOMB: INDIA AND THE ONTOLOGY OF AN "OVERPOPULATED" SOCIETY

Sankaran Krishna

We want the Nobel Prize. This is our only goal.

Professor Sanjay Dhande, Director, IIT-Kanpur

We are a nation of nearly a billion people. In development terms, we rank No. 138 out of the 175 countries listed in the UNDP's Human Development Index. More than 400 million of our people are illiterate and live in absolute poverty, over 600 million lack even basic sanitation and about 200 million have no safe drinking water. A nuclear bomb isn't going to improve any of this. . . . India's nuclear bomb is the final act of betrayal by a ruling class that has failed its people. However many garlands we heap on our scientists, however many medals we pin to their chests, the truth is that it's far easier to make a bomb than to educate 400 million people.

Arundhati Roy, "The End of Imagination"

In the literature about the Indian nuclear tests of 1974 and 1998, analyses that give priority to security threats, alliance politics, arms races, and related explanations from within the domains of security studies and international relations have jostled with others who accord primacy to the anxieties and insecurities of a postcolonial middle class that is tired of being ignored and belittled in the world comity of nations. One might describe this as a debate between security-centered explanations versus status-centered explanations for the Indian decision to nuclearize. While the former genre of explanation often has a difficult time squaring up to the fact that there were no imminent security threats from familiar regional adversaries—China and Pakistan—nor was there any dramatic deterioration in a wider geopolitical sense to which either set of tests could be seen as a response, the latter explanations are inherently "soft," making it difficult to establish with any finality the causal links between a perceived sense of ressentiment and the decision to test the bombs. The differing emphases in these two modes of explanation for Indian nuclearism will likely endure for some time, as they represent fairly divergent epistemologies in understanding social reality.[1] This paper locates itself within the latter genre of explanations for Indian nuclearism. Its focus is trained on the distinctive evolution of a colonial middle class, its science and insecurities, as the primary factors in the emergence of India as a nuclear weapons state in contemporary times.

A significant number of Indians—both within and outside the governing elites—see the bomb redressing a disjuncture between India's actual status in the comity of the world's nations and its desired or deserved status. Critical to this disjunction is the idea that India is an overpopulated society. Many middle-class Indians believe that they are not given due respect and appreciation for what they have accomplished, because their attainments are literally drowned in a sea of humanity. The bomb, therefore, is not only an entity within an economy of threats, security concerns, alliances, and arms races; it also inhabits another realm, one embedded in the desire for respect, status, attention, and appreciation. An analysis of the bomb thus demands a wider focus that extends beyond conventional security studies or international relations and looks at the multiple meanings of the bomb as well as the many anxieties it seeks to quell.

I undertake this analysis through three overlapping but analytically distinct sections. I begin by outlining theoretical literatures on the social nature of things as a means to understand the global semiotic economy in which the Indian nuclear tests of 1974 and 1998 make sense. I next examine the special significance of science in a colonial context and its entailments for a postcolonial society, especially the need for spectacular state effects through science. I then turn to the distinctive characteristics of the Indian middle class and its relationship to both the political realm and the larger population that constitutes the "silent nation." I show how the push for nuclearization has a complex and disturbing relationship to electoral democracy, the changing nature of access to political power in recent decades, and middle-class attitudes toward the people and their perceived superfluity in an era of economic liberalization. Overall,

I argue that the desire of the Indian middle class to occupy center stage in a world of nations is inseparable from its desire to be seen as developed or advanced, and to be rid of a large section of fellow citizens viewed as irrelevant and an impediment to its own enjoyment of the nation.

Objects as Incarnated Signs

The title of this essay is clearly inspired by Arjun Appadurai's work on the semiotics of commodities and consumption.[2] Following a long and distinguished tradition within cultural anthropology, Appadurai argues that in assessing the value of commodities we have been overly enamored of their use or functionality, and have ignored or underestimated the role of exchange, social interactions, fetishization, thwarted desire, and the symbolic realm in general. He reminds us that a commodity should be seen more as a social signifier whose possession or lack stratifies individuals, classes, and cultures as it circulates through a space. Indeed, any rigid separation between use- and exchange-values of commodities is difficult to sustain as they leak into one another at the very outset of their definitions. In other words, the status of things is determined as much in a social and symbolic economy of signs, signifiers, and desires as in their putative use-value defined narrowly in terms of their functions. In a significant passage, Appadurai notes,

> Economic exchange creates value. Value is embodied in commodities that are exchanged. Focusing on the things that are exchanged, rather than simply on the forms or functions of exchange, makes it possible to argue that what creates the link between exchange and value is *politics,* construed broadly. This argument . . . justifies the conceit that commodities, like persons, have social lives.[3]

Besides emphasizing social exchange as critical to the determination of value, and the centrality of politics to this process, Appadurai's work also has an insightful discussion of a special section of commodities, namely, luxury goods. Goods such as these are distinguished even more by their distance from common utility, and they are freighted with an excess of social significance. I suggest that nuclear weapons might be regarded as exemplars of this special class of luxury goods in an international symbolic and security economy. Appadurai outlines a list of attributes of such luxury goods:

(1) *restriction,* either by price or by law, to elites;

(2) *complexity of acquisition,* which may or may not be a function of real "scarcity";

(3) *semiotic virtuosity,* that is, the capacity to signal fairly complex social messages (as do pepper in cuisine, silk in dress, jewels in adornment, and relics in worship);

(4) *specialized knowledge* as a prerequisite for their "appropriate" consumption, that is, regulation by fashion; and

(5) a high degree of *linkage* of their consumption *to body, person, and personality.*[4]

These attributes of luxury goods whose purpose is primarily "rhetorical and social" is extraordinarily appropriate in a discussion of the global system of signs that has governed nuclear weapons since 1945. The nonproliferation regime that has tried to control nuclear weapons can easily be seen as an effort of a small handful of nuclear powers to deny the same to latecomers. The operative concepts here are "restriction" and "complexity of acquisition," both of which endow the Indian nuclear pursuit with a scientific and social significance it would otherwise lack. What imputes any scientific value or salience to the bomb in the postwar world is the difficulty of acquiring the fissile materials and some of the necessary technological nuts-and-bolts—an artificial scarcity engineered by the nuclear haves through the Nuclear Nonproliferation Treaty and the sanctions consequent upon its violation.

The clearly neocolonial character of an international regime obsessed with horizontal proliferation (to Third World societies) and blind to vertical proliferation (within the members of the nuclear weapons club) generates a field of value in which India's nonparticipation can be narrated as anticolonial resistance and the assertion of national sovereignty.[5] Moreover, the restrictions on the mobility of materials and technology allow Indian scientists and the political establishment to portray this reinvention of a sixty-year-old wheel as pathbreaking, an insignia of scientific originality and acumen. As the nuclear scientist and peace activist Pervez Hoodbhoy demonstrates in his careful study, while the nuclear tests in India and Pakistan reflect at most a certain degree of engineering or organizational skills on the part of certain state bureaucracies, they have "little to do with cutting-edge science, original scientific research, high technology, or the country's general scientific progress. . . . [N]uclear weapons and missile development is today a second-rate science. The undeniable fact is that the technology of nuclear bombs belongs to the 1940s, and the furious pace of science makes that ancient history."[6]

The international nonproliferation regime further creates a theater in which the outsmarting of Western intelligence agencies' surveillance and monitoring of the Indian nuclear establishment becomes an occasion of rejoicing and pride. The tests of May 1998 gained salience and value in part because, on at least one prior occasion (when Narasimha Rao was prime minister in the first half of the 1990s), everything was supposedly in place and ready to go when American detection and pressure forced the Indian regime to abort the tests. Intermixed here is a sense of achievement at having outfoxed the Americans, along with pleasure in the fact that one is considered worthy of surveillance rather than being, as it were, "off the radar."

In the short-lived euphoria following the tests of May 1998, issues of national masculinity, self-esteem, and anger over Western indifference were prominent. As Bal Thackeray, leader of the Shiv Sena Party (a right-wing Hindu fundamentalist organization based largely in the western state of Maharashtra, and an ally of the Bharatiya Janata

Party), famously declared: the bombs had proved that "we are not eunuchs anymore." There were many such statements that saw the tests as a counter to self-perceptions of Indian effeminacy, weakness, and a historical record of repeated subjugations.[7] They show the constant juxtaposition of insecurities about national masculinity—as indexed in statements such as Thackeray's above—and the hope that nuclear weapons would conclusively demonstrate their irrelevance. The bomb's literal links to the body and personality of the desired hyper-masculine Indian is palpable in such discourses.

This perceived Western indifference, if not contempt, toward India is one of the most consistent themes underlying middle-class support for the tests, and for India's nuclear program in general. The feeling was that this would awaken the West to India's development, her successes and accomplishments, and her real status as a world power—and counter a media obsession with rail accidents, natural disasters, poverty, dowry deaths, and the caste system. Achievement of "great power status," membership in the UN Security Council, recognition as a "global player"—these are repeatedly touted as the desired outcome of, and reason for, the tests of 1998.[8] The bomb has a polyvalent quality in such discourses—what Appadurai calls "semiotic virtuosity"—wherein it stands for a number of things simultaneously. It is regarded as a sign of India's advancement and equality with the Western developed countries, a negation of stereotypes about the effeminacy and historical weakness of the nation, and an argument against the mimetic and derivative nature of its science and technology.

Inescapable in these links between the bomb and a refashioned national self is the element of fetishization. Evoking the cargo cults of South Seas islanders in the aftermath of their "discovery" by the Western nations in earlier centuries, Indian supporters of the bomb seemed to believe that its mere acquisition would magically bring all the other accompaniments of "development"—affluence, status, recognition, and, most of all, respect. The sheer possession of something owned by the West is seen as synonymous with the re-creation of the structures of "advanced" production, lifestyles, histories, and societal contexts within domestic space. The talismanic appropriation of Western military uniforms, spent bullets, decrepit weapons, discarded artifacts, and their revalorization as symbols of status and substance within South Pacific societies, is not that different from the ways in which a poor and underdeveloped country such as India seeks to recalibrate its position in the global order of nations through detonating a few bombs.

The bomb continues to be seen as an instant antidote to a certain narration of history in which India was a supine and pacific victim of invaders from the outside, a long-suffering civilization that had now finally asserted its manhood. The historical veracity of this narrative of victimhood and the image of a peaceful civilization is rarely questioned within middle-class India; indeed, it is one of the enduring staples of journalistic and historical narrations of the nation.[9] Such a self-understanding is something which India's Dalits and Adivasis, for all too long the victims of development, as well as its smaller neighboring countries, would find ludicrous. That there is something truly pathetic in longing for Western attention, and that attention garnered under such circumstances could not possibly be authentic or real, seems not to matter in the least. In a concise summary of the bomb as fetish, Amitav Ghosh notes that "it is a great vessel filled with all the unfulfilled aspirations and thwarted dreams of the last fifty years—ambitions of a larger and grander place in the world, for a rearrangement of global power, for a rebirth of national pride."[10]

Underlying the adulation of the scientific enclave following the 1974 and 1998 tests is a theme elaborated in the rest of this essay: in the view of significant sections of the middle class, Indians excel when they are insulated from the corrosive influence of politics, and when merit is given its deserved rewards. The figure of the scientist becomes merit incarnate, and the bomb represents the achievement of a mind unburdened of political interference. The politicians standing alongside the scientists around the craters in Pokhran gain symbolic capital through a strange and ironic reversal: they are effective politicians because, under their regime, India's nuclear scientists have the necessary insulation, secrecy, and autonomy from politics itself in order to succeed. In other words, the political regime seeks legitimization for having acted in ways that are apolitical—or, more precisely, above politics. The very brevity and matter-of-factness that characterized Vajpayee's announcement of the successful May 1998 tests, the careful choice of words presenting it as a national achievement of "our scientists"—rather than a partisan one—were all calibrated to gain political capital from an event coded as simultaneously anti- and supra-political.[11]

India was the 6th nation in the world to conduct a nuclear test, and is currently the 127th nation (out of 177) in the latest World Bank's Human Development Index, flanked by countries like Botswana and Namibia, and behind Gabon and Mongolia. The symbolic field of value created by the nonproliferation regime allows Indian elites to offer the "achievement" of nuclear power status as a response to the abysmal state of development indicated by such rankings. Some of the questions that are inadequately entertained within Indian media coverage and debates on the bomb are these: If so many other countries have the technical and scientific capacity to test and acquire weapons (as noted by Hoodbhoy above), why have they chosen not to do so? Why do so many ex-colonial countries, as sensitive as India to the issues of neocolonialism, not find it problematic to sign the nonproliferation treaty? If this truly is a sign of a country's scientific acumen and talent, what does Pakistan's emulation of India's tests a few weeks later in 1998 tell us, especially given the extremely poor state of scientific institutions in that country? Could the obsession of some in India to acquire nuclear weapons not be read as a sign of continued colonization rather than as the means to escape that status? Why must we seek to be equal to the best in the art of killing large numbers of people—and not similarly prioritize feeding, clothing, housing, and educating them? The vehement anger and sexist disparaging that the author Arundhati Roy faced for posing a version of such questions in her widely publicized essay are indicative of a postcolonial insecurity that deserves more inquiry.[12]

Science and Postcolonial Space: The Politics of the Spectacular

In his first book, Ashis Nandy examined the lives and careers of the Bengali scientist Jagadish Chandra Bose (1858–1937) and the Tamil mathematician Srinivasa Ramanujan (1887–1920).[13] In an insightful analysis of the extent to which familiarity with Western education, culture, and civilization simultaneously enabled and enfeebled the creativity of the two men, Nandy argues that Ramanujan's self-confidence, in contrast to Bose's insecurities, arose precisely from the fact that the former was less versed in discourses of colonialism and nationalism, less familiar with Western traditions of inquiry and scientific legitimating processes, and, to put it differently, less obsessed about decolonization and his own originality. Ramanujan's virtually autodidactic learning, his very Hindu religiosity, and his immersion in a highly orthodox Tamil Brahmin household left him relatively less concerned about his place in a "universal" (read: Western) hall of scientific fame. He was not as concerned as Bose about nationalism or disproving notions of Western superiority and the inferiority of "Indian" science. Ramanujan's un-self-reflective location of his own genius in visions and mystic relations with God made his introspections orthogonal to a colonial intelligentsia's usual preoccupations about mimesis and originality that could and did paralyze someone such as Bose. Nandy outlined the contrast between the two men:

> Bose's science, on the other hand, was coloured by the psychology of subjecthood and feelings of personal inadequacy. It allowed him neither enough autonomy nor flexibility. Unlike the European scientists of the age of faith and other Indian scientists more immersed in traditions, Bose in his science could not take advantage of the integrative strengths and range of his personality. . . . This was unavoidable. For the very sensitivities that made Bose creative also made him sensitive to his colonial status. If his nationalism was a straitjacket, it was one that he could not help wearing. *One could even speculate that it was this sensitivity to issues of dominance and submission, and not any actual interference in the processes of research, which was often the main contribution of colonialism to intellectual decay.* . . . Bose's modern nationalism bound him too closely to the West, both in admiration and in hatred.[14]

Characteristically, Nandy privileges the psychological over the material in assessing the impact of Western colonialism on Indian science. The combination of admiration of the West and hatred, which he discerns in Bose and rightly regards as a straitjacket, would have a profound impact on the evolution of both science and the middle class in the post-independent period.

During the colonial period modern science served as a critical differentiating principle between rulers and ruled.[15] Western mastery over space and time—revealed by the railway, the telegraph, the bridges that spanned raging rivers and the dams that controlled them, trigonometric land surveys, archaeological excavations, epidemiology, immunization, and multiple other scientific achievements—stood in contrast to native awe and surrender to the forces of nature.[16] The "civilizing project" that redeemed colonialism was predicated on the assumption that science (emergent from Western rationality) and education would eventually awaken the native from his sloth and slumber.

As Gyan Prakash notes, however, colonial science was always underlain by an important contradiction.[17] On the one hand, the rationality and grandeur of colonial science presumed an intelligent and discerning native capable of comprehending the magnitude of what was being achieved. On the other, colonial rule, based as it was on a notion of irreversible civilizational superiority over the native, also had to believe that he was irremediably unscientific and irrational, and hence incapable of serving as the discerning audience that could offer any admiration that was genuine. It was the native's inherent inferiority that necessitated colonial rule in the first place and justified its continuance in the second. Among other things, this contradiction or paradox resulted in a translation of colonial science into the realm of the spectacular, critical to efforts at legitimating alien rule in a largely illiterate society. Further, it resulted in science becoming a definitive icon of power, wealth, intelligence, success, and rank. Science was not only statist from its very inception—in the sense that science in the colonies was primarily conducted under state auspices—but it was statist in that it was always also about legitimating (alien) political rule. Finally, the dissemination of science through society aimed not so much at the molecular transformation of ways of thinking among the "population" (itself a novel category at this time, as Foucault reminds us), the inculcation of scientific rationality or scientific temper, but focused on spectacular demonstrations of what one might term "state effects," that is, the legitimation of the state through the staging of scientific spectacles or events under its auspices. This cluster of attributes that characterized Indian science during the colonial period—its spectacular quality, its iconic status, its statism, and its intimate relationship to the production of state effects—would remain intact to a substantial degree after independence.

The democratization of science that had occurred in the West—with mass literacy, free public education, rising standards of living across all classes—bypassed colonial and independent India. In the well-worn cliché of science studies, science in the West owed more to the steam engine than the steam engine owed to science. What is conveyed by this cliché (alongside the old saw about necessity being the mother of invention) is that many an early inventor was not a scientist but rather a craftsman, an artisan, an improviser or innovator trying to find a way around a practical problem in production in an industrializing society. The contrast with the emergence of science in a place like colonial India could not be more profound. The social base of the scientist here was overwhelmingly the literati, a group quite unaccustomed to working with their hands. Science emerged in a colonial political-economy trapped in technological stagnation, deindustrialization, and the freezing of social relations in the agricultural sector that produced and further aggravated the idea of a "surplus" population. The state was focused on extraction of land revenue, maintenance of a captive market for

British manufactured goods and raw material sources, and maintenance of law and order (defined minimally as the protection of settler property and lives). The linkages between science, society, and economy that characterized the early industrializers were not merely absent in India but were systematically distorted and extraverted into a classically colonial pattern, to use terms from a now unfashionable political economy literature.

Just as Hamza Alavi spoke of the overdeveloped state as a postcolonial legacy in South Asia,[18] one can similarly talk of a distorted and "overdeveloped" science there. The problems that Indian science set for itself reflected metropolitan necessities rather than homegrown ones. It is not that there was no awareness or resistance to such a form of intellectual colonization; rather, as in other realms, it was colonialism's ability to present a certain understanding of the present and a certain desired vision of the future as a *universal common sense* (despite its provincially Western provenance) that has proved to be so enduring and difficult to overturn. To use Partha Chatterjee's framework, Indian science often constituted a form of resistance at the level of the problematic ("we, too, can do what you have done") but seemed incapable of conceptualizing an alternative at the level of the thematic of a discourse of nationalism ("we can do what we need to do for ourselves").[19] The forgotten Luddites of alternative sciences in India—the Kumarappas, Gandhis, and others who argued for technologies appropriate to one of the most labor-abundant economies in the world—testify to the degree to which Indian science responded to alien puzzles and extraneous material requirements.

Given the very limited ambit of formal education (at independence about 15% of the population was literate), proficiency in science, and fluency in the English language more generally, served as the marker separating the native middle classes from the people. Sections of the native middle classes took to science in the late nineteenth century, and their enthusiasm for the scientific method, deductive logic, positivism, and other accompaniments of the modern temper are indexed in journals, literature, scientific societies, social movements, religious reformations, and, increasingly, in domestically owned and operated textile mills, chemical plants, research laboratories, locomotive factories, steel mills, and the like. Science and nationalist politics came to be intertwined from the outset, as scientific acumen was one of the prominent signifiers of readiness for self-government and independence. As I have argued elsewhere, for Indian nationalists, science was the definitive marker separating the colonizer from the colonized, and also the source of redemption for the colony once independence had been achieved. Nehru, for example, systematically sets aside one reason after another for the conquest of India by the West and ultimately settles on two: first, India's political disunity and disintegration following the last of the great Mughal emperors; and, second, the fact that modern science and reason emerged initially in the West, allowing it to qualitatively distance itself from the rest of the world, and indeed colonize it. It was the twinning of these two historical events that explained the meteoric rise of England in the centuries after the Industrial Revolution, and the concomitant fall of a once-rich culture and civilization such as India.[20]

Science by the late colonial period was therefore burdened with an unrealistic set of expectations. It came to be regarded as the means by which India would reverse centuries of underdevelopment and speedily gain its rightful place in the comity of nations. As Prakash notes, "Introduced as a code of alien power and domesticated as an element of elite nationalism, science has always been asked to accomplish a great deal—to authorize an enormous leap into modernity, and anchor the entire edifice of modern culture, identity, politics, and economy."[21] In some senses, this was the temper and spirit of the early decades after independence—the Nehru years—as India sought to transform itself into a modern society through science, planning, and a state-led public sector. Yet, given the sharp disjunction between the material culture of an "overpopulated" and largely poor society, and a scientific culture that had emerged in the shadow of a Western, colonial form of education confined to the literati, this transformation was always going to be very difficult.

What emerged was one of the most dedicated and ascetic attempts by an upper-caste elite to develop an entire country while bypassing the social. The focus on science, planning, a controlled industrial state-sector (financed largely through external aid), and the relative neglect of the agrarian sector (in terms both of state investment and effective land reforms) obviated the need to encounter the domestic social too closely. The Nehruvian state was a quintessentially pedagogical state that spoke at and for the nation—it rarely ever spoke to it or with it.[22] This was a form of development that abhorred contact with the masses, the soil, and the tools and machinery necessary for development, while emphasizing rhetorical exhortations, elegant planning models, and nuanced argumentation. India remains one of the most assiduous efforts to theorize one's way to development.

The specific characteristics of Indian science—its limited ambit within society, its often derivative and extraverted character, its emphasis on spectacular effects—were fundamentally at odds with expectations that it would be the redemptive source of widespread development. The failure of the postcolonial nation to come into its own—in the sense of sufficient numbers of peoples seeing a tangible improvement in their lives as a consequence of independence—has meant that science remains an academic practice divorced of any organic linkage with the material requirements of the nation at large. It is an arcane practice of urban, educated, upper-caste middle classes locked in a competition for recognition and rewards by an ostensibly international but overwhelmingly Western jury. The tendency to confuse such recognitions and prizes with the real thing—meaningful change in the lives of a significant number of Indians—occasions one of the epigraphs at the head of this essay. Shiv Visvanathan notes the alienation of Indian science from a context-bound, socially relevant, problem-solving enterprise to an obsession with recognition from Western scientific forums when he recounts how Atma Ram, a rarity among Indian scientists given his early work experience on the shop floor of a sugar factory,

> ... asked again and again, "Why is it that science in independent India, despite all the investments in it, is not the potentially creative force it threatened to be during the nationalist period?" He then provided part of the answer. He confessed that the Nehruvian dream was to make India win Olympic medals in science: "we really believed that Nobels in science went hand in glove with rise in GNP." He then added that it was a race in which we will always be poor thirds, or at best glorified seconds.[23] Atma Ram's critique of Indian science encapsulates the limitations of a prize-wanting science as distinct from a problem-solving science.[24]

To understand the 1974 and 1998 nuclear tests, and the inevitable slide into weap-onization and more tests in the future, we have to place it in the context of the failure of the postcolonial middle class to deliver on its promise of general social development and rising standards of living for the people at large. For close to four decades after independence, economic growth rates averaged just over 3 percent per annum, which, once deflated by population growth rates of over 2 percent per annum over this same period, brought per capita annual growth rates to a glacial 1.4 percent or so. Given the abysmally low starting points and widespread poverty in 1947, this meant entire gen-erations have lived and died without reaching the Promised Land. Although many nar-ratives seek to explain this failure—export pessimism, a rent-seeking over-regulatory state, failure of land reform, urban bias, a monopolistic private sector, Hindu or Indian fatalism, flawed developmental models, overpopulation, wrong priorities—they all agree that postcolonial India missed the development bus. The masses—and their im-minent development—had always constituted both the silent referent and the alibi of the postcolonial middle class. As country after country sped by India in the 1970s and 1980s, there seemed nowhere to hide. This failure of the Indian middle class to deliver on development is an important constitutive element of its identity in the last quarter of the twentieth century—and is crucial to understand its nuclear politics.

The 1974 and 1998 tests were perverse insignia of the failure of the middle class's self-defined historical mission. As Abraham's landmark work shows with careful at-tention to detail, the impetus to produce the bomb occurred in a context where the privileged enclave of scientists within the country's Atomic Energy Commission (AEC) realized they were not going to be able to deliver on the promise of cheap and efficient nuclear energy to the nation. The switch to the bomb within the AEC was a way to ensure the continued legitimacy and stature of a strategic enclave that could not have withstood a social and political audit within a democratic society. This shift on the part of the scientific elite dovetailed with the conjunctural needs of state elites faced with problems regarding their own political and electoral legitimacy.[25] While the connections between developmental failures, the burden of over-expectation, and the decision to test the bomb were by no means direct and unmediated, the former constituted the historical context within which the latter gained a semblance of rationality. Not for the first time in a postcolonial context, the response to a failure on the part of elites to deliver on the material front came through the staging of a symbolic and spectacular state effect, namely, the testing of nuclear bombs.

The Indian Middle Class, Population, and Politics

In his now classic formulation on state power and social classes in India, Pranab Bardhan outlined a thesis that has found many takers and few dissenters.[26] He argued that by virtue of its education, and by its disproportionate presence in the state bureaucracy, the public sector, and the professions more generally, the Indian middle class was one of three "dominant proprietary classes" that constituted the ruling elite. That neither of the other two dominant classes—the industrial bourgeoisie or the rich farmer class—was able to decisively establish its hegemony over the nation augmented the power of this middle class, and was the chief source of the relative autonomy of the Indian state which "formulated goals and pointed policy directions, neither at the behest of nor on behalf of the proprietary classes"[27]

Bardhan's formulation (which owes much to Alavi's piece cited above on the overdeveloped state in postcolonial South Asia as well as to an earlier literature on "intermediate regimes") merits reproduction:

> It is not customary to include them [professionals and state bureaucrats—S.K.] among proprietary classes, but if physical capital can be the basis of class stratification, so can be human capital in the form of education, skills and technical expertise.... In a country where the overwhelming majority are illiterates or drop-outs at the primary education level, the educated elite enjoy a high scarcity value for their education and profession. By managing to direct educational investment away from the masses, they have been able to protect their scarcity rent.... Brahmins and other upper castes are disproportionately represented.

The prominence Bardhan accords to the middle class in the governing of India has historical antecedents. In an insightful work on the colonial origins of this middle class in northern India, Sanjay Joshi observes a number of factors crucial to its formation. The colonial middle classes fashioned themselves as cultural entrepreneurs who were the native interlocutors to a desired and superior modernity. They emphasized proficiency in education, especially Western education, and attributes such as personal discipline, effective time management, ambition, deferred consumption, and diligence. The emergence of new public spheres (in part by their own activities) created a stage on which this middle class stood as the "new arbiters of appropriate social conduct and establish(ed) new modes of political activity that empowered them at the expense of the traditional elites of the city, less powerful social groups, and ultimately also the

British rulers. Much of the power of this group of men, and later women . . . came from their claim to emulate an ideal-typical modernity first appropriated to similar projects by their counterparts in the West."[28]

These new cultural entrepreneurs were by no means rich (they had neither inherited wealth nor could they afford not to work for a living) and were not at the apex of society. They were overwhelmingly upper caste, and in the case of Muslims were Ashrafs. In the rapidly changing circumstances of the late nineteenth century, and the enlarging public political sphere of the early twentieth century, they increasingly emerged as representatives of a desired future, as arbiters to a rational and scientific modern, and, increasingly, as legitimate spokesmen for the nation.[29] Extending Joshi's analysis, the self-fashioning of this middle class emphasized its merit within modernist discourses of achievement and rationality, and implicitly contrasted these with inheritance and 'traditional' ascription. That this emphasis on "merit" was itself premised, especially in a largely poor, illiterate, and deeply hierarchical society, on a favorable set of circumstances within a colonial sociopolitical economy was not often realized. Obviously a key historical reason for the prominence of the middle class in postcolonial India was its very centrality during the nationalist movement for independence, wherein it constituted the social base both of the leadership of the anticolonial movement and the colonial administrative apparatus that ran the country. The highly protracted and legalistic nature of the nationalist struggle, the slow devolution of power into Indian hands, the careful shepherding of the anticolonial movement away from "divisive" social and class-based antagonisms, and the unbroken continuity in the Indian Civil Service after independence essentially meant that middle classes were disproportionately represented among the political elite that ran the country in the early years of independence.

In India, for all these reasons, it is logical to conflate the ruling class and middle class and speak interchangeably of the two, especially in the decades immediately after independence. It was for all practical purposes the attendant public of the Indian political sphere, and had an inordinate degree of influence in what happened therein. The self-construction of this middle class, its changing attitude toward "politics" and the "masses" in the postcolonial period, the impact of economic liberalization, and the links of these processes to nuclear politics are critical to the rest of this essay. To anticipate (and greatly adumbrate) the argument, I suggest that in the era of mass democratic politics and economic liberalization, the Indian middle class has grown increasingly alienated from the larger population that constitutes the rest of the country, and that this alienation manifests itself, among other arenas, most significantly in its nuclear politics.

First, *pace* Joshi, this middle class sees its rise to prominence during the late colonial period and in the postcolonial era as essentially meritocratic. It was the ability of this class to master the new language of administration (English), its capacity for hard mental work, and its felicity with the emerging modern disciplines—law, science, engineering, accountancy, economics, medicine, literature, history, and so on—that accounted for its rise. Its success was based neither on the accident of inherited wealth as landed property nor through practices traditionally regarded as suspect (for example, mercantile trade, investment and speculation, profiteering, and moneylending). The Indian middle class would like to be evaluated as a successful instance of a modernized and developed segment of the world, one that has played the game of Western modernity—with its emphasis on achievement rather than ascription—dexterously and with poise. A large portion of its sense of ressentiment vis-à-vis the Western world comes from its perception that it is not given its due, that it is literally invisible because the focus is trained exclusively on the poverty-stricken masses and on natural disasters.

Second, to this ruling/middle class, "politics" is increasingly regarded as the domain of the profane and the dirty: politics is that which intervenes to prevent a meritorious person from earning what is rightfully his. The middle class today defines politics as uneducated legislators and ministers, criminals in legislatures, statist inefficiency and corruption, reservation programs for underprivileged groups, and criminalization of public life. Mass politics emerged in the post-independence period when India went in for universal adult franchise, and the world's largest electoral democracy has steadily eroded the unwritten privilege of the middle class. As previously excluded sections have translated their larger numbers at the polls into demands for greater access to opportunities in education, employment, state subsidies, and other entitlements that were hitherto the exclusive privy of the middle classes, "politics" has become the name for the process by which this middle class feels marginalized. As Kaviraj, among others, has noted, in India the liberal democratic ethos of this middle class (which was quite shallow to begin with) has shrunk even further as mass politics and elections have steadily broadened—and coarsened—political participation.[30] In an unusual reversal, democracy means far more to the rural and urban poor than it does to the educated middle classes today, as was witnessed during the Emergency and in the elections that followed its lifting in 1977. One might say that, for many in India's middle class, democracy is to be valued only because it gives the country an exalted status compared to the rest of the Third World (and especially neighboring Pakistan). This limpid commitment is also revealed in the consistently higher turnouts for elections among the poor and the rural, in contrast to the urban middle classes.

Third, and closely related to the above point, is the notion dear to the middle class that there exists an extra- or supra-political sphere from where ethical interventions to cleanse public life of corruption and graft might emerge.[31] This transcendent, moral, antipolitical space has a long tradition in Indian thought, and has been occupied for varying lengths of time in the last century by figures as diverse as Mohandas Gandhi, Jayaprakash Narayan, Vinobha Bhave, Arun Shourie, T. N. Seshan, Rajiv Gandhi, B. G. Khairnar, V. P. Singh, Medha Patkar, Kiran Bedi, Abdul Kalam, and Harsh Mander. It reflects the desire of the Indian middle class for a knight in shining armor who will restore merit to its righteous place in the distribution of rewards—and put politics in its proper place. Crucially, it allows for the possibility that bypassing the political can itself be an ethical act. An individual sees his actions as ethical precisely because they refuse to be bound by the injunctions of a state that is no longer committed to meritocracy and captured by those who can commandeer large numbers of people to the hustings. Bypassing the state can also be seen as a form of resistance to its excessive bureaucratization, and a means to escape the effects of dirty politics on actions taken in the "national" interest.

Such an understanding of ethical politics as antipolitics can, among other things, justify a strategic enclave's secrecy and its desired insulation from politics and social audits. This idea of governance by a supra-political scientific and technocratic elite is greatly appealing, as it stands as proof of what "ordinary" middle class Indians can achieve if only they were unimpeded by the messy politics of Indian democracy and an inefficient state. Inter alia, it can also justify this same enclave's cavalier dismissal of a citizen group's demands for environmental impact assessments of a nuclear plant, or an intrepid journalist's request for information regarding safety records and radiation levels around a reactor, or mobilization by Dalits or tribals against the latest developmental project that threatens their homelands and livelihood.

And, finally, the Indian middle class's distaste for mass politics is accompanied by an ardent desire for technological solutions to socioeconomic and political problems. In an insightful passage, Suhas Palshikar outlines this antipolitical common sense:

> At the basis of these sentiments there lies a firm belief (in middle-class minds) that social issues can have a technocratic solution. . . . The middle classes believe that politics is irrelevant; solutions to various issues are either "economic" or technology based . . . Issues concerning public policy are not seen as contestations of competing interests because the middle classes do not recognize contestability of policies. Policies are understood as universalized wisdom based on "knowledge" and "expertise." The distrust of politicians and the notion of policy as the business of objective experts push the middle classes into the direction of bureaucracy and judiciary. The former is seen as the non-partisan and legitimate centre of decision making and the latter as neutral arbiter. Politics and politicians do not have a respectable place in the world view of the middle classes.[32]

The historical alienation of this middle class from the rest of the nation has sharply intensified in recent decades with economic liberalization, as well as the increased movement of Indians to the West and elsewhere. Under presently hegemonic neoliberal developmental models, the responsibility that the state and middle class feel for the rest of society is palpably diminishing. The benchmarks for consumption and desired lifestyles are set from outside India. The guilt associated with anything bordering conspicuous consumption—a guilt that was almost the habitus of being middle class and Indian in the 1950s and 1960s—has been replaced by an emphasis on enjoying the present. Although it is true that Nehruvian rhetoric regarding socialism and responsibility of elites for poorer sections of the country was overblown, at least it indexed a guilty conscience. In its hypocrisy lay a tacit acknowledgment that the poorer country cousins were nevertheless a part of the national family.[33] Today, it is as if many in the middle class wish that the poor would simply go away or disappear (but only after making the morning cup of tea and taking the kids to school), for they impede the enjoyment of the nation so desperately desired by the middle class.[34]

As always, Nandy's triangulation of the modern ideology of development, science, and security allows him to put his finger on what one has to describe as the genocidal impulse that has come to characterize many in India's middle class:

> There are a lot of Indians now who are willing to sacrifice the unmanageable, chaotic, real-life Indians for the sake of the idea of India. They are miserable that while the Indian democracy allows them to choose a new set of political leaders every five years, it does not allow them to choose once in a while the right kind of people to populate the country. Instead, they have to do with the same impossible mass of 950 million Indians—uneducable, disorganized, squabbling, and, above all, multiplying like bed bugs. For in the Indianness of Indians who are getting empowered lies, according to many learned scholars, the root cause of all the major problems of the country.[35]

Many have remarked on the lack of concern in the Indian press, and in the South Asian nuclear debate in general, with issues like mass casualties, breakdown of services, lack of hospitals with burn treatment centers, and the impossibility of even basic forms of civil defense (gas masks, stored potable water, bomb shelters, evacuation plans) in the event of a nuclear exchange. This is part of a larger story of wanton or deliberate neglect that has characterized India's nuclear establishment: the overwhelming negative fallouts—radiation; poisoning of land, water, and the atmosphere; birth defects; and cancers and other illnesses—have been preponderantly visited upon Adivasis, Dalits, and the poorest sections of people.

Such lack of concern for those least able to protect themselves is by no means new. It stems from a widely accepted "reality" within India's middle class that we as a society are overpopulated. As far back as 1959, in a speech to a conference on population and family planning, the father of India's atomic program, Homi Bhabha (himself a bachelor with no issue, as we say in India) suggested funding for research into a substance that would reduce the fertility of people by 30 percent when mixed with rice.[36] Such statements often disguised as jokes, accompanied by a rueful laugh to indicate that one is not fully serious, are a commonplace of Indian middle-class life. Yet one cannot help but feel that they also articulate a barely repressed desire to be rid of a substantial number of one's countrymen in order to better enjoy the nation. Quite often, the one issue that is seen as separating the Indian middle class from joining the ranks of the advanced, developed nations of this world is India's "surplus" population.

Amitav Ghosh recounts an Indian army officer telling him of a secret plan to win the war against Pakistan which he wished to communicate to the (then) Defense

Minister George Fernandes. Essentially it involved detonating a nuclear bomb a mile-deep within the Siachin glacier causing it to melt and simply drown Pakistan.[37] I was recently conversing with a fellow Indian and well-published security studies specialist employed in a defense think tank. As we talked about a recent earthquake in Kashmir, he wished a quake of over 9.0 on the Richter scale would hit Pakistan and "solve that problem for us permanently."

Some may point out that such comments are made about a neighboring country and not indicative of a genocidal impulse toward one's own citizens. Setting aside the problematic ethic which excuses contemplating genocide simply because it is across a recently drawn line on a map, what such arguments fail to notice is one is often talking about oneself when ostensibly talking about the "enemy." There is a displacement of attributed traits about the poor, the Muslim, and, by extension, the Pakistani in Indian discourses: they are all seen as hyper-fertile, unconcerned about family size, incapable of deferring present enjoyment in the interests of the future, and the main impediment to national enjoyment. Their presence both produces Indian-ness and ensures its incompleteness. The genocidal impulse voiced in the context of nuclear war with Pakistan, from this angle, is part of an impulse directed at one's own countrymen. Or, as the final sentence of Amitav Ghosh's *Countdown* would have it: "The pursuit of nuclear weapons in the subcontinent is the moral equivalent of civil war: the targets the rulers have in mind for these weapons are, in the end, none other than their own people."[38]

Conclusion

This essay has tried to connect the evolution of a postcolonial middle class in India and the decision to take up nuclearization in recent decades. Put most bluntly, it has argued that the historical alienation of this middle class from the vast majority of Indians has now manifested itself in a desire to be rid of them altogether. While the bomb is an important manifestation of this desire, it also congeals within itself the complex history of derivative science in a colonial society, the role that spectacular science has played in legitimizing the state and elites of a postcolonial society, and its salience as a resistant symbol against Western neocolonialism and indifference to Indian aspirations. In some way, this essay also represents an effort to answer a simple question: Why does one of the poorest and most populous nations in the world wish to join a small handful of nations that have the capability of annihilating this planet?

About twenty-five years ago, at the onset of the European movement for nuclear disarmament, Edward Thompson suggested (following Marx) that if the hand-mill epitomized feudal society and the saw-mill that of industrial capitalism, then perhaps the nuclear bomb—and the attendant category of exterminism—best represented our own times.[39] In a highly significant passage, Thompson elaborates:

By "exterminism" I do not indicate an intention or criminal foresight in the prime actors. And I certainly do not claim to have discovered a new "exterminist" mode of production. *Exterminism designates those characteristics of a society—expressed, in differing degrees, within its economy, its polity and its ideology—which thrust it in a direction whose outcome must be the extermination of multitudes.* The outcome will be extermination, but this will not happen accidentally (even if the final trigger is "accidental") but as the direct consequence of prior acts of policy, of the accumulation and perfection of the means of extermination, and of the structuring of whole societies so that these are directed towards that end.[40]

In the last few decades India has embarked on a set of policies in the nuclear realm that decisively move us forward on an exterminist path. When the annihilation of large numbers of people as a result of a nuclear exchange in South Asia occurs, it will have been a result of our present actions, of policies being shaped as we speak. Their foretold deaths cannot be expiated at the altar of the "accident." Some accidents, perhaps, better reveal our innermost desires than do our plans for our country.

Notes

Epigraphs from, respectively, Sanjay Dhande addressing U.S. alumni during the 50th anniversary celebrations of the Institutes and quoted in Rohit Chopra, "Neoliberalism as Doxa: Bourdieu's Theory of the State and the Contemporary Indian Discourse on Globalization and Liberalization," *Cultural Studies* 17, no. 3/4 (2003): 443; Arundhati Roy, "The End of Imagination," *Frontline* 15, no. 16 (August 1–14, 1998).

1. A useful collection of recent essays that reflects the range of opinion within this Indian debate can be found in D. R. Sardesai and Raju G. C. Thomas, eds., *Nuclear India in the Twenty-First Century* (New York: Palgrave Macmillan, 2002).

2. See Arjun Appadurai's introduction, "Commodities and the Politics of Value," in his edited volume, *The Social Life of Things: Commodities in Cultural Perspective* (New York: Cambridge University Press, 1986), 1–48.

3. Appadurai, *The Social Life of Things*, 3 (emphasis in original).

4. Ibid., 38 (emphases mine).

5. For the importance of the neocolonial character of the global proliferation regime in impelling India's nuclearization, see George Perkovich, *India's Nuclear Bomb: The Impact on Global Proliferation* (Berkeley: University of California Press, 2001).

6. Pervez Hoodbhoy, "Bombs, Missiles, and Pakistani Science," in Smitu Kothari and Zia Mian, eds., *Out of the Nuclear Shadow* (Delhi: Oxford University Press, 2003), 153, 156–157. Hoodbhoy goes on to note that at the present time at least sixty countries that currently do not have nuclear weapons have the necessary scientific and engineering skills to easily assemble one if they wanted to. Another recent work that demystifies the scientific aura attached to India's accomplishments in the nuclear arena is M. V. Ramana, "La Trahison Des Clercs: Scientists and India's Nuclear Bombs," in M. V. Ramana and C. Rammanohar Reddy, eds., *Prisoners of the Nuclear Dream* (Delhi: Orient Longman, 2003), 206–244.

7. One of the more interesting collections of such material can be found in Anand Patwardhan's documentaries, especially his *Father, Son, and Holy Bomb* and *Jang Aur Aman* (*War and Peace*).

8. George Perkovich argues that such status-related considerations were of paramount importance in India's decision to go nuclear. See idem, *India's Nuclear Bomb*. A clear delineation of the importance of such factors, converging with strategic considerations and nuclear apartheid, written soon after the tests, can be found in Pratap Bhanu Mehta's "India: The Nuclear Politics of Self-Esteem," *Current History* 97:623 (December 1998): 403–406.

9. For a clear description of this argument in the context of nuclear politics, see Achin Vanaik, "Unravelling the Self-Image of the Indian Bomb Lobby," *Economic and Political Weekly* (Bombay), November 20–27, 2004. Available at http://www.epw.org.in/epw/uploads/articles/1399.pdf (accessed April 14, 2008). In the more general Indian context, see my essay, "Boundaries and Violence: Postcolonial Ruminations on Space," in John Agnew, Katharyne Mitchell, and Gerard Toal, eds., *A Companion to Political Geography* (London: Blackwell, 2002), 302–314.

10. Amitav Ghosh, *Countdown* (Delhi: Ravi Dayal, 1999), 18.

11. The brief footage in Patwardhan's *Jang Aur Aman* showing the cluster of scientists and politicians around the bomb site in Pokhran a few days after the May 1998 tests, along with the segment of Vajpayee's speech, bears out the analysis I offer here. The career of someone such as Raja Ramanna, who at various points in his life was close to Mrs. Gandhi and to the Janata regime that appointed him scientific adviser to the cabinet of Prime Minister Morarji Desai, and who ultimately became a minister of state for scientific affairs under the Prime Ministership of V. P. Singh in the late 1980s, indicates the nonpartisan and supra-political value attached to the person of the scientist in postcolonial India. For an analysis of Ramanna's autobiography as an exemplary text revealing the zeitgeist of the Indian middle class and nuclearism, see my essay, "The Bomb, Biography and the Indian Middle Class," in *Economic and Political Weekly*, (Bombay): June 10–16, 2006. Available at http://epw.org.in/showArticles.php?root=2006&leaf=06&filename=10191&filetype=pdf (accessed August 4, 2006).

12. See Roy, "The End of Imagination." Much of the criticism of Roy's essay within India questioned the right of a female author of a fiction novel to hold forth on matters of national security, international affairs, and nuclear weapons. For two fairly typical examples of this reaction, which often borders on misogyny, see Anil Nair, "The Idea of Apocalypse," http://www.rediff.com/news/1999/aug/19anil.htm; and Sadanand Dhume, "Rekindling the Imagination," http://www.littleindia.com/archive/Nov98/Imagin.htm (both accessed November 7, 2005).

13. Ashis Nandy, *Alternative Sciences: Creativity and Authenticity in Two Indian Scientists*, 2nd ed. (Delhi: Oxford University Press, 1995). Original: Delhi: Allied Publishers, 1980.

14. Ibid., pp. 141–143 (emphasis mine).

15. One of the best general introductions to the ways in which machines and technology served as icons of colonial superiority remains Michael Adas's *Machines as the Measure of Men: Science, Technology, and Ideologies of Western Dominance* (Ithaca, N.Y.: Cornell University Press, 1989).

16. See Rudyard Kipling's "The Bridge Builders" for a stunning evocation of the contrast between colonial scientific rationality and native superstition. As often with Kipling, the neat dichotomies are considerably muddier by the end of the story and intimations of hubris haunt the margins (in idem, *The Day's Work* [London: Macmillan, 1945], 1–47).

17. Gyan Prakash, *Another Reason: Science and the Imagination of Modern India*, (Princeton, N.J.: Princeton University Press, 1999).

18. Hamza Alavi, "State and Class under Peripheral Capitalism," in Hamza Alavi and Teodor Shanin, eds., *Introduction to the Sociology of "Developing" Societies* (New York: Monthly Review Press, 1982), 289–307.

19. Partha Chatterjee, *Nationalist Thought and the Colonial World: A Derivative Discourse* (Delhi: Oxford University Press, 1986).

20. See my *Postcolonial Insecurities: India, Sri Lanka, and the Question of Nationhood* (Minneapolis: University of Minnesota Press, 1999).

21. Prakash, *Another Reason*, p. 12.

22. While many have previously noted Nehru's forms of address to the Indian peasantry—and the ways in which it positioned them as helpless recipients of his, and his government's, noblesse oblige—a recent work emphasizing this is Benjamin Zachariah's *Nehru: A Biography* (London: Routledge, 2004).

23. Shiv Visvanathan, *A Carnival for Science: Essays on Science, Technology, and Development* (Delhi: Oxford University Press, 1997), 5.

24. Many works have recently explored the impact of colonial rule and political economy on the emergence and character of "Indian" science. I have learned much from Deepak Kumar's excellent *Science and the Raj, 1857–1905* (Delhi: Oxford University Press, 1995), besides the works of Nandy, Visvanathan, Prakash, and Abraham cited elsewhere in this chapter.

25. Itty Abraham, *The Making of the Indian Atomic Bomb: Science, Secrecy, and the Postcolonial State* (London: Zed, 1998).

26. See Bardhan, *The Political Economy of Development in India*, rev. ed. (Delhi: Oxford University Press, 1998); original, 1984. A recent work describes Bardhan's thesis on the Indian state as the "prevailing consensus." See C. J. Fuller and John Harriss's introduction to *The Everyday State and Society in Modern India*, ed. C. J. Fuller and Veronique Benei (London: Hurst, 2001), p. 7. Another significant work that echoes Bardhan's thesis regarding the class character of the state in India is Achin Vanaik's *The Painful Transition: Bourgeois Democracy in India* (London: Verso, 1990).

27. Bardhan, *The Political Economy of Development*, p. 38.

28. Sanjay Joshi, *Fractured Modernity: Making of a Middle Class in Colonial North India* (Delhi: Oxford University Press, 2001), 2–3. For a similar, but less thoroughly worked out understanding of the emergence of a fractured modern within Bengal, see Sumit Sarkar's essays "Renaissance and Kaliyuga: Time, Myth, and History in Colonial Bengal" and "Kaliyuga, Chakri, and Bhakti," in idem, *Writing Social History* (Delhi, Oxford University Press, 1997).

29. For a parallel, and in important ways distinctive, set of issues in the emergence of a public sphere and a high-caste Brahmanic middle class in southern India, in contrast to Joshi's context of Lucknow, see M. S. S. Pandian's "One Step Outside Modernity: Caste, Identity Politics, and the Public Sphere," *Economic and Political Weekly* (Bombay), May 4, 2002. Available at http://epw.org.in/showArticles.php?root=2002&leaf=05&filename=4425&filetype=html (accessed August 4, 2006).

30. Sudipto Kaviraj, "The Imaginary Institution of India," in Partha Chatterjee and Gyanendra Pandey, eds., *Subaltern Studies VII* (Delhi: Oxford University Press, 1–39).

31. See Thomas Blom Hansen, *Wages of Violence* (Princeton, N.J.: Princeton University Press, 2002), for a fascinating discussion of this antipolitical space as the ground for varied kinds of interventions in Indian politics, most notably in his analysis of the rise of the Shiv Sena in Bombay and Maharashtra in recent decades.

32. Suhas Palshikar, "Politics of India's Middle Classes," in Imitaz Ahmad and Helmut Reifeld, eds., *Middle Class Values in India and Western Europe* (New Delhi: Social Science Press, 2002), 178.

33. As late as 1971 Mrs. Gandhi built her electoral platform on the slogan "Garibi Hatao" ("Abolish Poverty"), indexing this rhetorical commitment. Yet, by 1975, under the cloak of the Emergency, her son Sanjay Gandhi was already implementing what we know to be the

secret dream of many a middle-class Indian: mass sterilization of the poor, along with their physical relocation out of sight. See Emma Tarlo, *Unsettling Memories: Narrative of the Emergency in India* (Berkeley: University of California Press, 2003), for a substantiation of the points I make here about the Emergency, the complicity of the middle class in its excesses, and the worldview it entails.

34. Thomas Hansen captures the dispensability of the masses in the eyes of middle-class India when he notes in the context of urban planning in Mumbai that "the most striking feature of these plans, however, was the extent to which they were marked by a distinct upper middle class view of the overwhelming part of the city, namely, vast expanses of slum or ordinary neighborhoods that one must drive through on new expressways, drive under on a new metro, fly over in helicopters, or avoid altogether in hovercraft services that would take the upper middle class from their homes in the western suburbs to the city center without ever having to pass through the congested city" (*Wages of Violence,* pp. 207–208). A whole story can be told about the links between economic liberalization, the media revolution, changes in consumption, and the recent resurgence of Hindutva and majoritarianism. I can do no more than point to recent works such as Leela Fernandes, *India's New Middle Class: Democratic Politics in an Era of Economic Reform* (Minneapolis: University of Minnesota Press, 2006); Arvind Rajagopal, *Politics after Television: Hindu Nationalism and the Reshaping of the Public in India* (Cambridge: Cambridge University Press, 2001); David Ludden, ed., *Making India Hindu: Religion, Community, and the Politics of Democracy in India* (Delhi: Oxford, 1996); and Achin Vanaik, *The Bourgeois Transformation.*

35. Ashis Nandy, "The Twilight of Certitudes," *Postcolonial Studies* 1, no. 3 (1998): 293.

36. See Zia Mian, "Homi Bhabha Killed a Crow," in idem and Ashis Nandy, eds., *The Nuclear Debate: Ironies and Immoralities* (Colombo: Regional Center for Strategic Studies, 1998), p. 17.

37. Ghosh, *Countdown,* p. 43.

38. Ibid., p. 106.

39. Edward Thompson, "Notes on Exterminism, the Last Stage of Civilization," in Edward Thompson et al., *Exterminism and Cold War* (London: Verso, 1982), pp. 4–5.

40. Ibid., p. 20 (emphasis mine).

5

PRIDE AND PROLIFERATION: PAKISTAN'S NUCLEAR PSYCHE AFTER A. Q. KHAN

Ammara Durrani

If nuclear weapons can come to acquire the same "profound value" as the sacred symbols that supposedly condense the meaning and purpose of a religion, and if the discourse surrounding them can seem as arcane and complex as the higher reaches of religious philosophizing can be for the ordinary believer or the uninitiated, then we have surely succeeded making the politics and ideology of the possession of nuclear weapons virtually incontestable. After all, to sacralize something is precisely to remove it from the domain of normal contestation except for the "qualified" few!

Praful Bidwai and Achin Vanaik

In February 2005 Pakistan's former president Pervez Musharraf became accessible to the Pakistani people and the world at large on his very own personalized Web site, launched (and now managed) with much fanfare by the country's Inter-Services Public Relations (ISPR) Department of the Pakistan Army.[1] The "Personal Life" page of this Web site features a list of questions and answers pertaining to the president's life and person. In answer to a question as to what was "the most embarrassing moment" of his life, General Musharraf answered: "Discovering the involvement of Dr A.Q. Khan in the nuclear proliferation scandal."[2]

Musharraf's remark may be taken as reflective of the shock and humiliation experienced by the Pakistani government, media, intelligentsia, and the general public at the exposé of the A. Q. Khan nuclear proliferation affair hitting international news headlines. In February 2004 Pakistanis began tuning into sensational news reports on the country's pioneering nuclear scientist, Abdul Qadeer Khan. The "father" of the nation's highly revered and much touted nuclear program came under government investigation; he was subsequently arrested for allegedly running an international nuclear proliferation network, selling sensitive information and knowledge to "rogue" states—North Korea, Iran, and Libya—for personal profit. A year down the line, the issue remains a top story both at home and abroad. Given ongoing national and international political developments, the issue carried grave implications for the future of Pakistan's nuclear program.

The Khan controversy opened a Pandora's Box, and all pandemonium broke lose within and outside Pakistan. It created a political commotion enough to send jitters down the country's power corridors. Not since the 1998 explosions had the country's nuclear program captured so much national and international attention from the public, the media, and the international community. The two events in Pakistan's nuclear history could, in fact, be compared for identification of commonalities and differences, which span their respective timeframes and circumstances.

The strongest—and perhaps the only—commonality between the two events was their immediate and powerful reactions from governments and publics alike. The surprise may be attributed to the element of secrecy surrounding both events, taking most by surprise. Here, however, the similarity ends. The reactions caused by Pakistan's 1998 nuclear tests and those ignited by the 2003–2004 revelations have been hugely different in both nature and proportion.

The politico-strategic, economic, social, and cultural implications of the nuclear tests conducted by India and Pakistan in May 1998 have been analyzed from both ends of the nuclear spectrum by proponents of weaponization as well as advocates of disarmament. In essence, the 1998 tests pushed the debate out of the "nuclear ambiguity" paradigm and into the domain of overt weaponization, closest to the zero-sum status quo of nuclear deterrence reminiscent of the Cold War years.

Compared to an abundance of traditional security discourse on the post-1998 nuclear scenario in South Asia, dissenting discourse from a nontraditional security perspective has been quantitatively less but argumentatively authoritative and no less convincing, espousing a strong case for the region's de-nuclearization. Pathbreaking studies have identified the issues and problems, and also examined public opinion.[3] There have also been a few, though acclaimed, initiatives to present the antinuclear perspective to larger audiences through the electronic media.[4] The binding thread of all these works is their subscription to a politics of pacifism, philosophical and political positioning against nuclear weapons which they see as detrimental to the political, social, and economic well-being of the people of South Asia.

Barring differences of country-specific factors, nearly all these studies—produced prior to the Khan affair—on the nuclear weapons of India and Pakistan share contextual approaches; they examine similar factors that inform their prognosis and prescriptions, albeit carrying some shades of philosophical and theoretical differences of opinion. Studies by Pakistani scholar-activists depict a narrower difference in methodological and conceptual approaches.

This similarity of approach and argument mainly stems from a common understanding of the geopolitical conditions prevalent in the region between May 1998 and September 2001. The factor of timing is crucial here: following the end of the Cold War, the larger international system had still not taken the shape of the present times. On the eve of the 1998 tests the global influence of military and nuclear power was considered diminished in contrast to economic, technological, and cultural factors, which had assumed increased significance. Hence the higher emphasis on developing and applying a nontraditional security paradigm for international relations, particularly in protracted conflict zones like South Asia.

However, a persistent frost in India-Pakistan relations on the question of Kashmir meant that the nuclear weapons option remained "under active consideration" in South Asia, showing little sign of receding. The questions generally examined by most of the Pakistani studies, therefore, revolved around issues of policy history and options for Pakistan (sustained nuclear ambiguity, renunciation of the nuclear option, capping the nuclear program, and overt weaponization), domestic politics, public opinion, access to information, economic and social costs, command and control concerns, international arms control and disarmament concerns, and humanitarian and environmental issues. The 1998 tests only magnified these concerns, with a heightened awareness of the role of public opinion and domestic politics in paving the way for the development of nuclear weapons in the region.

Much to the horror of peaceniks, the 1998 tests created a national sense of pride, accomplishment, strength, and defiance within the Pakistani government and the public, while causing an international scare. In stark contrast, however, the Khan controversy created a backlash of largely defensive, apologetic, retaliatory, and accusatory responses by the state, experts, political groups, the press, and sections of the general public. Matters were not helped by the condescending U.S. tone in the backdrop of Pakistan's frontline role in the war against terror; of particular irritation was India's smirking and patronizing jibes at the controversy. As opposed to 1998, the Pakistani nuclear psyche has taken a jolt in the wake of the proliferation scandal and A. Q. Khan's exit from the national nuclear scene. The nation's nuclear ego—bloated full-scale in 1998—has visibly been punctured.

But could it also have led to an introspective sobering of attitudes, particularly from a denuclearization perspective? One can answer this question by analyzing shifts in prevailing attitudes and opinions, including those against nuclear weapons. One notes with concern that far from any increase in the marginal antinuclear sentiments existing in the country, the new responses depict complex new realities. These realities point to a predominant acceptance and adoption of traditional notions of "national security" as opposed to their critical questioning from an antinuclear position. Gaps previously existing on the subject between experts, the general public and political powers have narrowed in favor of keeping nuclear weapons. It seems that the case against nuclear weapons is decidedly becoming a distant and increasingly irrelevant idea in Pakistan.

Despite the proliferation embarrassment and security concerns caused by the Khan controversy, Pakistan's nuclear weapons now stand as an accepted and least challenged reality of the country's security apparatus. The debate has clearly entered the next stage: today it is no longer about whether or not to have nuclear weapons; rather, it is about their effective and responsible management and unthreatened possession. To the government, the political parties, the experts, and the general public, the world seems perpetually hostile and biased toward, and inconsiderate of, Pakistan's security needs—even when it is a frontline ally in an allied war.

This essay looks at the sociopolitical shifts caused by the Khan controversy and its impact on the nuclear debate in Pakistan. Locating itself in the history of the 1998 nuclear tests and responses to it, the paper examines how these have culminated into new realities in the wake of the Khan affair. In this context, it analyzes the respective roles of expert knowledge, social distance, and political power; how these have interplayed during and after the proliferation controversy; and what new attitudes they have created. Conceptually the paper relates its arguments to concerns of traditional and nontraditional security, power politics and patriotism, access to information, accountability, and peace. Finally, it discusses the possible future scenario of the nuclear issue's qualitative and quantitative thrust in Pakistan, and what it could mean for those espousing a nuclear-free South Asia.

Beyond Pokhran-II and Chaghai

The Terror Factor

It took the attack on the Twin Towers of the World Trade Center in New York on the morning of September 11, 2001, to redefine and set a new context for nuclearism and nuclearization across the world. South Asia was no exception. Both India and Pakistan were still trying to comprehend the meaning and potential of the bilateral Agra Summit (July 2001) when they were sucked into a new international system aggressively driven by the dynamics of the U.S. war on terror and George W. Bush's doctrine of preemptive strike.

The U.S. war on Iraq, on the pretext of nabbing that country's alleged weapons of mass destruction (WMDs), forced India and Pakistan to review their own equations—both political and military-nuclear. The contemporary India-Pakistan détente—initiated by A. B. Vajpayee's famous extension of a "hand of friendship" in Srinagar (April 2003)—had significantly altered bilateral relations between the two countries. The Composite Dialogue following the historic Islamabad Declaration (January 2004) had become what could best be described as something akin to an "institutionalization of peace" between the two countries.

But what impact could such peace initiatives have on South Asia's nuclear equation? Praful Bidwai and Achin Vanaik had this to say on the nuclear component of the India-Pakistan Composite Dialogue on the eve of the Khan affair's exposure:

> [The Lahore Declaration] . . . contained not one serious measure or even promise of nuclear restraint. Indeed, the agreement reached at the poorly prepared Summit, on extremely limited confidence-building (or rather, transparency) measures like informing each other beforehand of ballistic missile tests, effectively legitimized the very process of both countries' further nuclearization! On future bomb tests, the left hand took what was presumably given with the right—e.g., the moratorium on further nuclear tests in both the countries would continue unless the "national interest" dictated otherwise![5]

How true, for both countries continue to conduct their "routine" missile tests while simultaneously engaging in active multi-pronged diplomacy for peace! Clearly this is a peace that the two governments are proudly negotiating while basking in the glory of a successful nuclear deterrence. They would like their publics and the world to believe that both are responsible nuclear states, and that nuclear weapons remain prime national assets and guarantors for peace between the two countries.

Nuclear Pride

This mind-set of "nuclear pride" is well grounded in Pakistan's nuclear psychology as described by several analysts. Pervez Hoodbhoy counted it as one of the three "critically important" elements of the imperatives for the Pakistani bomb, the other two being the "nuclear shield" doctrine and military dominance of Pakistani decision making:

> Growing institutional malfunction and a feeling of collective failure have understandably led to a steadily deepening crisis for the Pakistani nation. Pride and confidence follow from real achievement; conversely absence of achievement inexorably leads to diminished self-esteem . . . More and more Pakistanis in the English language press ask what was gained from partition, although this question still cannot be asked

in the conservative Urdu press. The psychological anguish must somehow be made bearable. Enter the bomb.

He observed further that the Kahuta Research Laboratory (where the Pakistani nuclear program is institutionalized) has helped create a "sense of achievement" in an otherwise bleak environment, and many Pakistanis take "mental refuge within its four walls." No longer just a secret laboratory, Hoodbhoy said, it has become a "sacred symbol" which must be protected at all costs. The atomic weapons said to be produced there are "glittering objects" that symbolize mastery of the most sophisticated technology. A country that can manufacture them has presumably proved its mettle. With Kahuta, Pakistan is "safe," he noted, adding that "it cannot be pushed around, called backward, or sent to the bottom of the pecking order of nations":

> It is important to understand the extraordinary sense of desperation felt by most Pakistanis as they reel before the rapacity of political and economic elites, and see concern for the common good evaporate. Citizens have become cynical and increasingly disappointed at their historical fate, resulting in a collective loss of confidence in the state. The bomb provides to the masses a refuge from reality and an antidote to collective depression.[6]

Pakistan's Moment of Truth

Confessions

At the time when the A. Q. Khan nuclear proliferation affair became public, Pakistan was well on its way to negotiating peace with India, and receiving international accolades and financial aid for its role as a frontline ally in the U.S. war against terrorism. General Musharraf and his government highlighted ad nauseam these foreign-policy achievements to the public in efforts to garner public legitimacy and support. In this scenario of high politics and reinforcement of the traditional security paradigm—especially in the wake of the Afghanistan and Iraq wars—the notion of national security became the exclusive concern of Pakistan's military establishment, defined and applied as it deemed fit.

An effective nuclear balance with India served as the backbone of this national security doctrine, as Pakistan continued to test its ballistic missiles capable of carrying nuclear warheads while talking peace across the border. Pakistan's nuclear confidence and pride was at its comfortable peak. So confident was the Musharraf government that on the eve of the then Indian premier A. B. Vajpayee's visit to Islamabad for the South Asian Association for Regional Cooperation (SAARC) Summit in January 2004, it removed a replica of Pakistan's Ghauri missile from its prominent display point in the capital city.[7]

When investigations began in late 2003 into allegations of proliferation activities of six Pakistani nuclear scientists of the Khan Research Laboratories (KRL), the nation viewed the "debriefing" of these scientists with confusion and suspicion. Non-attributable gossip—especially in Islamabad's elite social circles—about Khan's dubious business interests had been around for several years. But the scientist was a sacred cow, and therefore the "inside story" was not known to the general public. Before the outbreak of the proliferation scandal, Khan's most recent brush with controversy had occurred in late 2002 when he was embroiled in a legal dispute over ownership of the Institute of Behavioral Sciences (IBS) in Karachi.[8] Not until the government removed Dr. Khan from his post as adviser to the prime minister on the country's strategic program in order to "facilitate" the ongoing "investigations in a free and objective manner" did people realize the gravity of the situation. The cat was finally coming out of the bag.

With the outbreak of the Khan scandal, the nuclear equation for Pakistan changed completely. Among other things, the traditionally comparative approach vis-à-vis India could no longer be applied as comfortably as in the past. Reminiscent of global criticism and the chiding of India for its 1974 nuclear tests, this time "nuclear guilt" had come to Pakistan. In the past Pakistan had sought legitimacy for its nuclear program by pointing the finger at India and accusing it of "forcing" Pakistan to go nuclear because India had upped the ante in the regional security balance. The Khan scandal, however, provided India—and the rest of the world—a way to reproach Pakistan for its inability to handle its nuclear assets responsibly. Once again, Pakistan's nuclear program was facing tough questions about its legitimacy and viability. Ironically the Khan scandal also gave India a perfect opportunity to seek legitimacy for its own nuclear program by showing the world that it was a more "responsible" nuclear power than Pakistan—since its scientists or government had not committed proliferation crimes like Khan—and therefore deserved to be in league with the nuclear club of the world.

Nevertheless, the Pakistani government tried to dispel fears "in the strongest terms" that it would ever compromise on its nuclear capability, and asserted that "far from rollback or freeze, Pakistan would continue to undertake qualitative and, if necessary, quantitative upgrades with the objective of consolidating the national deterrence in line with its minimum deterrence needs."[9]

The next day Pakistani newspapers reported that Dr. Khan had "admitted" to having transferred nuclear technology to North Korea, Iran, and Libya during "four intense sessions of two hours each," and the National Command Authority (NCA) would "decide whether to formally charge Dr. Khan and try him in court or simply take administrative steps."[10] On 4 February 2004, in a televised address to the people of Pakistan, Dr. A. Q. Khan admitted his "error of judgment" and sought "pardon," after which he submitted a "mercy petition" to General Musharraf.

Notwithstanding the shame and regret evident in his speech, Dr. Khan's words are interestingly illustrative of his knowledge and understanding of the public psyche and pride in the country's nuclear program:

I am aware of the vital criticality of Pakistan's nuclear programme to our national security and the national pride and emotions which it generates in your hearts. I am also conscious that any untoward event, incident or threat to this national capability draws the greatest concern in the nation's psyche. It is in this context that the recent international events and their fallout on Pakistan have traumatized the nation.[11]

For the father of Pakistan's nuclear weapons, the sum total of this controversy amounted to Khan's personal fall, and not the end of the grand idea of nuclear weapons as guarantors of the country's national security or as evidence of its national progress and a source of national pride. Khan may also have banked on his televised "performance" as a check against anticipated public backlash. As national reactions reveal in the following section, his speech actually elevated his status in the public eye as a "martyr" who had willingly sacrificed his position and privileges to protect the country's security assets.

Reactions

Dr. Khan's confessions were followed by a spate of strong, yet mixed, reactions from the government, political parties, the general public, the media, and experts alike. The responses were indicative of the changes that Pakistan's nuclear psyche had undergone because of this controversy. Interestingly Khan's speech received little or no press or academic analysis for its content and delivery. Rather, most recorded reactions revealed a rush to pass moral judgment—one way or the other—on Khan's failings and to prescribe methods of damage control. Though confronting the same crisis, the Pakistani elite and the masses reacted with subtle differences. For the former, Pakistani's national security and nuclear program was now vulnerable at a crucial point in international history. For the latter, on the other hand, Pakistan's image as a proud, moral nation equipped with nuclear might was tarnished forever. But the predominant opinion held by both is that, despite the loss of national prestige, protecting the country's nuclear assets must be the nation's top priority at all costs.

To monitor and analyze their reactions, I scanned Pakistan's largest and most influential daily newspapers, the English daily *Dawn* and the Urdu daily *Jang. Dawn* is generally considered to be a liberal newspaper to which the country's educated elite subscribe; daily *Jang* is generally perceived as a conservative newspaper and has the largest national circulation among the popular masses of all walks of life. Narrowing my focus to February 2004, when the controversy reached its peak and ignited the highest wave of recorded reactions, I categorized the following regular newspaper sections as reflective of corresponding perspectives of certain social segments. The section "Letters to the Editor" was a measure of public opinion; opinion articles corresponded to expert knowledge; and editorials reflected media influence.

Table 5.1

Distribution of Views by Category and Language

	Dawn	Jung
A. Letters to the Editor	**30**	**7**
a. Supportive of Khan and the Pakistani nuclear program	20	6
b. Critical of Khan but supportive of the nuclear program	4	0
c. Neutral	3	1
d. Against nuclear weapons	3	0
B. Opinion Articles	**18**	**56**
a. Supportive of Khan and the Pakistani nuclear program	5	38
b. Critical of Khan but supportive of the nuclear program	0	2
c. Neutral	4	12
d. Against nuclear weapons	9	4
C. Editorials	**7**	**5**
a. Supportive of Khan and the Pakistani nuclear program	4	2
b. Critical of Khan but supportive of the nuclear program	1	0
c. Neutral	1	1
d. Against nuclear weapons	1	2

Source: Collected by author from February 1 to February 29, 2004.

I also perused these newspapers for news items and reports on political statements and activities of political parties and interest groups concerned with the issue and its fallout. Political parties were studied as examples of how the Khan controversy influenced political power, how it was used to manipulate opinion, and for what ends and purposes. Interest groups were examined to identify indications of social assertion—or distance—on this contentious issue, and what it meant for public opinion on the nuclear weapons program.

A total of thirty-seven letters to the editor, seventy-four opinion articles, and twelve editorials specifically related to the A. Q. Khan scandal were published in the two dailies during February 2004. An analysis of all these pieces revealed multiple shades of intricately linked and sometimes self-contradictory opinions (Table 5.1).

Public Opinion

The Pakistani journalist Zubeida Mustafa dissected the very notion of public opinion and its relation to the bomb in an article published shortly after the Khan issue became public. She noted that, as the proliferation saga unfolded in Islamabad, the government sought shelter behind so-called public opinion, making it sacrosanct in this case, which was intriguing since usually military rulers worry least about that.[12] "The question, however, arises," wrote Mustafa, "whether the public in Pakistan at all holds an opinion on such complex issues as nuclear weapons and proliferation. And if it holds a vague opinion on the matter, can it actually be measured?"

Mustafa's observations may be valid. Nevertheless, the common people made themselves heard in various public forums on the issue of the Khan affair, notably in the form of letters to the editors of the major dailies. Even after the advent of survey polls, the world press has continued to regard the Letters to the Editor section as representative of ordinary readers' views and opinions on any particular issue. Despite their inherent lack of a scientific methodology to gauge public reaction, these letters have traditionally been considered by policy makers, intellectuals, and the press as a window into public opinion. Particularly for want of a survey in the wake of the Khan scandal, I have relied on these letters as useful tools for gaining insight into the minds and hearts of the public.

Most of the letters published in *Dawn* and *Jang* during the period under study are supportive of both Khan and the nuclear program. The views and emotions expressed in the following excerpts range from outright denial of the crisis at hand to falling back on faith in times of distress.

Far from either acknowledging the hard reality of Khan's involvement in the crime of nuclear proliferation, calling for his accountability, or showing a serious introspection about the costs of this issue for Pakistan, the dominant view in these letters reflects a scant disregard for these considerations. Instead, Khan is upheld as a "genius" who stands above the law because he is Pakistan's "saviour" and no one must hold him responsible for any wrongdoing. Those who do are themselves criticized as "traitors" and "anti-Pakistan." Patriotism is linked to calling for protection of the country's nuclear assets against global conspiracies hatched by the enemies of Islam against whom God's help is needed. Consider the following excerpts from sample letters expressing support:

> The people of Pakistan are proud of their nuclear achievement. Dr AQ Khan and his colleagues achieved "mission impossible" by setting up a uranium enrichment plant and giving the nation the much-needed nuclear deterrence and fortified its defence ... Dr Khan, a DJ College alumnus, has celebrity status. He is the greatest genius the country has ever produced. Please stop giving a bad name to the nation's benefactors and take steps to re-establish their dignity.[13]

> To safeguard the honour and liberty of Dr. Khan, I suggest parliament should resolve that no government agency and no court of law will proceed against him and that he will enjoy permanent immunity from legal action for charges in question. The matter of granting immunity should be kept above party politics.[14]

> Today we have been forced to make ourselves accountable to such an extent that we have rounded up our defense benefactors and are questioning them ... While it is

equal to a national disgrace for us, we must remember that this is part of the many challenges that the Muslim Ummah is presently facing. May God bring the Ummah out of this calamity soon.[15]

The way the issue of nuclear scientists has been given negative coverage has harmed the national interest. It has caused a lot of pain and sadness for every patriotic Pakistani. Today, we have to protect our independence not only for ourselves but also for our future generations. But if we start bargaining on our national interests today, then who will protect us tomorrow?[16]

These views represent the largely emotional and parochial view held by most Pakistanis. It is generally believed that because the Pakistani nation is at the mercy of oppressive international powers and corrupt governments, its people can turn only to Allah for help at a time when its territorial and political integrity is threatened by Western and anti-Islam entities. The general argument is that protection of Pakistan's nuclear weapons and its "creator" is the nation's only salvation, and therefore it is every Pakistani's responsibility to safeguard this national asset at all costs.

A second category of letters were critical of Khan but supportive of the nuclear program. Criticism of Khan was mild, expressing disappointment at his "human error" of succumbing to personal greed. Elements of shock and embarrassment were more pronounced but by no means prompted a rethink over nuclear weapons and their costs. On the contrary, that was secondary to serious concerns about the safety of the nuclear program which called for urgent government measures to protect it. Although a number of such letters were published in *Dawn*, no critical letters were published in *Jang*. Consider the following sample:

To cope with a situation like this the government and the opposition need to take a joint stand against any foreign pressure to close down our nuclear programme. The government should call a roundtable conference of all opposition parties and make it clear to the world that for Pakistan its nuclear assets are indispensable and Pakistan cannot cap its nuclear programme.[17]

The number of neutral letters (so-called because they did not express a strong view in favor or against Khan or the nuclear program letters) in both *Dawn* and *Jang* were almost even and made up only a fraction of the total number. They served more as inquiries, raising questions about an issue shrouded in mystery, while expressing concern for a confusing situation.

A small number of letters expressing opinions against nuclear weapons were published in *Dawn; Jang* carried none. Consider the following sample:

Unhappily, one cannot escape the frightening apprehension, with all the fissile material, treaty bound or not, but bristling around us, that Tony Blair may at least once be right that to stem the movement of the world to horrific self-destruction a return to basic values may indeed be imperative. To me the first international step in this direction would be to convene the moribund Disarmament Conference at Geneva.[18]

This illustrates that the constituency for an antinuclear perspective remains small and marginalized in Pakistan. For all its gravity, even the Khan scandal did not lead to an alternative view on these weapons. On the contrary, the numerous letters in support of the scientist and the weapons show a hardening of nuclear attitudes, never mind their disappointment. No longer necessarily defined by opinions for or against the bomb, these attitudes are located in the well-argued dominant discourse of the elite that puts nuclear weapons at the center of Pakistan's national security paradigm.

Expert Knowledge and Opinion

Standing at the lowest rung of the country's social hierarchy, the general public can only express opinions of shock, anger, humiliation, or condemnation; or, at the most, it can demand redress. In large part, the burden to explain, justify, or critically question an event falls on those who are knowledgeable and skilled at analysis. In the Khan affair, Pakistani politico-strategic and scientific experts suddenly found themselves facing a situation that had put the sanctity of the country's nuclear program in a compromising position. In the expert analyses that followed, the moral aspect was marginally addressed, relatively more so in *Jang* articles than those in *Dawn*. However, opinion articles published in the two major dailies mainly considered the political and geostrategic implications for Pakistan and what problems it could face from the international community.

Most of these expert arguments centered around questions of the West's biased approach toward nonproliferation issues, the security of Pakistan's nuclear program, its rationale, corruption, and accountability of those responsible for its management, parliamentary evaluation of the scandal, the government's handling of the crisis, and what new challenges might the government face in fending off intense international pressure. The dominant thinking and normative paradigm was that of exercising political realism. Though there were differences of perceptions on the issues involved, most analyses took the reality and acceptance of nuclear weapons as a given for Pakistan's security apparatus, the possession of which—as opposed to their governance and safety—were unquestionable. They had to be retained at all costs, no matter the sacrifice—even if it meant the shame of the "national hero." In fact, adequate governance and foolproof security became the new subject for concern and debate for most experts. Voices questioning their very existence were few and far between.

Dawn published the most opinion articles against the idea of nuclear weapons, whereas *Jang* predominantly featured articles supportive of both Khan and the nuclear program, the latter far outnumbering *Dawn*'s neutral and antinuclear articles combined. Furthermore, although *Dawn* did not feature any article critical of Dr. Khan, *Jang* did run a small number of articles that criticized Khan but supported the nuclear program. Consider the following excerpts:

The extent of autonomy that the nuclear related organizations enjoyed in the past needs to be curtailed now by balancing with greater measure of accountability.[19]

Qadeer Khan's past activities are . . . woven into Pakistan's memory and trying to de-link the two is an exercise in futility. It's also an exercise in some dishonesty for what it shows is a whole phalanx of once-eminent men scurrying for cover as the blame for a large slice of national history is shouldered by one individual.[20]

The nuclear game is beyond the means of the poor countries . . . It is therefore recommended for the poor countries like Pakistan to strictly adhere to the golden principle of "mind your business." The business in such cases is to work hard to provide the basic necessities of life to the people of their countries, and leave the luxury of going nuclear for those who can afford it.[21]

Despite the seriousness of A. Q. Khan's televised *mea culpa* and its implications for Pakistan, many people—and not just those in government—are still in deep denial. They feel Pakistan is being unfairly targeted, and moan about how other countries like Israel indulged in secret and illicit purchases to develop their nuclear weapons.[22]

Pakistan today is caught in a predicament and the only way out is its accession to [the] NPT [Nonproliferation Treaty] so that it can rehabilitate its credentials as a responsible and law-abiding member of the international community.[23]

Whatever mistake has been committed will have to be accepted. Those held responsible will have to be punished and foolproof security will have to be provided in future . . . Two things are more important than any individual: Pakistan's nuclear program that has to be saved at all costs, and Pakistan's national interest and dignity.[24]

If you are interested in ending corruption in the country then instead of targeting Dr. Qadeer Khan, first pursue those who ate the nation's resources and didn't do a dime's worth of work for the nation.[25]

This is not an ordinary case and neither is the culprit an ordinary man. This is the man about whom the nation has a united judgment that Quaid-e-Azam made Pakistan and Dr Qadeer Khan saved it. If there is any doubt in that then a referendum should be held and a verdict on this culprit should be taken from the nation . . . This is a case and decision of life and death.[26]

[Khan] gave nuclear technology to Pakistan, which shocked the developed world. His brilliance and success galvanised the Zionist and Christian lobbies and they all have become enemies of Dr. Qadeer Khan and the nuclear program . . . We are so foolish that we are giving our weaknesses to our enemies so that they attain these very objectives.[27]

[Government] should take the Parliament into confidence on the whole issue, so that the dangers facing the country and the nation could be met adequately.[28]

[The] hateful weapon that the nation had made in a condition of absolute helplessness almost became a source of idolatry for extremists. The more these people protest against Basant and Valentine's Day, with the same intensity they express their love for the atomic bomb. In a religion that was declared the religion of moderation by the Almighty, what is the capacity of hating flowers and loving bombs?[29]

As evident in these excerpts, most views fall between open criticism of the government for exposing its weaknesses to international powers working against the interests of Pakistan and a grudging acceptance of and disappointment at Khan's stumbling. Views openly questioning the viability of nuclear weapons for a poor and troubled country like Pakistan are few. Despite the experts' perception of the negative fallout for Pakistan as a result of the Khan controversy, however, their predominant concern revolves around how best to control the damage, quickly move on from the point of embarrassment, and protect the program from future leaks or attacks.

Media Influence

A look at the editorials published in the two major dailies during this time largely depicts a national press caught between expressing bemused shock and providing advice on damage control. *Dawn* wrote the largest number of editorials supporting Khan and the nuclear program, not only compared to its number of critical or neutral editorials but also outnumbering *Jang*'s supportive editorials. *Jang*'s high score is evenly split between editorials supporting Khan and the nuclear program, on the one hand, and those critical of nuclear weapons, on the other. No editorial in *Jang* was critical of Khan but supportive of the nuclear program.

This latter pattern stands in stark contrast to the high number of pro-Khan and pro-nuclear opinion articles published in *Jang*'s editorial pages. Similarly, *Dawn*'s numerous pro-Khan and pro-nukes editorials do not correspond with the many neutral and antinuclear opinion articles published in its editorial pages. Consider the following excerpts from editorials published in both the papers:

> It is reassuring to hear from the president that there will be no rollback of Pakistan's nuclear programme. However, Islamabad must move ahead in a way that combines the dictates of security with credible guarantees against proliferation . . . What is involved is not just the fate of a few individuals but the very future of Pakistan's nuclear programme. (*Dawn*)[30]

> Proliferation of weapons only occurs when countries are locked in an arms race in an effort to gain strategic and political superiority over one another . . . Moreover, the time has come for India and Pakistan to focus on the development of their human resources. This is possible only if they reduce their exorbitant defence expenditures and channel their financial resources towards socio-economic sectors. (*Dawn*)[31]

> Circumstances demand that all those heads and concerned officials of sensitive and secret institutions should strictly be scrutinized during whose tenure the technology transfer evidence has surfaced. Because this case can temporarily be pushed under the carpet, but not forever. (*Jang*)[32]

> Spread of nuclear weapons or transfer of nuclear technology is a sensitive and dangerous issue. No one should consider himself as the ultimate authority on it, neither should one-sided statements be issued on it. Nuclear assets are assets of the whole

nation; therefore, the whole nation should be united for their security ... Through our thought process and consensus we have to prove that the Pakistani nation has not made this mistake. (*Jang*)[33]

That *Dawn* mainly took a position supportive of Khan and the nuclear program is thought provoking, as is the observation that *Jang's* editorial position is split between supportive and critical views on Khan and nuclear weapons. As noted, a traditionally held notion among our elite is that *Dawn* represents liberal and progressive politico-economic positions on issues, whereas *Jang* represents a conservative viewpoint. But our findings point to a think-shift in both major papers. It seems that even the most liberal Pakistani paper holds views not unlike the dominant elite view of supporting the Pakistani nuclear program and calling for its protection at all costs. The issue of whether it is for or against the bomb is either no longer valid or has been submerged in the larger question of safeguarding Pakistan's nuclear program from a hostile international environment.

On the other hand, *Jang's* criticism of the lopsided global arms regime is no less surprising. Conventional antinuclear wisdom has long dubbed the conservative Urdu press as a major actor in advocating nuclearism through its hawkish positions on the India-Pakistan conflict. But our findings suggest a more globally refined editorial position adopted by *Jang* on this issue. Particularly noteworthy is the absence of emotional vitriolic or inflammatory language in its editorials on the Khan issue, even in contrast to some of its well-known columnists. Instead, *Jang's* editorials are couched in a language of cool political realism. Unlike *Dawn,* it even moves a step further by framing the Khan issue in the larger context of the global problem of nuclear weapons and the proliferation regime, and how that hinders the progress in eliminating global poverty and world conflicts.

For the Pakistani press, these views represent important intellectual departures showing an interesting switching of roles. While the liberal English press is found conforming to the establishment's views on national security, the conservative Urdu press has adopted a more internationalist politically realist view.

Political Parties

When the Pakistan government sacked Dr. Khan from his advisory post, the action was greeted by strong discontent and disapproval by most of the country's major political parties, save the ruling Pakistan Muslim League (Quaid-e-Azam Group), known as the "King's Party" for its subservience to General Musharraf and his policies.[34] A report filed in *Dawn* illustrates the positions taken by several shades of political parties. According to the report, leaders of various political parties "criticized" the government's action and said that "this would cause irreparable damage to the country's integrity":

Chairman of the PML-N Raja Zafarul Haq, in a statement, said: "Wittingly or unwittingly, under pressure, the rulers of Pakistan today are hurtling the country to a very dark end" . . . He said it was time for all political parties, irrespective of their past or views on different issues, to plan a unified action to stop the process of causing irreparable damage to the country's integrity . . . People's Party Parliamentarians (PPP) Senator Farhatullah Khan Babar said the party was of the view that scientists were being made scapegoats and the decision to remove Dr. Khan from his post of adviser strengthened this viewpoint . . . Chairman [of the] Pakistan Tehrik-i-Insaf (PTI) Imran Khan . . . termed the sacking of Dr. AQ Khan the beginning of the end of the nuclear programme . . . The PTI chief alleged that under the conspiracy, the nuclear programme was being systematically destroyed by first undermining the credibility of the nuclear scientists. This would in turn lead to complete crippling of nuclear organizations thus leading to a total freeze of nuclear weapons development . . . PML-Q Senator Tariq Azeem said . . . services of Dr Khan for the country would always be remembered. He asked other political parties to keep this issue above their personal politics. He said all facts would be laid before the nation in due course of time. On the other hand, spokesman for the Communist Party of Pakistan Engineer Jameel Malik has asked the government to arrest Dr. AQ Khan and give punishment to all those responsible for transfer of nuclear technology to Iran and Libya . . . Mr. Malik asked other political and religious parties not to politicize the issue as it was a sensitive matter. He said at present over 6,000 scientists and 60,000 other staff members were working in various sensitive institutions and they had no role in the sale of nuclear technology as only a few persons were involved in this act.[35]

Consider another report published the following day in the same paper:

Politicians representing a cross section of the population have condemned the removal of the famous nuclear scientist Dr AQ Khan from the position of adviser to the prime minister on the strategic programme. Terming the step a shameful action, they said Dr. Khan was a national hero whose contribution to the defence of the country made it invincible. Senator Prof Ghafoor Ahmad, the deputy chief of Jamaat-i-Islami, said that under foreign instructions the saviour of the nation was being declared guilty. Its attitude had transformed the government into something which threatened the good name as well as the nuclear capability of the country. Prof Ghafoor demanded that before taking further steps the government should take the parliament into confidence and also present its case before the higher judiciary . . . Meraj Mohammad Khan said let the government point its fingers towards Dr Khan for alleged proliferation, links with the underworld and corruption. The people of Pakistan would never accept all this because he is their hero. Referring to the threat given by the US to Zulfikar Ali Bhutto, he said if anything happens to Dr. Khan it would be another great tragedy in Pakistan's history. Speaking of the possibility that Dr. Khan will be murdered, which could be termed a suicide, Mr Khan appealed to the Supreme Court and other patriotic forces in the country to take note of the situation.[36]

The report quotes a top leader of the ultra-conservative Jamaat-e-Islami Party and veteran politicians belonging to the major liberal parties sitting in the opposition. In the following weeks these positions hardened, with the opposition parties criticizing the government and the ruling party justifying Khan's removal and the investigations, and also asking the opposition parties "not to politicize the issue" out of concern for preserving the national interest and unity. Of the opposition parties, the stance of the Muttahida Majlis-e-Amal (MMA) was most active: it called for a nation-wide strike "to express complete solidarity with the nuclear scientists and condemn those who had put the country's integrity at stake." MMA's top leader, Qazi Hussain Ahmed, even asked General Musharraf to leave office for taking Dr. A. Q. Khan's issue to the controversial National Security Council (NSC) instead of parliament, saying that "this step had proved that General Musharraf was not ready to go along with the constitution and the democratic system given by himself," and accusing the president of "exposing Dr. Qadeer to media trial, and assassinating the character of a great nuclear scientist."[37] Besides such political rhetoric aimed primarily against General Musharraf and the West, opposition parties also linked the issue to questions over the president's power to grant such a pardon, debate in the parliament and senate, the legal lacunae of the "pretrial" pardon, and the role of the army in proliferation activities.

Social Assertion

Another manifestation of public opinion on the Khan issue, in addition to letters to the editor discussed above, was the participation of rights and advocacy groups in the debate, bringing in a rights perspective. For instance, the Human Rights Commission of Pakistan (HRCP) urged the government to observe due process of law during the scientists' probe:

> Saying no citizen can be treated as over and above the law of land, or seen as being exempt from its provisions, the Human Rights Commission of Pakistan has reiterated its demand that the scientists currently being detained be treated in accordance with the law ... "The scientists, and indeed any other person kept in detention, must be allowed to meet their families and counsel and must be produced before courts. They must not be humiliated and must be treated with respect, like any honourable citizen of the country," the statement said. It said: "In all matters such as the current investigation that is under way, it must be noted that transparency can help remove many doubts about the nature of the action taken. The right of the people to information about the findings must not be denied. This process can also remove lingering suspicions about innocence and guilt, and set a precedent for future investigation into national issues, ending the tendency to keep them overt and shrouded from the public eye."[38]

Similarly, a newly formed Parliamentarians Commission for Human Rights (PCHR) reportedly submitted an adjournment motion to the National Assembly secretariat on detention of KRL scientists, saying "detention of the nuclear scientists had created resentment in the country, especially among professionals who now felt insecure":

"Disgracing of nuclear scientists in the name of debriefing is a condemnable act. Media trial of nuclear scientists has spread panic among the common man," they said. Stressing the need to handle the matter with caution, the PCHR members said the case should be discussed in the parliament so that people could become aware of the truth and taken into confidence by revealing the names of those involved in "leaking nuclear capability" to others.[39]

The legal community also played its role by reportedly observing a partial strike to express solidarity with nuclear scientists put in custody on "the pretext of debriefing," and demanding their immediate release.[40]

Such advocacy by the rights groups on a highly sensitive issue concerned with national security is unprecedented in the country's history. In the past, rights groups remained on the margins of mainstream socio-politics, as they are concerned more with leftist issues such as poverty, labor, gender, and violence. The significant change marked by the Khan episode came from the identity of the rights groups, not from the antinuclear groups, with patent differences between the two. This raises an important question: how has the rights discourse, unlike the antinuclear discourse, managed to negotiate its space in mainstream Pakistani politics?

The popularity of human rights discourse can be gauged from its effective use by an unusual social group that asserted itself during the Khan controversy. This group represented the families of the detained scientists. A news report quoted the daughter of one such scientist saying that her colleagues at college wanted to know the wrong her father had done: "She regretted that her father had used all his waking hours in making the country invincible and he got medals on his good performance. However, now the government was humiliating him."[41]

The families quickly organized themselves into interest groups and adopted the usual tactics of activist groups. They protested against the scientists' detention in front of important government buildings and press clubs; filed writ petitions in courts against detentions; called press conferences and issued press releases; liaised with political parties, parliamentarians, lawyers, and rights groups; and campaigned for the release of prominent scientists. At least two new interest groups were formed as a result of this new kind of social assertion: the Pakistan Professional Forum (PPF)[42] and Khan's Release Liaison Committee.[43] The following text of a statement issued by PPF at the end of a peaceful demonstration in Islamabad reflects a sense of sophisticated political awareness and an assertion of rights not usually associated with civilians in Pakistan:

[The] [n]uclear programme is [an] indispensable organ of Pakistan's national security. [The] Pakistani nation, for the last three decades, has been contributing to the country's nuclear programme in the form of taxes paid to the government despite severe economic hardships. The programme has been the target of negative propaganda by the hostile countries and Western media right from its inception. The latest allegations of the nuclear proliferation are part of the same negative media campaign that is designed for the purpose of depriving Pakistan of its most vital strategic asset and to force [the] Pakistani nation into subjugation.[44] According to one report, participants in the demonstration—mostly belonging to the professional class—protested against the government attitude that they said, "had sent shock waves among Pakistani intellectuals at home and abroad."[45]

The extent to which the families' reactions exposed the divisions within the national security establishment in the wake of the Khan controversy is important to consider. After all, these families have been part of the security establishment for as long as Pakistan's nuclear program has been operational. They have provided strong evidence of how the Pakistani professional class has seldom made distinctive political choices—such as being for or against the bomb—instead choosing only to protect its professional and economic interests. It becomes doubly interesting, therefore, to note that in the present environment, when the interests of this professional class are at stake, it has chosen to use the highly political rhetoric of rights for its case, knowing full well that it is taking on the very establishment that, for decades, has been its benefactor. This shows, perhaps, the coming of age of Pakistani society on the basis of increased access to information and media knowledge, on the one hand, and exposure to political advocacy by non-state actors, on the other. If they choose to, Pakistanis can use these tools to make a socio-political stand against state policies.

Whither the Antinuclear Movement?

The social landscape of Pakistan was set abuzz by the new controversy. Political parties and groups manipulated the issue as a good opportunity for social mobilization and political activism, primarily to score political points against General Musharraf. A number of organizations and groups played their role in presenting a civic perspective, showing a new form of social assertion as displayed by the families of the scientists.

But in this lively social milieu, the antinuclear movement appeared conspicuous by its near silence on the Khan controversy. Pervez Hoodbhoy wrote some articles referring to the issue, but most were analytical opinion articles, similar to those discussed earlier. In one of these articles, however, Hoodbhoy linked the Khan issue to the larger question of the value of nuclear weapons:

> Pakistan will have to put its nuclear house in order. Anything less than strict and complete accountability, regardless of rank or reputation, will leave the door open for those who may wish to try their luck, or in whom the fire of faith burns brighter. My country's loose nukes underscore a global danger that may already be out of control. Nuclear secrets will keep leaking as long as the bomb has value as a currency of power and prestige. Humanity's best chance of survival lies in creating taboos against nuclear weapons, much as those that already exist for chemical and biological weapons, and to work rapidly toward their global elimination. To do away with the bomb, bomb technology and the menace of their proliferation will require the

United States, as the world's only superpower, to take the lead by reducing its own nuclear arsenal, as well as dealing with all proliferators, including its ally Israel, at the same level.[46]

To a keen observer of the antinuclear weapons movement in Pakistan, it appeared that it did not address the A. Q. Khan nuclear proliferation controversy as it should have. Thus the antinuclear movement lost an important opportunity to strike home their point. In an interview published in the *News on Sunday,* I questioned the Pakistani physicist and antinuclear activist A. H. Nayyar as to whether he agreed with this observation. Disagreeing, Nayyar replied:

> The peace movement has always warned of the many dangers of Pakistan's nuclear weapons programme . . . Many of these fears have been realised, including the A. Q. Khan affair. Sadly, those in power in Pakistan do not yet understand the full seriousness of the harm the nuclear programme has done to us. The peace movement has a long way to go.
>
> Many of us in the Pakistani peace and anti-nuclear movement who have followed our nuclear weapons programme closely over the past three decades were not surprised by the revelation that A. Q. Khan was running an international network selling nuclear information and technology . . . Many of us have long worried about the growing presence of radical Islamists in our society and seen it happen in the nuclear complex.[47]

Nayyar's opinion reflects an intelligent calculation about nuclearism and its politics in Pakistan but also shows the limitations that continue to confront the antinuclear weapons movement in the country. The Khan scandal brought all its previous concerns to the forefront of national politics. Yet the movement seemed at a loss on how best to assertively, effectively, and influentially place itself in its center.

Conclusion

Dr. A. Q. Khan remains a figure of intense curiosity, not least because of the Pakistani government's insistence that no one speak to him. Political implications aside, it is of note that in a span of one year of the controversy, Pakistan's nuclear program has become a source of embarrassment and concern for its people, a far cry from the great pride it generated in the past. In this essay I have tried to analyze how this transformation occurred and how various segments of the national spectrum responded to the issue. My primary concern is whether this discomfort can translate into disillusionment with nuclear weapons? Based on the data and observations presented here, one can draw some basic conclusions on the status of Pakistan's current nuclear psyche and the impact it could have on the prospects of its nuclear program and the antinuclear movement.

First, the Khan scandal has completely changed the politico-strategic equation for Pakistan's nuclear program. It has particularly affected the traditionally comparative approach vis-à-vis India that can no longer be applied as comfortably as in the past. As opposed to India's nuclear program, Pakistan's has become politically vulnerable to international pressure. This has generated an automatic defensive posture among its managers, who are currently busy controlling the damage. The government continuously reassures the people that it will not roll back the nuclear program.

Second, the controversy has thrown the nation into a myriad of shocked confusion and outrage at the irresponsible management of its nuclear "assets." By and large, however, the sum total of this controversy has *only* amounted to Khan's personal fall and not the end of the grand idea of nuclear weapons as guarantors of the country's national security, evidence of its national progress, and a source of national pride.

Third, the dominant thinking evident in public opinion, expert analyses, and media influence is that of accepting the reality of nuclear weapons as a given for Pakistan's security apparatus. Elite discourse, whether for or against the bomb, has remained consistent. Popular voices have joined this discourse not necessarily from reducible positions of "for or against" but from the perspective of saving Pakistan's security assets from a hostile international environment and anti-Islam/anti-Pakistan conspiracies.

However, one sees interesting think-shifts in the positions of the mainstream national press. Contrary to popular perceptions, the "liberal" English press—in this case, *Dawn*—has shown an increased conformity with the establishment's views on national security and the nuclear program. On the other hand, *Jang,* one of the leading Urdu newspapers and traditionally known for its political conservatism, shows a remarkable intellectual departure by voicing concerns about the fate of world peace in the presence of nuclear weapons and their proliferation. But one clear reality emerges out of this mix. For all these segments, the *possession* of nuclear weapons—as opposed to their governance and safety—is now largely beyond question. Voices questioning possession remain rare. The national psyche understands that weapons must be retained at all costs, no matter the sacrifice—even if it means the disgrace of the "national hero." In fact, adequate governance and foolproof security have become the new subjects for concern and debate.

Fourth, Pakistan's major political parties have manipulated the Khan issue to score political points against General Musharraf's government. For them, the Khan issue is yet another vulnerable area for the Musharraf government, an issue they want to push for creating oppositional political pressure for their own parochial interests. However, the consensus of the past remains intact on the subject of nuclear weapons, namely, that nuclear weapons are the most important asset for Pakistan's security and national integrity, and anyone compromising their status will face collective political opposition.

Fifth, a new form of social assertion—as witnessed in the formation of groups campaigning for release of the scientists—is now operating *within* the paradigm of nuclearism while incorporating a new language of rights. This new activism accepts and propagates nuclear weapons as precious assets of Pakistan, as it campaigns to protect the people associated with their manufacture and management. Thus we see a narrowing of any previous gap between perspectives of the public, the experts, and political parties: no harm to or compromise on nuclear weapons is acceptable to Pakistani society.

Given this scenario, the kind of renewed challenges the country's antinuclear movement now faces are obvious. The national hero may have fallen, but, in so doing, he has actually become a martyr for many, which has only served to strengthen nuclearism in Pakistani society.

Notes

The source of the epigraph to this essay is Praful Bidwai and Achin Vanaik, *South Asia on a Short Fuse: Nuclear Politics and the Future of Global Disarmament* (New Delhi: Oxford University Press, 1999), 1–2. The contents of this essay are the sole responsibility of the author and do not necessarily reflect the views of the organization she currently works for.

1. http://www.presidentofpakistan.gov.pk/ (accessed 14 April 2008).

2. http://www.presidentofpakistan.gov.pk/PersonalLife.aspx

3. David Cortright and Amitabn Mattoo, eds., *India and the Bomb: Public Opinion and Nuclear Options* (Notre Dame, Ind.: University of Notre Dame Press, 1996); Samina Ahmed and David Cortight, eds., *Pakistan and the Bomb: Public Opinion and Nuclear Options* (Notre Dame, Ind.: University of Notre Dame Press, 1998); Praful Bidwai and Achin Vanaik, *South Asia on a Short Fuse: Nuclear Politics and the Future of Global Disarmament* (New Delhi: Oxford University Press, 1999) (published in the U.S. as *New Nukes: India, Pakistan, and Global Nuclear Disarmament* [Northampton, Mass.: Interlink, 1999]); Haider Nizamani, "Whose Bomb Is It Anyway? Public Opinion and Perceptions about Nuclear Weapons and Policy in the Post-Explosions Phase in Pakistan," Occasional Paper, Social Science Research Council, New York, 2001;Yogendra Yadav, Oliver Heath, and Anindya Saha, "Issues and the Verdict," *Frontline,* November 13–26, 1999; and Smitu Kothari and Zia Mian, eds., *Out of the Nuclear Shadow* (New Delhi: Rainbow, 2001).

4. These include *War and Peace/Jang Aur Aman*, a documentary film by Anand Patwardhan (30 minutes, color, 2002); *Pakistan and India under the Nuclear Shadow*, a documentary film by Pervez Hoodbhoy (35 minutes, color, 2001); and *Roz-e-Qaza: Hibakusha ki Aapbeti* (*The Last Day: Story of a Hibakusha*) a documentary film by Ayesha Gazdar (45 minutes, color, 2003).

5. Bidwai and Vanaik, *South Asia on a Short Fuse,* p. viii.

6. Pervez Hoodbhoy, "Pakistan's Nuclear Future," in Ahmed and Cortight, *Pakistan and the Bomb,* pp. 70–74.

7. *Agence France-Presse,* 9 December 2003. In May 2005 replicas of the Chaghi Hills along with the Ghauri missile were removed from their display point in a public park near the Lahore Railway Station. Government functionaries gave no explanation for this removal and even claimed that they had no knowledge of the removal operation. For details, see "Govt. Disowns Replicas Removal Responsibility," *The Nation,* 9 May 2005.

8. See Ardeshir Cowasjee, "The Depths of Degradation," *Dawn,* 22 December 2002.

9. "Dr. Qadeer Khan Removed to Facilitate Probe: Govt. Dispels Fears of N-Plan Rollback," *Dawn,* 1 February 2004.

10. "Dr. Khan Admits He Transferred N-Technology: Action to Be Decided by NCA," *Dawn,* 2 February 2004.

11. For details and the complete text of A. Q. Khan's statement, see *Dawn,* 5 February 2004.

12. *Dawn,* 18 February 2005.

13. Chairman, D. J. College Alumni Foundation, Karachi, *Dawn,* 5 February 2004.

14. *Dawn,* 10 February 2004.

15. Translated from *Jang,* 1 February 2004.

16. Translated from *Jang,* 14 February 2004.

17. *Dawn,* 23 February 2004.

18. *Dawn,* 28 February 2004.

19. Talat Masood, "Countering Proliferation," *Dawn,* 2 February 2004.

20. Ayaz Amir, "Khan, Scapegoat or Magician Extraordinary?" *Dawn,* 6 February 2004.

21. A. Rashid, "The Nuclear Question," *Dawn,* 7 February 2004.

22. Irfan Husain, "The Atomic Arms Bazaar," *Dawn,* 7 February 2004.

23. Shameem Akhtar, "NPT Authors and Proliferation," *Dawn,* 25 February 2004.

24. Irshad Ahmed Haqqani, "Nuclear Technology: Pakistan's Serious Imbroglio," translated from *Jang,* 1 February, 2005.

25. Nayyar Zaidi, "Security Should Be Provided to Those Serving the Nation," translated from *Jang,* 1 February 2004.

26. Abdul Qadir Hasan, "I Have Not Done Anything Wrong," translated from *Jang,* 5 February 2004.

27. Agha Masood Husain, "Do Not Divide the Nation Further," translated from *Jang,* 6 February 2004.

28. Shahid Hasan Siddiqui, "Highlights of Economy," translated from *Jang,* 10 February 2004.

29. Nazeer Naji, "Flowers and Bombs," translated from *Jang,* 16 February, 2004.

30. "Powell's Positive Stance," *Dawn,* 8 February 2004.

31. "Proliferation Issues," *Dawn,* 10 February 2004.

32. "Demand for National Preservation: An Extremely Cautious Strategy," *Jang,* 6 February 2004.

33. "Nation or Hero: Realism or Emotionalism?" *Jang,* 7 February 2004.

34. The Pakistan Muslim League-Nawaz (PML-N), Pakistan Peoples Party (PPP), and Pakistan Tehrik-i-Insaf (PTI) are opposition parties, whereas the Communist Party of Pakistan represents the extreme Left that sits on the margins of the country's political spectrum.

35. "Govt's Decision to Remove Dr. A. Q. Khan Criticized," *Dawn,* 1 February 2004.

36. *Dawn,* "Qadeer's Removal Criticized," *Dawn,* 2 February 2004.

37. *Dawn,* "Qazi Asks Musharraf to Quit," *Dawn,* 5 February 2004

38. *Dawn,* "HRCP Urges Due Process of Law for Scientists," *Dawn,* 27 January 2004.

39. *Dawn,* "KRL Scientists: PCHR Submits Motion to NA," *Dawn,* 29 January 2004.

40. *Dawn,* "Lawyers Demand Release of Scientists," *Dawn,* 24 January 2004.

41. Ibid.

42. See "Professional Forum Calls for Release of Scientists," *Dawn,* 30 January 2004.

43. See "Detained KRL Officials' Family Members Form Body," *Dawn,* 7 February 2004. Also see "Decision on KRL Men's Plea Today," *Dawn,* 9 February 2004.

44. *Dawn,* "Professional Forum Calls for Release of Scientists," *Dawn,* 30 January 2004.

45. Ibid.

46. See Pervez Hoodbhoy, "The Nuclear Noose around Pakistan's Neck," *Washington Post,* 1 February 2004. Also see idem, "Pakistan: Inside the Nuclear Closet," www.chowk.com (14 April 2008), http://www.chowk.com/show_article.cgi?aid=00003200&channel=civic%20center&start=0&end=9&chapter=1&page=1.

47. Ammara Durrani, "AH Nayyar: Pacifism with a Method," *News on Sunday,* 30 January 2005.

6

THE POLITICS OF DEATH: THE ANTINUCLEAR IMAGINARY IN INDIA

Srirupa Roy

It is one of those cases where the art of the reasoner should be used rather for the sifting of details than for the acquiring of fresh evidence. The tragedy has been so uncommon, so complete and of such personal importance to so many people, that we are suffering from a plethora of surmise, conjecture, and hypothesis. The difficulty is to detach the framework of fact—of absolute undeniable fact—from the embellishments of theorists and reporters. Then, having established ourselves upon this sound basis, it is our duty to see what inferences may be drawn and what are the special points upon which the whole mystery turns . . .

"Is there any point to which you would wish to draw my attention?"

"To the curious incident of the dog in the nighttime."

"The dog did nothing in the nighttime."

"That was the curious incident," remarked Sherlock Holmes.

Arthur Conan Doyle, "Silver Blaze," in *The Memoirs of Sherlock Holmes*, 1892

Why has there been no significant antinuclear movement in India? Like Conan Doyle, my attempt to answer this question foregoes the search for "fresh evidence" such as surveys on public attitudes toward the bomb, ethnographies of existing antinuclear movements, or analysis of media coverage of nuclear politics and India-Pakistan relations. I settle instead for the more limited task of simply (re)"sifting the details" of the mystery at hand. In what follows, I focus on one particular detail of the antinuclear movement, what we might call its "apocalyptic imaginary" or the rhetoric of mass death and destruction that antinuclear groups in South Asia have advanced in attempting to mobilize citizens of India and Pakistan since the nuclear tests of 1998.

The foundational premise of an antinuclear movement is a commitment to prevent mass annihilation. Toward this end, they reproduce cautionary specters of mass death and destruction that contrast markedly with the promise of life that has energized all modern political ideologies and social movements, including the nationalists' natalist fantasies and the socialists' utopian desires, the religious traditionalists' conservationist efforts and the liberals' guarantee of individual protection.[1] I argue here that the antinuclear symbolic repertoire of mass death and destruction does not have a radical political charge within the existing ideological terrain in postcolonial India; that (and to mix metaphors) the attempt to center a transformative politics on idioms and images of mass death and destruction is *necessarily* doomed.

The "curious incident" I investigate in this essay is, accordingly, the political limitations of mass death narratives in late modern India. What explains these limitations? What are the theoretical and political-ethical lessons to be learned from investigating the limits of dystopian and apocalyptic narratives? These questions inform this chapter, and, in addressing them, I carry forward the overarching theme of this volume, which is understanding South Asian nuclearization through the lens of socio-cultural and historical analysis. A counterpart to the examination of "how we have come to love the bomb," or the complex constellation of national fears and longings that underpin the nuclear testing decision of 1998, this essay explores the contours of the antinuclear imagination and asks whether, how, and why we have come to hate the bomb.

The notion of a transformative politics requires elaboration. Social movements are instances of collective action undertaken to bring about significant social and political change.[2] They are ideologically quite varied; for instance, a social movement inspired by Hindu nationalist ideology clearly subscribes to a very different vision of social and political transformation compared to a left social movement.[3] Despite these ideological variations, they all share a common goal of achieving substantial sociopolitical transformation and a common mobilizational strategy based on radical critique or a thoroughgoing interrogation of the existing sociopolitical order through what I call a "politics of anger." I contend that mass death narratives are unable to elicit and harness such a radical or transformative politics, and thus they cannot facilitate the emergence of a social movement. To use the language of social movement theory, the apocalyptic imaginary invoked and sustained by narratives of mass death has not led to an effective "injustice frame" or fostered an effective "insurgent consciousness."[4]

In focusing on the apocalyptic imaginary as the key to the puzzle of why a sustained antinuclear movement has not emerged in India, I subscribe to the school of social movement theory which holds that collective action of any kind can only be understood by exploring the symbolic-cultural landscapes within which individuals and groups act (or fail to act). From this perspective, the very notions of "action" and "movement" require us to engage with more than the macro-structural variables that shape social movements. Thus accounts of mass deprivation or transformations in political opportunity structures are only partial explanations for why social movements emerge at particular moments in time. The political resources and opportunities available to social movements are integral to an explanation but they do not exhaust the explanatory factors. Also required is an investigation of how social and cultural meaning is produced by individuals and groups. Analytical attention must be directed toward practices of meaning making—the particular "cultures of protest" and "symbolic repertoires" that are produced by social movements,[5] and to how these symbolic and cultural interventions relate to or resonate within the wider field of public culture. This calls for an exploration of the particular symbolic-cultural imaginary elaborated by a social movement and the field of engagement, or the symbolic-cultural landscape of contemporary public life. The following sections take up this task.

The first section locates the apocalyptic imaginary of the antinuclear movement within the new alignments of order and opposition that were formed in the aftermath of the nuclear tests of 1998. I show how the reconfiguration of India as a nuclear weapons state created new opportunities, as well as new political burdens, for the antinuclear movement, and I examine the different vocabularies of antinuclear protest that emerged in this context. The second section situates the apocalyptic imaginary within the wider field of postcolonial public culture. I examine the proliferation of mass death narratives around events and issues unrelated to nuclearization, and I argue that the imaginary of nuclear destruction is refracted through these depoliticized, even "anti-political," narrative lenses. The essay concludes with a consideration of whether, and how, an alternative antinuclear imagination might emerge.

Order and Opposition in Nuclear India

New Political Orders

The formal announcement of India's successful testing of the nuclear bomb on May 11, 1998, and Pakistan's declaration of a similar test a few days later, marked a significant disjuncture in South Asia's material and symbolic-ideational engagement with the nuclear bomb. The formal-legal shift from an antinuclear policy to a pro–nuclear weapon policy stance, and the structural realignments in the character of state authority in both India and Pakistan as a result of the unfettered ascendancy of "national security" as the dominant vocabulary of governance after May 1998,[6] also had counterparts in the realms of public culture and political discourse. The long-standing official moral condemnation of nuclear weapons in the first few decades after independence, and the more prevaricating stance of "nuclear ambiguity" that had characterized establishment discourses following the "peaceful nuclear explosion" under the Indira Gandhi regime in 1974 were now supplanted by a very different set of laudatory discursive constellations.

Starting in the summer of 1998, competing imaginaries of nuclear India as both a feared dystopia and a desired utopia would jostle for recognition in public cultural landscapes and media worlds, as the moral condemnation of nuclear weapons was joined by its opposite: exuberant proclamations of nuclear pride. A new set of triumphalist-celebratory representational repertoires[7] now emerged around the nuclear bomb, from Bal Thackeray's infamous declaration, "We have to prove that we are not eunuchs," to reports that Hindu nationalists were distributing sweets to celebrate the achievement of the tests, to the proud comments of bureaucrats, scientists, and civilians about India's new identity as a global player that led the writer Amitav Ghosh to conclude that India's nuclear bomb was the product of a "status-driven," not a "threat-driven," quest.

At stake here was not simply the novelty of these positive commentaries on the bomb, nor the resulting reconfiguration of the national imagination around the achievement of what state elites had denounced just a few decades earlier for economic, strategic, and moral-humanist reasons. Of significance as well were the transformed meanings, and the qualitatively different kind of affective-political work that negative and dystopian imaginaries of nuclear weapons and technologies had to undertake after May 1998.

As noted above, the denunciation of state efforts to possess nuclear weapons as immoral and illegitimate had been an enduring trope of postcolonial political discourse. Following independence, Gandhi's emphatic and unambiguous opposition to nuclear science and technology (and, in fact, to modern science and technology in general) was modified by Nehru's concession to the possibility that certain situations justified, even necessitated, the acquisition and use of nuclear technology, particularly if it could further the development of the newly sovereign nation-state.[8] This exemption did not apply, however, to military uses. The state's possession of nuclear weapons continued to be the target of moral-legal opprobrium, although this sanction against the present acquisition of nuclear weapons did not rule out the possibility of their acquisition or use in the future.[9]

The existence of such oppositional discourses about nuclear weapons was not itself a remarkable or distinctive phenomenon. After all, vocabularies of antinuclear protest were an integral part of social movement repertoires in many contemporary nation-states, particularly in those that already possessed nuclear weapons.[10] What distinguished postcolonial antinuclear discourses prior to the 1998 tests was their intimate relationship with state power, namely that the critique and condemnation of nuclear weapons was intrinsic to the language of governance in postcolonial India.

Nehru's emphatic condemnations of the destructive potential of nuclear weapons, Indira Gandhi's reassurance that the 1974 nuclear test was not at all connected with the ultimate evil of weaponization,[11] and, as recently as 1998, foreign policy officials' public endorsement of global nuclear disarmament—these are only a few examples of the tireless, repetitive statist disavowal of nuclearization in bureaucratic and policy circles throughout the half-century of independent India's existence, even though the official antinuclear mantra might have been disingenuous and ultimately hollow.

The transformation of this statist character of the antinuclear imagination in the post-1998 period, and the subsequent relocation of antinuclear discourses from the domain of state power to that of social protest amounted to the most politically consequential shift in the public cultural landscape of post-Pokhran II India. The dystopian imaginations of nuclear worlds were now radically disengaged from, and in fact deployed *against,* state institutions and government regimes. This meant that after May 1998 the antinuclear imagination had to harness two very different affective registers. The current impasse of antinuclear politics may be traced to the difficulties of this affective negotiation, as I explain below.

In the first instance, the task at hand was a continuation of the earlier effort to convey the sense of horror, despair, and disbelief over the enormity of the mass destruction that would result from a nuclear bomb. But where such a *politics of horror* was the only goal of the pre-1998 state-authorized antinuclear imaginary, a second and equally pressing imperative emerged once antinuclear vocabularies were decommissioned or dissociated from state power.

With the condemnation of nuclear weapons now serving as an expression of dissent rather than consent vis-à-vis the existing regime and the political status quo, antinuclear discourses were invested with an additional and radical charge, namely, a *politics of anger.* Henceforth the antinuclear imagination would have to respond to both these imperatives—to elicit the chilling, numbing, and paralytic horror that leads to moral revulsion and condemnation of nuclear weapons, and also the outrage that can lead to a purposive and concerted struggle against the illegitimate and undemocratic actions of the state.

Could this be achieved? To what extent did the antinuclear imagination in the wake of the 1998 tests respond to the new imperative of a politics of anger—a response that would have entailed modifying and even supplanting existing antinuclear lexicons of horror and moral condemnation?

Antinuclear Imaginaries

In recognition of the multiple stakeholders and arenas of late-modern politics, opposition to the 1998 tests took different forms addressed to diverse audiences. Protest and resistance were expressed through the familiar institutional routes and corporatist structures of civil society, such as political parties, trade unions, professional associations, and civic groups, and through decentralized insurgencies of political society and spontaneous mass action engendered by new social movements.[12] At once reaffirming and transcending the state's presentation of nuclearization as a nationally specific phenomenon (the bomb as the site and means for asserting a new definition of national identity), antinuclear activists addressed domestic audiences as well as international intergovernmental and nongovernmental constituencies. Alliances were forged both with global social movements of nuclear prevention and disarmament, and with local/national cultures of protest around issues as varied as environmental degradation, indigenous rights, popular science education, social and economic justice, secularism, and South Asian regional peace.[13]

This diversity would split the antinuclear opposition, so that the Pokhran tests would be criticized differently by left parties such as the Communist Party of India (Marxist) and Gandhian social movements such as the National Alliance of People's Movements, but several common clusters of antinuclear discourses and symbolic repertoires also emerged, each facilitating a distinctive strategy of political mobilization and opposition.

Initially *public good arguments* of antinuclear campaigns drew attention to the considerable social opportunity costs of nuclear weaponization. As the pithy text of a placard at an antinuclear protest in Delhi on Hiroshima Day in 1998 expressed it: "No Water, No Electricity, No Jobs, No Problem: We Have the Bomb!" The antinuclear arguments in the pamphlet, "The Buddha Would Not Have Smiled," that was distributed in the course of a public rally in Delhi on May 16, 1998, was another example of such reasoning:

> The process by which this decision was taken has been secretive and clearly undemocratic, and once again, the priorities of common people have been set aside for spurious considerations. In different parts of our country, people are struggling against poverty and deprivation, while so-called development projects displace millions of toiling people. The diversion of resources to a mutually destructive arms race on the subcontinent is insane, unjust and inhuman.[14]

As the above quote indicates, the trade-off between human security and national security was a primary focus of public educational campaigns. Campaign material highlighted the interested/selective rather than disinterested/neutral provenances of nuclear weapons policy, that this was a policy choice driven by narrow elite interests rather than by considerations of the "greater common good." When viewed against the backdrop of the considerable social and economic inequality that pervaded the subcontinent, and the fact that millions of citizens were presently denied access to basic essentials of life such as safe and adequate drinking water, shelter, education, and sanitation, the folly of investing state resources in the development and acquisition of nuclear capability was especially pronounced.

Further, this trade-off between national security and human security was described to be a zero-sum game. For instance, at a public demonstration on Calcutta's College Street immediately after the Indian nuclear tests, protestors "raised slogans demanding that the social issues like education, food, clothing, shelter should be given priority over the N-bombs. Comparing the cost of each Hydrogen Bomb they claimed that at least two lakhs [*sic*] primary schools can be set up or six hundred poor children can have one-time meals against the cost of a single H-bomb."[15] Such arguments emphasized the considerable opportunity costs of nuclearization. It was not just that national security expenditures took precedence over human security expenditures, but that every rupee spent on the nuclear project effectively reduced social spending. By questioning the existing priorities in state expenditures, the debate over nuclearization versus the public good brought the issue of the state's democratic accountability and legitimacy into the political-cultural arena. For the opponents of nuclear policy, the state's decision to engage in nuclearization violated the first principles of democratic governance: to oppose nuclear weapons was to indict the state for its unrepresentative, even illegitimate, policies and its manifest failure to secure the lives of its citizens.

Arguments about national history and ideology animated additional antinuclear campaigns. Here, the emphasis was on the fact that the nuclear tests were a departure from India's proclaimed commitment to normative principles of nonviolence and pacifism. References to Gandhian ideals, Nehru's rejection of nuclear weapons, and the loss of India's "moral stature" in the international community were the mainstay of this line of reasoning. The following extract from a press statement issued by the National Alliance of People's Movements (NAPM), a Gandhian umbrella organization representing local social movements from all across India, illustrates the logic of presenting the nuclear tests as a radical break in the otherwise pacifist course of Indian national history:

> After Independence, India has taken a principled stand against nuclear weapons and general militarization of the globe. India's moral and political power in international politics was largely dependent upon such principled stand and pursuit of a new international economic and political order. This stand has been paying short term and immediate dividends to our country in the international community. All along these years, [the] international community has been taking the Indian view seriously and has mostly adopted a tough posture towards the tantrums by Pakistan. That apart, India has forfeited the opportunity and historical responsibility to lead the march towards a more humane, peaceful world. We too have become ... part of the Global Market of Military-Industrial complex.[16]

Attention was also directed at the ideological motivations and implications of the nuclear tests which, according to Hindutva ideology, were yet another example of the radical reconfiguration of Nehruvian secularist India. From this perspective, the opposition to nuclear weapons was a key and necessary component of a larger and ongoing ideological and political battle against the ascendancy of Hindu nationalism in the postcolonial polity.

Strategic-realist arguments against nuclearization constituted a third strand of antinuclear opposition. In contrast to efforts to link antinuclear opposition to broader national political and social movements that worked toward other goals unrelated to nuclearization, such as social and economic justice or the defeat of Hindu nationalism, these oppositional discourses addressed official nuclear weapons policy on its "own" terms. Whether through countering official claims about the effectiveness of nuclear deterrence in securing strategic goals, or by establishing that India's effort at "nuclear blackmail" would not impact the existing hierarchies of power, antinuclear activists harnessed the strategic-realist idioms of nuclear scientists, bureaucrats, and foreign policy experts to argue against nuclearization. Although this form of argument was most commonly found in editorial comments by nuclear policy and strategic studies experts opposed to nuclear tests (for example, the Jawaharlal Nehru University professor Kanti Bajpai, the retired naval admiral Laxminarayan Ramdas, and the journalist-activists Achin Vanaik and Praful Bidwai), it was also endorsed by activist organizations such as the Delhi-based Parmanu Bomb Virodhi Andolan (PBVA):

> The earlier stand that the tests are meant to be a deterrent has proved to be false. We now fear that when the BJP [Bharatiya Janata Party] says that its nuclear policy stands vindicated they will use the excuse of the Pakistani tests to induct and deploy nuclear warheads, This will only lead to the escalation of tensions and the beginning of a nuclear arms race that no one can afford.[17]

Finally, a dominant theme was what I referred to earlier as the *apocalyptic imaginary,* or the specter of the mass destruction that would inevitably result from a nuclear war between India and Pakistan. The South Asian reproduction of this mid-century antinuclear leitmotif from Europe and the United States, with distinctly Judeo-Christian eschatological resonances, was not simply a modular replication or a mimetic replay of a "derivative discourse," to borrow Partha Chatterjee's leading phrase.[18] The nuclear nightmares haunting "our modernity" both mirrored and departed from the dystopias of nuclear Armageddon that had haunted public culture and political discourse in other parts of the world since the bombing of Hiroshima and Nagasaki in 1945.[19]

For instance, the chilling descriptions of the enormity of death and destruction that would surely result in the event of "bombing Bombay,"[20] or Amitav Ghosh's somber remapping of the ruins of Lutyens' Delhi in the aftermath of a nuclear disaster,[21] echoed the dark scenarios of Cold War nuclear dystopias and reproduced several of the iconic visions and metaphors commonly associated with nuclear death and destruction: the mushroom cloud, the death of time, the unbearable brightness of a "thousand suns."[22]

The political charge of these dystopian visions, however, reflected the unique imperatives of the postcolonial context. Thus, unlike the literary-aesthetic contours of Western nuclear horrors, Indian Armageddon had a resolutely scientific lineage. The frightening visions of the end of the world were unadorned by rhetorical excess and were presented instead in the methodical and measured language of scientific research.

Deliberately designed to be transformative interventions that could effectively question establishment certitudes, these chilling scenarios of nuclear devastation pitted careful scientific calculations against the scientific bombast of the state. A paradigmatic example of this is the "Bombing Bombay" report, produced by the physicist and antinuclear activist M. V. Ramana, which presented meticulous scientific calculations of the death and destruction that would follow a nuclear attack on Bombay. In contrast to the "artistic" approach of the West in its engagements with the nuclear imagination, where mostly novelists, poets, filmmakers, and artists invoke specters of mass destruction to dismantle the pretensions of nuclear science, in South Asia it was scientists who advanced conflagrationist visions of nuclear destruction: modernity's excesses called into question by archetypical modernists themselves.

Apart from their rational-scientific constitution, nuclear dystopias failed to resonate politically as a result of several other symbolic and affective features related to the eventual political non-resonance of this imaginary. To begin with, they were highly abstract. As the "Bombing Bombay" report clearly illustrated, the nuclear apocalypse was effectively a thought experiment: a "what if" series of events, in this case a scientific simulation or set of mathematical predictions. Although descriptions of what would happen during and after a nuclear explosion were horrific, the scenarios were strangely unreal in that the highly technical and totalizing imagery of nuclear destruction did not convey the individual and visceral phenomenology of pain and suffering attending the "mortification of the body."[23] Their effect was more metaphysical than somatic, with the experience of death and destruction temporally and spatially distanced from the immediate present. The eventual end of the world, and not the dangers and inequities of the here-and-now, was the focus.

Second, and related to this effect of distancing, was that, as in all doomsday prophesies, the postponement of disaster in the apocalyptic imagination had the unintended effect of deflecting attention from the urgent need for political action in the present. The implicit teleological determinism of nuclear dystopias—the emphasis on the inevitability of mass destruction in a nuclear age—also contributed to this effect. A telling comment by a citizen at an antinuclear rally in Delhi in May 1998 captures this effect all too well. "We are suffering and dying every day," noted the pedestrian, bemused and perhaps also annoyed by the traffic-stopping exertions of anti-nuclear activists at a busy street corner in the city. "A nuclear bomb will kill us all together one day, at the same time. So what's the difference?"[24]

Third, the heightened prominence of visibility, spectacle, and scale in these conflagrationist imaginaries, whose affective charge was based on the horrific sight and enormity of nuclear destruction, effectively foreclosed political action directed against the everyday, invisible, and structural inequities of power. The iconic representation of the mushroom cloud that circulated in pamphlets, posters, and other print material, along with the grainy, black-and-white images of a Hiroshima in ruins that haunted the cinematic productions of antinuclear activists, were undoubtedly chilling in their depiction. At the same time, however, the very enormity of destruction conveyed by these visual representations—for, indeed, it was the apparent, demonstrable, and visible quality of nuclear devastation to which they repeatedly drew attention—constituted the violence of nuclearization in exceptional terms, considerably removed in scale, scope, and intensity from the structural violence of "normal" politics-as-usual in South Asia. In the "apocalyptic imagination," as the term itself implies, the object of contemplation was the sociopolitical exception or the aberration of the once-in-a-lifetime nuclear apocalypse; the default or benchmark condition of the political norm did not fall under equivalent critical scrutiny.

With all this, the abstract, deferred, determinist, and spectacular constitution of the antinuclear movement's imagination of mass death and destruction had a constraining effect on the exercise of transformative political action in the present. Although it effectively elicited a "politics of horror," providing moving and compelling evidence about the totalizing devastation that a nuclear bomb would surely cause, it failed to enable the emergence of a "politics of anger" that could translate this moral shock and horror into a purposive struggle against the peremptory and undemocratic actions of a national security state.

An analysis of the internal logic and symbolic structure of the antinuclear imaginary, however, can only provide a partial explanation for its political effect. A comprehensive understanding requires investigation of the larger material and discursive universe within which it circulates, and the existing narrative frameworks and "theodicies" or rationalizations of suffering, death, and destruction that refract and modulate the idioms and images of Kali Yuga.[25] The following section addresses this task.

Mass Death Narratives in Postcolonial India

The apocalyptic imaginaries of the antinuclear movement do not exist in isolation but are refracted through other specters of mass death that saturate contemporary public culture. Since its inception, the antinuclear imagination has had to negotiate a dense representational terrain saturated with images, texts, historical experiences, public memories, institutional structures, and policy regimes about mass death. At least three different specters of mass death have haunted the postcolonial political-cultural field over the past fifty years, each structuring the public imagination in a distinctive way. Let us examine these in detail.

The first is the considerable death toll resulting from cyclones, earthquakes, volcanic eruptions, tsunamis, and other "natural disasters." The physical occurrence of natural disaster deaths is universal and random, as they can happen anytime, anywhere, to anyone, leveling prosperous urban populations in industrialized nations as well as impoverished fishing communities in the developing world.[26] However, the representational grammars that translate these lived experiences of death, destruction, pain, and suffering into a socially intelligible category of "natural disaster deaths" vary considerably across cultural and historical contexts, as do the repertoires of responses such deaths elicit—whether institutional, moral, or aesthetic.[27]

In postcolonial India the dominant understanding of mass deaths caused by natural disasters is that, in fact, they are sudden or unforeseen, aberrant, and unrelated to any form of human, social, cultural, or political agency. Unlike the politicized bodies of those who died in a riot, where death is inevitably an event of social, communal, and national significance, the most memorable feature of the lives felled by a "random act of God" is their political innocence and purity.

As Hendrik Hertzberg acidly observed in explaining the astonishing levels of global concern, sympathy, and grief over the death and devastation of the Asian tsunami disaster of December 2004, the "tsunami has no politics."[28] This aptly captures the pervasive tendency to represent natural disaster deaths as universal-human rather than socially or politically circumscribed tragedies. The peculiar quality of the "simple," "bare," or "unqualified" death that results from natural disasters can be extended to other events as well that, unlike the global spectacle of the tsunami, have remained within national frames of significance.

Thus, long before the tsunami crashed to shore, media reports and legislative discussions about the Andhra cyclone of 1977 and the West Bengal floods of 1978[29] were framed in virtually identical terms, with the horror of the death toll established through repeated assertions about the hapless innocence of the victims. More recently, the narratives of mass death in the context of the Gujarat earthquake of January 2001 provide another telling example of this practice of mourning "nonpolitical" mass deaths following natural disasters.

The depoliticized imagination of the Gujarat earthquake becomes all the more evident if we compare it to representations of another kind of mass death that took place in the same state a short while later, when at least three thousand people were killed during the anti-Muslim pogrom of March 2002. The universal humanity of the dead in the former case contrasts sharply with the communalized extinction of the latter, as the "human" corpse and the "Muslim" corpse are witnessed and mourned in very different ways.

The Gujarat earthquake victim, like the tsunami victim, was raised as a subject of general and unqualified empathy. The savagely mutilated bodies from Modi's Gujarat, like the Iraqi war dead or the torture victims in Abu Ghraib prison, were caught in the fury of ideological partisanship and subjected to the calculus of "deserved" and "undeserved" death, deaths to minimize and deaths to mourn. Initially, this differential valuation of dead bodies was even the subject of state policy, as Hindu victims of the Godhra "terrorist" attack were promised the sum of Rs.200,000 as ex-gratia compensation, whereas Muslim "riot victims" were offered exactly half that amount.

In sum, narratives and representations of mass disaster death in India have the effect of naturalizing and depoliticizing death. They depict mass death as an externality, thus disallowing questions of agency and culpability, institutional accountability, and democratic responsibility.

Riot victims are the subject of the second major narrative of mass death in postcolonial India, namely, that of "riot deaths." Like the discourses surrounding natural disaster deaths, these are produced by a range of both state and non-state (media and civil society) actors.

Official representations of riot deaths are governed by familiar narrative-symbolic conventions shaped by the legacy of colonial rule.[30] The exceptionalism of these deaths—the riot as a discrete eruption—is a ubiquitous trope. The metaphor of riots as tinderboxes that burst into flames, accompanied by descriptions of the chaos, confusion, and general social and moral panic and dissolution that prevails when things fall apart all of a sudden, are but some of the ways in which the discrete drama of the riot has been conveyed. Similar to the representation of natural disasters, riots are thus also represented as events that can be located within a bounded space and time. There is always a then and there for a riot, and, conversely, times and spaces that are declared to be riot-free.[31]

The other metaphor commonly evoked in official representations of riot deaths is apposite as well: the riot as the visible symptom of a disease plaguing the body politic reconstitutes the meaning of a riot in significant ways. The riot as a mysterious disease that "strikes" and "infects" society naturalizes what is actually a complex social process shaped by the interplay of human agency and socio-historical structures. The frequently invoked "virus of communalism" furthers this naturalizing logic, as the spread of a riot from one locale to another is seen to occur naturally. Riots are like diseases, the argument goes, and will run their infectious course.

Paradoxically, although riot pathologies have a naturalizing effect, they also authorize the agency and efficacy of institutional intervention. As Paul Brass pointed out in his provocative examination of dominant riot "texts" in postcolonial India, official discourses about riot pathologies hold out the hope that, like diseases, riots can be "cured"—that their contagious effect can indeed be kept at bay by the ministrations of experts, that it may even be possible to prevent riot deaths by "inoculating" society against future outbreaks.[32]

With these discourses of prevention, riot death narratives authorize the managerial interventions of the state. Indeed, as Thomas Hansen has noted, although commonly characterized as a momentary social and political collapse, a riot is, in fact, the (literal) site upon which the "myth of the state" is resurrected and its bureaucratic, legal, policy, and disciplinary powers are put on display.[33]

The official representation of a riot inevitably represents the state as the authoritative problem solver: the neutral, objective, and "sublime" institutional entity that comes to the aid of individual victims and of the nation as a whole in the aftermath of a riot.[34] Charges of state complicity, or the long-standing inequities and discriminatory policies that caused the riot, are inadmissible. Instead, the political imaginary of riot deaths locates the cause in "social evils" such as communalism, which can be eradicated by "better and more" intervention[35] rather than a critical questioning of state power.

Riot death narratives "foreclose multiplicity,"[36] replacing the complex and context-specific reasons for mass violence with a simplistic and invariant account of how "communal mind-sets" are manipulated by "power-hungry politicians" and "antisocial elements." Not only does such an explanation absolve the state of involvement and responsibility, it also endorses an explicitly anti-political stance. Thus, in the wake of riots, laments about the "dangers" and "evils" of political life and action dominate official discourse.

Ever since the Jabalpur riot of 1961—codified in state and academic circles as the first major riot after independence—citizens have been exhorted to transcend politics and return to the harmonious truths of Indian culture and history. The task at hand is not political organization and the assertion of transformative political agency but "recuperating" the ethos of intercommunal harmony and emulating the folk syncretisms practiced by communities that have "resisted the temptations" of modern politics. The haunting image of the riot dead thus turns us toward the nostalgic utopias and "golden ages" of history and myth, away from the risks and uncertainties of political engagement in the present.

The examination thus far has focused on state-produced narratives of riot deaths, such as the reports of official commissions of inquiry, parliamentary debates, police reports, and judicial decisions. As instances of "state propaganda," their failure to investigate state complicity in riot deaths is only to be expected. What is surprising, instead, is that narratives about riots produced by a variety of non-state actors are also shaped in similar ways. Thus, as Brass's investigation of the different riot texts in postcolonial India has established, reports in the independent print media have shored up the official truth on riots by reproducing the naturalizing, depoliticizing thesis of the "communal virus" and its spread.[37] And although civil society organizations have made concerted efforts to draw attention to the complicity of state actors and structures in riots, the primary long-term solution for preventing future riot deaths is the familiar call to "transcend politics" and return to the norms and ethos of peaceful coexistence that forms the "authentic" core of Indian culture.[38] Even in instances when civil activism targets state actors, the indictment in most cases is of the particular governing party (e.g., the Congress in the case of the anti-Sikh riots of 1984; and the BJP and

Sangh Parivar in the case of anti-Muslim riots after 1990) rather than the underlying structures of state power.[39]

Do narratives about mass deaths caused by industrial and technological accidents offer a different understanding of causality, institutional responsibility, and politics? Does the ability to identify a definite, named agent of mass death—for example, Union Carbide, Northern Railways, and Ansal Properties (the Delhi corporation that owned Uphaar Cinema, the site of a massive fire in 1997)—shift the representational terrain and enable the emergence of new political and ethical visions and practices? By way of answering these questions about the third major mass death narrative that has an enduring presence in postcolonial India, let us briefly consider the symbolic and material terrain of a paradigmatic industrial accident, the "Bhopal tragedy" of 1984.

On December 3, 1984, at least two thousand residents of Bhopal were killed by the accidental release of lethal methyl isocyanate gas from a pesticide plant. Foreshadowing the "instant death and endless devastation" scenarios of the antinuclear imaginary, even larger numbers suffered protracted illnesses, foreshortened life spans, and the loss of livelihood and economic security in the years to come.[40] The Bhopal disaster attracted considerable national and global media attention in the immediate period after the accident.[41] Even after the media spotlight moved on, the Bhopal tragedy continued to circulate in the public domain as a result of the legal and judicial actions undertaken by the Indian state over the following decade, and the activism of advocacy groups and victims-survivors groups in Bhopal such as the Gas Peedith Mahila Udyog Sangathan.[42]

These narratives of social suffering, as already noted, diverged from existing vocabularies of natural disaster deaths and riot deaths. Unlike the naturalized provenance of those types of events, the mass deaths in Bhopal were linked to the actions and decisions of one identifiable agent—Union Carbide, the corporation that owned and administered the industrial plant. This assignment of corporate responsibility meant that responses to the Bhopal disaster swiftly moved into the litigation arena, as post-disaster efforts involved not only relief and rehabilitation but the quest for punitive justice as well.

Another significant difference was the import assigned to the Bhopal deaths. With the passage of the Bhopal Act of 1989, the Indian government effectively nationalized the Bhopal disaster. Riot deaths were described in local terms, mapped onto specific urban spaces and memorialized as, for example, the "Ahmedabad riots" or, even more specifically, as "the violence at the Gulbarg housing complex." Bhopal, in contrast, was resignified as an *Indian* tragedy, pitting the Indian state, as the self-appointed legal guardian of the Bhopal victims—the infamous *parens patriae* government-as-parent clause—against an American corporation.

But even as the nationalization of the Bhopal disaster and the dominance of legal and medical relief and rehabilitation efforts set it apart from the usual responses to natural disaster deaths and riot deaths, the "state effect" of mass death narratives was preserved.[43] In fact, judicial-legal representations of Bhopal authorized the managerial interventions of the state with special vigor.

For instance, the view that mass death and destruction could be compensated, and that a "full and final settlement" for the Bhopal disaster was possible, consolidated social relations around the tutelary powers of the "guardian state," the definitive problem solver of the nation and its citizens. Moreover, as Kim Fortun, Ravi Rajan, and Veena Das pointed out in their critical investigation of the bureaucratic-legal discourses about Bhopal, the conflation of "justice" with financial compensation from Union Carbide, and the related assertion of an "end of suffering" once the legal battle was over and the monies awarded, disembedded the Bhopal disaster from a wider historical and social context of causes and implications.[44]

The varied forms and expressions of violence and injustice that led up to and followed Bhopal were elided in the dominant narrative that Union Carbide was the sole author of the disaster, and of that the disaster itself was confined to the dark night of December 3, 1984. The alliance between state and global capital, and the deals struck in the political marketplace that had allowed Union Carbide to repeatedly violate land-use and environmental safety regulations; the stark polarizations in the city that mapped suffering along class lines (an overwhelming proportion of the victims were those who lived in makeshift housing in poorer areas close to the plant); and, finally, the unintended ways in which concerned civil society organizations transformed the lived experience of pain into an abstract "categorical politics" of compensation for "victims"[45] put in place a rationalization of death and suffering that blunted the radical charge of a politics of anger.[46]

Conclusion

In keeping with the theme of this volume, that South Asian nuclearization requires a socio-cultural framework of explanation, this chapter has explored the symbolic landscapes of antinuclear protest in India. I have addressed the question of why an antinuclear movement has failed to take root in any sustained sense in India, and, by extension, the more general problem of how and why social movements emerge (or fail to emerge). Specifically I focused on one piece of the puzzle, namely, the political-cultural arenas or "fields" of discourse and ideology to which the antinuclear movement relates. I argued that although "opposition" may be common to all strands of antinuclear discourse, only certain kinds of oppositional discourse energize transformative social and political action. My contention here is that specters of mass death and destruction do not have a significant actional charge in postcolonial India. As the preceding sections have shown, the idioms and images of mass death that structure the ideological-political field horrify, shock, and sadden but do not anger. They reject the possibility that death from natural disasters and riots can be linked to the inequities of state structures, policies, and ideological practices. This forecloses the opportunity to hold the state accountable, to call for a more just, equitable, and substantively democratic political order, to *take present action.*

The apocalyptic imaginary of nuclear destruction, therefore, requires revision: specters of mass death are ineffective at best, and may even be counterproductive. Because apocalyptic scenarios reproduce the action-inhibiting representational logic of mass death, they inadvertently shore up the very features of state power that require dismantling if a nuclear-free South Asia is to emerge.

To conclude, there are three possible ways that an alternative "politics of anger" might take shape. The first would be a shift of mobilizational rhetorics from doomsday prophecies to current insecurities and injustices. This shift could possibly be achieved by diversifying the field of antinuclear protest beyond its primary preoccupation with nuclear weapons, and linking opposition to nuclear weapons with opposition to nuclear energy. Whereas the former defers death and destruction to the future, the latter brings into focus everyday, ongoing, and immediate instances of deprivation, injustice, and suffering. Such a shift calls for action protesting the human cost of nuclear energy, including the expropriation of land without compensation, the high incidence of infant developmental abnormalities among populations living in close proximity to nuclear power plants, the appalling lack of safety standards for workers in uranium mines—costs that are immediate and tangible, not hypothetical and abstract.

Second, instead of highlighting the horror of nuclear destruction, the "killing state" should take center stage. The object of opposition is not the bomb but its owner: the state that endangers the lives of its citizens. It may well be that the appropriate analogy for nuclear India is neither Hiroshima nor Chernobyl, but another kind of "curious incident" altogether: Jalianwala Bagh, Nellie, Trilokpuri, Bhagalpur, Naroda Patiya, Auschwitz, Diyarbakir, Wounded Knee, Tuskegee, Guantanamo Bay.

Finally, the "anti"-politics of the apocalyptic imaginary—its exclusively oppositional and dystopian stance—should be supplemented by positive political imaginaries, desires, and visions. As the rich legacy of social activism in India reminds us, movements for political and social transformation are built not on the fear that this world will end but on the hope that other worlds are possible.

Notes

1. Foucault's discussion of "biopolitics" is usually taken as the theoretical lodestone for discussions of how management (and indeed the production) of life ("the population") comes to be the primary focus of modern politics. See Michel Foucault, *Society Must Be Defended,* trans. David Macey (London: Penguin, 2003). For a different exploration of the relationship between politics, power, life, and death, see Giorgio Agamben, *Homo Sacer: Sovereign Power and Bare Life* (Stanford, Calif.: Stanford University Press 1998); Zygmunt Bauman, *Mortality, Immortality, and Other Life Strategies* (Stanford, Calif.: Stanford University Press 1993); Jean Baudrillard, *Symbolic Exchange and Death* (Thousand Oaks, Calif.: Sage, 1993); Lauren Berlant, *The Queen of America Goes to Washington City: Essays on Sex and Citizenship* (Durham, N.C.: Duke University Press 1997); Achille Mbembe, "Necropolitics," *Public Culture* 15, no.

1 (2003): 11–40; Anne Norton, *Blood Rites of the Poststructuralists: Word, Flesh, Revolution* (London: Routledge, 2002).

2. The vast sociological literature on social movements offers a wealth of interpretive paradigms to explain the emergence, dynamics, and eventual impact ("success" or "failure") of social movements. Although the definition of the phenomenon under consideration is varied, paradigms converge on a shared understanding of social movements as a form of concerted and visible collective action in the public sphere, which is undertaken in the effort to transform some aspect of the existing social, economic, cultural, and political status quo. The above discussion is based on this minimalist definition of a social movement. For a discussion of social movement theory, see, among others, Hank Johnston and Bert Klandermans, eds., *Social Movements and Culture* (Minneapolis: University of Minnesota Press, 1995); and Sidney Tarrow, *Power in Movement: Social Movements, Collective Action, and Politics*, 2nd ed. (New York: Cambridge University Press, 1998).

3. For an intriguing discussion of Hindu nationalism as a social movement, see Amrita Basu, "The Dialectics of Hindu Nationalism," in Atul Kohli, ed., *The Success of India's Democracy* (Cambridge: Cambridge University Press, 2001), 163–190.

4. I borrow these terms from William Gamson, "The Social Psychology of Collective Action," in Aldon Morris and Carol Mueller, eds., *Frontiers in Social Movement Theory* (New Haven, Conn.: Yale University Press, 1992).

5. On the symbolic-cultural dimensions of social movements, see Hank Johnston and Bert Klandermans, eds., *Social Movements and Culture* (Minneapolis: University of Minnesota Press, 1995).

6. This has been extensively documented. See Itty Abraham, *The Making of the Indian Atomic Bomb: Science, Secrecy, and the Postcolonial State* (New Delhi: Orient Longman 1998); Praful Bidwai and Achin Vanaik, *New Nukes: India, Pakistan, and Global Nuclear Disarmament* (New York: Olive Branch Press, 2000); George Perkovich, *India's Nuclear Bomb: The Impact on Global Proliferation* (Berkeley: University of California Press, 1999); and M. V. Ramana and C. Rammanohar Reddy, eds., *Prisoners of the Nuclear Dream* (Delhi: Orient Longman, 2003).

7. For a fascinating comparative case study of reimagination of French national identity in the post-nuclear age, see the classic study of Gabrielle Hecht, *The Radiance of France: Nuclear Power and National Identity after World War II* (Cambridge, Mass.: MIT Press, 2000).

8. The differentiation between the destructive power of nuclear weapons and the development of "peaceful" atomic energy for civilian purposes was a central pillar of Nehruvian nuclear doctrine.

9. In Itty Abraham's useful revisiting of "Nehruvian pacifism," the caveats about "possible use" that qualified the official stance on nuclear disarmament are brought into focus. See Abraham, *The Making of the Indian Atomic Bomb,* 1998.

10. See, for instance, Hugh Gusterson's ethnographic exploration of antinuclear activism in the United States in his *Nuclear Rites: A Weapons Laboratory at the End of the Cold War* (Berkeley: University of California Press, 1996).

11. For an extensive discussion of the policy discourses on the first Pokhran test, see George Perkovich, *India's Nuclear Bomb: The Impact on Global Proliferation* (Berkeley: University of California Press, 1999).

12. For a discussion of "political society" as the informal, non-elite zone of political engagement on the part of the mass public who are excluded from the rarefied domains of civil society and organized/institutionalized political formations such as parties and civic associations, see Partha Chatterjee, *The Politics of the Governed: Reflections on Popular Politics in Most of the World* (New York: Columbia University Press, 2004).

13. On this, see M. V. Ramana's discussion of a broad-based antinuclear movement committed to the realization of a "just peace" in "For a Just Peace: The Anti-nuclear Movement in India," *Items: Social Science Research Council Newsletter,* May 12, 1999.

14. Available online at http://pagesperso.fr/sacw/saan/buddha.htm (accessed April 17, 2008).

15. *Statesman,* May 17 1998.

16. NAPM Press Note, May 14, 1998. Available online at http://www.sacw.net.

17. PBVA Press Statement. Available online at http://www.sacw.net.

18. Partha Chatterjee, *Our Modernity* (Rotterdam and Dakar: SEPHIS-CODESRIA Publications, 1997).

19. For a discussion of nuclear dystopias in the West, see, among others, Paul Boyer, *By the Bomb's Early Light: American Thought and Culture at the Dawn of the Atomic Age* (Chapel Hill: University of North Carolina Press, 1994); Robert Jay Lifton, *Death in Life: Survivors of Hiroshima* (Chapel Hill: University of North Carolina Press, 1991); M. Susan Lindee, *Suffering Made Real: American Science and the Survivors at Hiroshima* (Chicago: University of Chicago Press, 1994); and Spencer Weart, *Nuclear Fear: A History of Images* (Cambridge, Mass.: Harvard University Press, 1988).

20. This was the evocative title of M. V. Ramana's estimate of the casualties of a nuclear explosion in Bombay. See M. V. Ramana, *Bombing Bombay* (Cambridge, Mass.: International Physicists for the Prevention of Nuclear War, 1999).

21. See Amitav Ghosh, "Countdown," *New Yorker,* October 26, 1998.

22. Ibid. See also S. Rashid Naim, "*Aadhi Raat Ke Baad,*" in Stephen P. Cohen, ed., *Nuclear Proliferation in South Asia: The Prospects for Arms Control,* 23–61 (Boulder, Colo.: Westview, 1991).

23. I borrow this phrase from James Der Derian, *Virtuous War: Mapping the Military-Industrial-Media-Entertainment Network* (Boulder, Colo.: Westview, 2001).

24. New Delhi, May 1998. Also cited in Srirupa Roy, "Nuclear Frames: Official Nationalism, the Nuclear Bomb, and the Anti-Nuclear Movement in India," In M. V. Ramana and Rammanohar Reddy, eds., *Prisoners of the Nuclear Dream* (Delhi: Orient Longman 2003).

25. For a discussion of narratives and policy practices that work to "rationalize" suffering, see Veena Das, "Sufferings, Theodicies, Disciplinary Practices, Appropriations," *International Social Science Journal* 49 (1997): 563–567.

26. See, for instance, Jared Diamond, *Collapse: How Societies Choose to Fail or Succeed* (New York: Viking, 2004); and Simon Winchester, *Krakatoa: The Day the World Exploded* (New York: Harper Collins, 2003).

27. The varied meanings of death across time and space is discussed in Philippe Aries, *Western Attitudes Towards Death: From the Middle Ages to the Present* (Baltimore: Johns Hopkins University Press, 1974); Rukmini Bhaya Nair, *Lying on the Postcolonial Couch: The Idea of Indifference* (Minneapolis: University of Minnesota Press, 2002); David Clark, ed., *The Sociology of Death: Theory, Culture, Practice* (Oxford: Oxford University Press, 1993); and Nancy Scheper-Hughes, *Death Without Weeping: The Violence of Everyday Life in Brazil* (Berkeley: University of California Press, 1993).

28. See Hendrik Hertzberg, "Flood Tide," *New Yorker,* January 17, 2005. The contrast between the global concern over the tsunami deaths and the relative global indifference following the deaths in the recent earthquake in northern Pakistan/India are another telling example of this phenomenon. In the current conjuncture of global Islamophobia, the Pakistani dead, one could argue, are politicized in ways that the "innocent tsunami victims" were not. Within India, a similar dynamic of politicization prevails, as the particular location of the earthquake in the "hotspot" of Kashmir has had a significant impact on public responses to the disaster.

29. See Stephen P. Cohen and C. V. Raghavulu, *The Andhra Cyclone of 1977: Individual and Institutional Responses to Mass Death* (New Delhi: Vikas 1979).

30. Paul Brass, *Theft of an Idol: Text and Context in the Representation of Collective Violence* (Princeton, N.J.: Princeton University Press, 1997); Gyanendra Pandey, *The Construction of Communalism in Colonial North India* (Oxford: Oxford University Press, 1990).

31. This argument is presented in Ashutosh Varshney, *Ethnic Conflict and Civic Life: Hindus and Muslims in India* (New Haven, Conn.: Yale University Press, 2002); and Steven Wilkinson, "Putting Gujarat in Perspective," *Economic and Political Weekly,* April 27, 2002.

32. Brass, *Theft of An Idol.*

33. Thomas Blom Hansen, "Governance and Myths of State in Mumbai," in C. J. Fuller and Veronique Benei, eds., *The Everyday State and Society in Modern India* (New Delhi: Social Science Press, 2000).

34. Thomas Blom Hansen and Finn Stepputat, eds., *States of Imagination: Ethnographic Explorations of the Postcolonial State* (Durham, N.C.: Duke University Press, 2001).

35. The call for state intervention is also produced by other policy discourses and practices. For instance, according to David Ludden, the call for "more and better" state intervention was a standard feature of developmental discourse in the colonial as well as postcolonial periods, enabling the developmental regime to consolidate its authority. See David Ludden, "India's Development Regime," in Nicholas Dirks, ed., *Colonialism and Culture* (Ann Arbor: University of Michigan Press, 2002).

36. I borrow this term from Kaylin Goldstein, "Secular Sublime: Edward Said at the Israel Museum," *Public Culture* 14, no. 1 (2005): 27–54.

37. Brass, *Theft of an Idol.*

38. Rustom Bharucha, *In The Name of the Secular: Contemporary Cultural Activism in India* (New Delhi: Oxford University Press, 1998).

39. For instance, the defeat of the Hindu right was a primary concern of civil society activists in the aftermath of the Gujarat pogrom of 2002. However, as the current impasse over securing justice for the victims of the anti-Sikh pogrom of 1984 demonstrates, the "secular victory" of returning a Congress government to power is a compromised one. While the Congress-dominated United Progressive Alliance (UPA) coalition has indeed condemned the Gujarat pogrom and declared its commitment to the swift pursuit of justice, the prosecution of the guilty parties (many of whom were Congress politicians) responsible for the carnage of Sikhs in 1984 has been repeatedly halted and delayed.

40. Kim Fortun, *Advocacy after Bhopal: Environmentalism, Disaster, New Global Orders* (Chicago: University of Chicago Press, 2001).

41. Lee Wilkins, "Media Coverage of the Bhopal Disaster: A Cultural Myth in the Making," *International Journal of Mass Emergencies and Disasters* 4, no. 18 (1986): 7–33

42. Ravi Rajan, "What Disasters Tell Us about Violent Environments: The Case of the Bhopal Gas Disaster," In Michael Watts and Nancy Peluso, eds., *Violent Environments* (Ithaca, N.Y.: Cornell University Press, 2001).

43. For a discussion of the state as an "effect" of discourses and practices rather than a reified entity, see Timothy Mitchell, "Society, Economy, and the State-Effect," in George Steinmetz, ed., *State/Culture* (Durham, N.C.: Duke University Press, 1999).

44. Das, "Sufferings, Theodicies, Disciplinary Practices, Appropriations"; Rajan, "What Disasters Tell Us."

45. Veena Das, "Suffering, Legitimacy, and Healing," In *Critical Events: Anthropological Perspectives on Contemporary Asia* (Delhi: Oxford University Press, 1995). Ravi Rajan, "Missing Expertise, Categorical Politics, and Chronic Disasters: The Case of Bhopal," n.d.

46. However, the ongoing interventions of survivors groups, such as the Gas Peedith Mahila Sangathan, suggest that the mass deaths of Bhopal can be remembered and represented in another way, one that has, in fact, rejected the rationalizations of the dominant narrative to offer a thoroughgoing interrogation of state power and social relations (Fortun, *Advocacy after Bhopal*). The consistent refusal of Bhopal survivors to accept the notion of a "final settlement" through monetary compensation, the contestation of medicalized determinations of victimhood, the efforts to highlight the antidemocratic constitution of the Bhopal Act and its *parens patriae* structure of justice, and the annual rituals of mourning and remembrance that convey the tangible immediacy of social suffering by locating the Bhopal tragedy in the living present rather than in the distant past are examples of how "angry" narratives can equally emerge around mass death.

7

PAKISTAN'S ATOMIC PUBLICS: SURVEY RESULTS

Haider Nizamani

Pakistani society is riddled with fissures on almost every aspect concerning the nature of the political system, nation building, the meaning of national identity and the means to ensure it. When it comes to the nuclear issue amid this cacophony and chaos, General Pervez Musharraf asserts that the nation is in complete consensus on Pakistan's nuclear program. Leaders of *Jamaat-e-Islami,* the most vocal political party in espousing the cause of nuclear Pakistan, argue that barring a few antinuclear individuals, the overwhelming majority of Pakistanis consider nuclear weapons essential for the country's security. But is there really a consensus in Pakistan regarding the nuclear option? Have people thought about their country's nuclear weapons program and policy? Have they considered the likely costs? Do they know who controls the country's nuclear infrastructure? These questions address the command-and-control dimension of the nuclear program, the role of nuclear weapons in current and future policy making, the probability of their accidental use, and scenarios in which Pakistanis might support their deliberate use. Probing these issues, which are the staple diet of traditional security studies, will help us understand the role played by nuclear weapons in the political sociology of Pakistan. Peoples' responses to Pakistan's nuclear weapons program will inform us about the nature of society and politics in that country.

In seeking answers to these questions, I conducted a countrywide survey, with the help of dedicated volunteers, between June and August 2000 to gauge the level of nuclear nationalism and its related aspects in the world's newest nuclear power, and to ascertain the reactions of ordinary men and women living in different parts of the country.[1] With illiteracy hovering at around 60 percent, the majority of people living in rural areas, and women often considered as silent spectators in the political culture, earlier surveys on the nuclear issue have only solicited the views of the elite urbanized section of the population. Although useful in some respects, those surveys tell us little about the presumed consensus on the nuclear issue. The present survey tries to fill that gap by also reaching out to the marginalized and rural sections of the population in order to elucidate the various public opinions and attitudes about Pakistan's security, with special reference to the different aspects of the nuclear issue in the post-Chagai period.

Pakistan: Profile and Context

To familiarize readers with Pakistan's political landscape, I begin with a brief profile of Pakistan, as well as a demographic breakdown of the survey respondents. Pakistan's whopping population clock was ticking at 157 million as of August 2006. According to a 1998 census, the population at that time was 132 million, with the majority (67%) living in rural areas.

Pakistan comprises four provinces (the Punjab, Sindh, North-West Frontier Province [NWFP], and Balochistan), the federal capital territory of Islamabad, and the federally administered tribal areas (FATA). The Punjab is the most populous province of Pakistan with a population of about 74 million, approximately 56 percent of the total population. For the purposes of this chapter, I include Islamabad, which is technically federal capital territory, in the Punjab, which today is seen as the region that most ardently supports the prevailing official vision of Pakistan. The Punjab is the big brother who bullies the smaller provinces of Pakistan because of its overwhelming presence in the armed forces—the institution that has directly ruled the country for almost half its existence. Like other provinces of the country, the Punjab is multilingual; the Siraiki-speaking population lives in the southern part of the province, whereas those who speak Punjabi are in the center and the north. The central districts of the Punjab were impacted the most by the 1947 Partition. Millions of Punjabi Muslim refugees arrived in this region of the newly carved-out Pakistan with stories of the atrocities committed against them in India. In subsequent years Partition has cast a long shadow on Punjab's political psyche, with India seen through the lens of the Partition tragedy.

Sindh, the second most populous province of Pakistan, has a population of about 29.9 million, approximately 23 percent of Pakistan's total population. There are two main linguistic groups in Sindh. The Mohajirs, which literally means "immigrants," speak Urdu and are mainly from Northern India, having arrived in the province during

Partition and in the years that followed. They are largely settled in urban metropolises such as Karachi and Hyderabad. Karachi, the country's largest city with a population of approximately 6 million, is considered a Mohajir stronghold. The Muttahida Quami Movement (MQM) disputes the 6 million figure, instead estimating Karachi's population as more that 10 million. Those living in the rural areas and small towns of the province predominantly speak Sindhi.

The Mohajirs have been electing the Muttahida Quami Movement (MQM) candidates as members of provincial and national legislatures in successive elections. The party, with its top leadership living in exile in London, has been vehemently against the "Punjabi Establishment." Altaf Hussain, the leader of the MQM, has gone so far as to declare the 1947 Partition as one of the greatest blunders in human history. He has challenged the validity of the "Ideology of Pakistan"—a pliable term in the dominant discourse in Pakistan carrying various meanings at different times. The Sindhi intelligentsia's anathema and mistrust toward Islamabad even predates the MQM's pronouncements. They have long viewed Sindhis as a wronged community in Pakistan.

The NWFP, with a population of 18 million, has about 14 percent of Pakistan's population. Its proximity to Afghanistan and its image as a sanctuary for alleged terrorists has put the region in the international headlines more than any other part of the country. The provincial government that came to power in 2002 was led by an alliance of assorted religious parties. This group's ascendancy to power is partly owing to its skillful use of anti-American sentiment in the wake of the 2001 military invasion of neighboring Afghanistan; it is also partly because the military-led government of General Musharraf disallowed Pakistan's two most popular personalities—Benazir Bhutto and Nawaz Sharif—to contest in the polls. NWFP is viewed as the junior partner in Pakistan's establishment because of its sizable share in the military top brass. Pashtun sub-nationalism, relying on the political legacy of Khan Abdul Ghaffar Khan dating back to pre-Partition times, has always challenged the proponents of Pakistani nationalism with some degree of success.

The sparsely populated province of Balochistan is Pakistan's largest province. About 5 percent of the country's people live in this mostly rugged area bordering Iran and Afghanistan. Within Balochistan, Balochi is the mother tongue of about 54.76 percent of the population, and 29.6 percent of the population there speaks Pashto. Baloch nationalists in Balochistan have been fighting pitched battles with Pakistani security forces for more than a year. During 2004 this struggle became more intense, causing the death of more than thirty soldiers and paramilitary personnel in attacks on troops and government installations, including the Sui Gas Complex. In January 2005, eight people were killed in fighting near strategic gas fields after a local doctor was raped, allegedly by an officer of the security forces. Since then there have been daily attacks on security forces, railways, and the power and communications infrastructure. The level of alienation from Islamabad and sense of deprivation is most acute among Balochs within Pakistan.

All these sub-national movements in Pakistan, taken together, do not necessarily echo the views of the dominant national discourse about the country's identity, security needs, and means to ensure national security.

Demographic and Sociopolitical Breakdown of Respondents

The sample size in the countrywide survey examined here was 801 respondents. Of these, 400 were from the Punjab, of which 68 percent were male and 31 percent female. There were 199 respondents from Sindh, 133 males (67 percent) and 66 females (33 percent), almost equally divided between rural and urban areas. Those polled in the NWFP numbered 150, 80 percent of them male; of the 52 respondents from Balochistan, about 88 percent were male. Although the ideal survey would have had equal numbers of male and female respondents, this was not possible because of the cultural impediments to interacting with women. This obstacle was most acute in the NWFP and Balochistan because of their more rigid cultural norms regarding gender segregation. Still, the percentage of women respondents in this survey is significantly higher than the survey commissioned by the Joan B. Kroc Institute and published in 1998 as an edited volume, *Pakistan and the Bomb: Public Opinion and Nuclear Options*. That survey was conducted prior to the May 1998 explosions, and only 7 percent of the respondents were female.

Pakistan is a society of young people—43 percent of Pakistanis are under the age of fifteen—and this is reflected in the breakdown of respondents by age. Seventy-five percent of those surveyed are younger than thirty-nine. Islamabad has persistently tried to create an overarching Pakistani identity at the expense of ethno-linguistic identities, but this survey shows that people in Pakistan can and do maintain multiple identities. The Punjab is perceived as the fortress of Pakistani nationalism where ethno-lingual identity has been superseded by pan-Pakistani identity. Of the 400 respondents, about 49 percent identified themselves as Punjabis and 18 percent as Pakistanis. About 5 percent from Punjab identified themselves as Baloch; this is explained by the sizable Siraiki- and Balochi-speaking population living in the southern part of Pakistan which considers itself as Baloch.

Sindh is an ethno-linguistic mosaic, and the manner in which people have defined their identities amply testifies to that: slightly over half of the respondents, or 55 percent, identified themselves as Sindhis. This shows the level of confidence in identifying oneself as a part of the Sindhi imagined community. The MQM has been in the forefront of creating a Mohajir sense of identity, but only 15 percent of the respondents identified themselves as Mohajirs, well below the projected percentage of the Urdu-speaking population in Sindh. The answer lies partly in the fact that 14 percent of the respondents identified themselves as Pakistanis, and, one can safely proffer, that most of these speak Urdu.

The bilingual feature of Balochistan is also evident in that 50 percent of the respondents identified themselves as Baloch and 33 percent as Pathans. The NWFP respondents are the most monolithic group in terms of their ethnic identity, as about 90 percent consider themselves Pathan.

The Countrywide Nature of Nuclear Nationalism

The responses to half a dozen selected questions posed in our survey provide a window into the national pulse regarding major aspects of Pakistan's nuclear policy and politics. An in-depth breakdown of additional questions regarding nuclear policy and politics along provincial lines will also broaden our understanding.

India's government, led by the Bharatiya Janata Party (BJP), in an operation codenamed *Shakti* (strength), conducted nuclear explosions on May 11, 1998. This decision determined the timing of the Pakistani explosions that followed on May 28. The question for the government of Nawaz Sharif was not whether it would authorize tests but when it would do so. After the explosions Sharif has claimed that Pakistan's defense had become impregnable. A couple of years after the tests, we asked the people of Pakistan if they shared Sharif's sentiment; 66 percent said yes, and 34 percent said no.

Greater honor, respect, and status are oft-repeated themes among proponents of the nuclear option in Pakistan. The leading lights of nuclear nationalism argue that Pakistan, as the first Muslim country to induct nuclear weapons into its armory, has earned the respect of the world and of Islamic countries in particular. Sixty-one percent think that nuclear weapons have earned Pakistan honor and respect, whereas 38 percent disagree.

Nuclear nationalists frequently refer to ordinary Pakistani's well thought-out adherence to the established parameters of the country's nuclear policy. Our survey showed, however, that that is not necessarily the case (see Table 7.1). More noteworthy is that only 51 percent of respondents said that they trust the government's official assertions about Pakistan's nuclear policy and program. Almost half the respondents either did not believe the government or were ignorant of the government's statements.

The Jamaat-e-Islami, arguably the most organized among Pakistan's Islamic parties, championed the cause of preventing the government from signing the Comprehensive Nuclear Test Ban Treaty (CTBT). To pressure the government, the Jamaat conducted what it termed a "nationwide referendum" on the CTBT in March 2000. The results, as the Jamaat predicted, showed that an overwhelming majority, almost 98.5 percent, of those who voted in the referendum were against Pakistan signing the CTBT. When we posed the same question in our survey, however, only 56.5 percent of respondents opposed the signing of the treaty, a far cry from the official claims of the Jamaat referendum. Thirty-six percent wanted Pakistan to sign the CTBT, and 6.5 percent had no opinion on the issue.

Table 7.1

Degree of Thinking Given to Pakistan's Nuclear Policy

	Number	Percentage
Serious	344	44%
Sometimes	300	38%
Don't care	140	18%

Another pillar of nuclear nationalism in Pakistan is the idea that these weapons are so crucial to the country's security that they should be retained at any cost. According to General Musharraf, safeguarding Pakistani nuclear weapons is a main reason for siding with the Americans in the "war against terror." Indeed, the "official" word is that about 72 percent of Pakistanis concur with retaining nuclear weapons at any cost, whereas 28 percent do not agree.

The countrywide aggregate figures are just the tip of the iceberg regarding the myth of national consensus on the nuclear issue. Pakistan since its inception has had trouble creating a democratic and federal polity. Proponents of Pakistani nationalism—of which nuclear nationalism is now an integral part—as mainly emanating in Islamabad has historically been problematic whose takers in various parts of the country have varied over the years. Therefore, by examining our nuclear survey on provincial grounds, it is my hope that students of contemporary Pakistan can learn much about Pakistani politics and society.

Provincial Perceptions about the Nuclear Program

The efficacy of nuclear tests as making Pakistan's defense "impregnable," to borrow former prime minister Sharif's term, is shared by a whopping 92 percent of people from the NWFP, followed by 84 percent in the Punjab. In Sindh, a majority (61 percent) replied in the affirmative, but as many as 31 percent did not think Pakistan was more secure after the nuclear explosions. Balochistan contrasted with this trend, with 73 percent of people believing that nuclear weapons have not made Pakistan safer. Thus the official claim of consensus on this aspect by the dominant discourse is echoed in the Punjab and the NWFP, finds reasonable support in Sindh, but lacks legitimacy in Balochistan.

Depicting the incorporation of nuclear weapons in its armory as a ticket to more respectful status in the comity of nations has over 90 percent of followers in the NWFP, followed by 75 percent in the Punjab. Fifty-four percent of people in Sindh believe this is so, and a meager 23 percent in Balochistan consider it to be the case. Seventy-three percent in Balochistan, 30 percent in Sindh, and 21 percent in the Punjab think that nuclear explosions have not earned Pakistan international respect or status. These figures shed light on the nature of the nuclear discourse in Pakistan.

Table 7.2
Degree of Thinking Given to Pakistan's Nuclear Policy

	Serious	Sometimes	Don't Care
Punjab	46%	42%	10%
Sindh	23%	46%	29%
NWFP	57%	39%	1%
Balochistan	46%	23%	30%

Contrary to the claims of the strategic elite, there is no national consensus regarding the honor and prestige value of Pakistani nuclear weapons. Surprisingly, the relevance of the prestige factor is highest in the NWFP and not in the Punjab. One-quarter of the Punjab respondents replying in the negative on the prestige question is significantly higher than what one might ordinarily assume. Balochistan's alienation from the official discourse is clear. Islamabad's image in the province has been undermined even further during the period since we conducted this in-depth survey.

The mainstream and undifferentiated accounts subscribing to the notion of a consensus in Pakistan about the nuclear issue assume that Pakistanis have reached this consensus after thoughtful debates about the country's nuclear program and policy. When probed on this issue, the results indicate that the majority of people either do not care about the nuclear policy or think about it only occasionally (Table 7.2).

Sindh appears to be least concerned about Pakistan's nuclear policy, and the thinking in Balochistan and the NWFP is diametrically opposed, with the former mainly not buying the official view and the latter accepting it almost uncritically.

Secrecy is the hallmark of the Indian and Pakistani nuclear programs with regard to their technical aspects and decision-making processes. Both governments have expected and assumed that their citizens believe in what they say about the nature of the nuclear programs and its policy directions. The myth of consensus also assumes a high level of trust between the government and ordinary people on this issue. Trust in the official assertion is highest among those in the NWFP, where more than about 87 percent strongly believe, and believe in, the government's claims about Pakistan's nuclear policy and program. A significantly lower percentage of Punjab respondents (56 percent) believe in the government. Almost half (45 percent) of those polled in Sindh do not believe what the government says about the country's nuclear program and policy. Another 20 percent were undecided as to whether they believed the government's word. Only 13 percent strongly believed the government, and another 18 percent generally believed the government's claims. Lack of trust in the government's word on the nuclear issue is highest in Balochistan, with 73 percent expressing doubts about the truth of the official policy. This finding further dents the dominant claims about a consensus on the nuclear issue as far as the overall country is concerned.

In the months this survey was conducted there was a lively debate, at least in the English-language media, about the pros and cons of Pakistan becoming a party to the CTBT. The Pakistani government's dithering on whether to sign the treaty purportedly was based on the argument that it was trying to build a consensus in the country on this fractious issue. The underlying assumption here is that ordinary Pakistanis have a say in determining the policy options in such matters. About 60 percent of people in Balochistan believe they have no say in shaping the country's nuclear policy. The majority of people in Sindh (46 percent) agree. Whereas 40 percent of Pashtuns strongly believe they can influence the country's nuclear policy, the number of Punjab respondents who follow their Pashtun compatriots is about 30 percent. Combining the views taken in all parts of the country, the lack of trust in the government's utterances about the nuclear policy and peoples' perceptions about their minimal say in forming this policy contradicts the claims of proponents of the dominant view on the nuclear discourse.

Another perception about nuclear weapons concerns their use as a way to prevent war between India and Pakistan. A favorite theme in the nuclear discourse in Pakistan is that with the introduction of the nuclear weapons in the strategic interaction between the two hostile neighbors, the probability of a major conventional war is now minimal. Some important assumptions on a number of issues may be drawn by looking at Table 7.3. First, there is a relatively high level of congruence nationwide, a rare occasion, regarding whether nuclear weapons will deter war. A high percentage of Pakistanis believe that there will never be a major conventional war between India and Pakistan. At the same time, a significant section of the population does not share the assumption that nuclear weapons are the ultimate deterrent, a pivotal point for those trying to rationalize their acquisition.

The traditional thinking on nuclear weapons is that they are there to avoid war, not conduct it. The belief is that the mere possession of nuclear weapons infuses responsibility in the relevant parties, in that they realize that these weapons are not a way to fight war. Only 54 percent of respondents in Sindh think there will never be a nuclear war between India and Pakistan, but 29 percent of them think there will be a nuclear war between the two countries in the next five to fifteen years. Even in the Punjab, 23 percent believe a nuclear war between India and Pakistan is likely in the next decade or so. The NWFP population is the most ardent believer that nuclear weapons are unusable, as 81 percent think that a nuclear exchange between India and Pakistan will never occur. Even 65 percent of Balochistan respondents think there is no likelihood of nuclear war between the two countries. The Baloch response to this question conveys that their opposition and lack of trust in the official Pakistani nuclear line is guided by factors other than the fear of nuclear holocaust between India and Pakistan.

An important question is whether those who think there will be a nuclear war between India and Pakistan have pondered ways to avoid this eventuality or prepared

Table 7.3

Views on When a Major Conventional War Will Erupt

between India and Pakistan

	5 years	10 years	15 years	Never
Punjab	14%	13%	12.5%	54%
Sindh	18%	13%	9%	45%
NWFP	20%	17%	13%	46%
Balochistan	17%	8%	10%	61%

themselves for the catastrophe. In my discussions with Pakistanis I have observed a severe lack of understanding about the actual destruction a nuclear war can cause. Rather, they see a nuclear confrontation as a somewhat refined form of conventional warfare. A major reason for this may be that previous conventional wars between the two countries have primarily been border wars, where civilians in what was then West Pakistan remained largely unharmed.

Nuclear Policy and Doctrinal Issues

Once nuclear weapons have been acquired, countries must grapple with questions concerning policy, doctrines, and command and control: "How and for what purposes should such weapons be used?" This question is at the heart of military doctrine that broadly consists of how and when to use military force. This section looks at peoples' responses to questions concerning the contours of Pakistan's nuclear policy and military doctrine.

Nuclear hawks have made effective use of the Jamaat's referendum verdict as a byword for anti-CTBT consensus in the country, declaring, in the words of retired general Hamid Gul, that the "entire Pakistani nation is against signing it." If one accepts uncritically the results of various national referenda, the otherwise fractured electorate of Pakistan would emerge as a homogeneous bloc. Fortunately the unrealistically one-sided results claimed by these referenda have always cast serious doubts about their validity. We need look no further than the April 2002 referendum that extended General Musharraf's presidency by five years.

The Pakistanis' response to our survey on the issue of the CTBT signing was nowhere near what the Jamaat claims it to be (see Table 7.4). The only region where the claims of Jamaat and other nuclear hawks will ring true is in the NWFP, where about 70 percent of Balochistan residents would like see Pakistan sign the CTBT. This stance, I argue, is not guided by actually weighing the pros and cons of the treaty. Plausible explanation for the high support among Balochistan residents lies in the region's extreme alienation from Islamabad and the dominant discourse.

Table 7.4
Should Pakistan Sign the CTBT?

	No	Yes	Don't Know
Punjab	68%	25%	5%
Sindh	48%	38%	13%
NWFP	85%	12%	3%
Balochistan	25%	69%	4%

Close to 40 percent in Sindh also suggested that Pakistan should sign the CTBT. Sindh residents' substantial support can be partly explained by the gulf between security perceptions in Islamabad and the province. Even in otherwise pronuclear Punjab, the level of support for signing the CTBT is surprisingly high with one-quarter of respondents expecting Pakistan to sign the Treaty.

Retaining the nuclear option has become an article of strategic faith in Islamabad. General Musharraf cited safeguarding Pakistan's nuclear program as the main justification for his decision to support the U.S. war on terror in the wake of 9/11. It is portrayed as one of those rare issues on which the entire Pakistani society agrees. The survey shows that 94 percent of people in the NWFP, 85 percent in the Punjab, and 72 percent in Sindh concur with the statement that nuclear weapons are important for Pakistan's security and that the nuclear option should be retained at any cost, which suggests that Islamabad has succeeded quite well in convincing ordinary citizens about the viability of the nuclear program and its importance for the country's security. This support will come as a surprise, however, to the cadres of ethno-national parties who imply that their views on national security are diametrically opposed to those of Islamabad. The only exception to the above is the public opinion in Balochistan, where 64 percent disagreed when asked if the nuclear weapons program is worth retaining at any cost.

The thinking of traditional security studies views nuclear weapons primarily as a political tool and sees deterrence weapons as an effective way to prevent war between India and Pakistan. To assure that these weapons continue to serve as deterrents, those who possess them must outline specific conditions under which their use would be deemed necessary. Unless the criteria of their usability is defined, the mere presence of nuclear weapons is unlikely to prevent war. "Counter-value" and "counterforce" are two euphemisms of the nuclear age devised by strategic experts to provide a sanitized version of specific uses of nuclear weapons. The former refers to the use of nuclear weapons against the adversary's population centers, and the latter means that their use is confined to the enemy's military-related establishments. Unlike the devastation experienced by Europe in the two world wars or the horrific atomic attack wreaked on the Japanese society, the India-Pakistan wars, as noted earlier, have been limited in scope and brief in duration. As a result, the ordinary Indian and Pakistani largely consider nuclear weapons as merely an extension of conventional weapons. Further, the marginal role played by the antinuclear weapons movement in these countries minimizes public awareness of the weapons' destructive capacity.

Regarding the use of nuclear weapons, survey respondents were given three choices: counter-value, counterforce, or never to use them. Balochistan residents topped the list with 79 percent responding that Pakistan should never use nuclear weapons. Even 42 percent of the NWPF respondents agree with that statement, which is surprising since that region's populace seems to accept nuclear lore more readily than any other segment of the Pakistani population. Also agreeing that Pakistan should never use the weapons were 38 percent of Punjabi residents and 36 percent in Sindh. Given the lack of public awareness about the inevitable, indiscriminate destruction of a nuclear exchange and an almost romantic, fetishistic official portrayal, the instinctive abhorrence toward the use of nuclear weapons by ordinary people might be construed as an innate sign of positive human quality. However, close to a quarter of the residents in Sindh and the NWFP, 19 percent in the Punjab, and a meager 3 percent in Balochistan believed that Pakistan should use nuclear weapons were India to "cross the line." Still, one can conclude that, overall, Pakistanis are not keen to lower the threshold regarding the use of nuclear weapons.

Although India has officially adopted a no-first-use policy, Pakistan retains the right to use nuclear weapons if its existence is threatened. In response to our question as to whether India would retaliate with a nuclear attack if Pakistan chose to use nuclear weapons against India first, 93 percent in the NWFP, 84 percent in the Punjab, 82 percent in Sindh, and 73 percent in Balochistan are convinced that were Pakistan to launch a nuclear attack on India, New Delhi would retaliate in kind. This response should come as a consolation to Indian policy makers, as it shows that ordinary Pakistanis take the threat of Indian nuclear retaliation seriously.

The draft Indian nuclear doctrine and subsequent assertions of New Delhi to eventually develop and deploy a triad-based nuclear arsenal is likely to evoke the call for a similar response from the military and "strategic enclave" in Pakistan. Prior to the 1998 testing, Indian and Pakistani strategic analysts extolled virtues of what came to be termed "the state of non-weaponized deterrence." The unconfirmed presence of nuclear weapons was seen as a stabilizing factor between the two regional rivals. The 1998 explosions changed the situation qualitatively, and analysts wondered whether the subcontinent would imitate the mindless arms-race experience of the East-West confrontation. Although it is too early to predict with any certainty the nuclear future of India and Pakistan, a staggering 90 percent of respondents in the NWFP, 68 percent in the Punjab, and about 54 percent in Sindh agree that if India develops more sophisticated nuclear weapons, then Pakistan should respond in kind. Barring overwhelming support from the NWFP, the number of nuclear enthusiasts in the country is not as high as officials in Islamabad generally claim. The Balochistan populace clearly disagrees, by 77 percent, with the proposition of matching India's nuclear weapons development. Islamabad's decision not to match India's resolve to raise its defense budget may be partly the result of Pakistan's ailing economy and partly the awareness of the lack of unqualified support for such an increase among the Pakistanis.

Command and Control of Nuclear Weapons

The aspects of Pakistan's nuclear program related to command and control have remained shrouded in secrecy, as the public continues to be fed symbols of nuclear nationalism. The controversy surrounding Abdul Qadeer Khan's alleged activities behind the facade of strict control (see chapter 5) may have come as a shock to analysts outside Pakistan, but our survey results show that, even before Dr. Khan's fall from grace, ordinary Pakistanis did not view Khan and his scientist cohorts as the ones controlling Pakistani nukes.

More than 60 percent of Pakistan's populace believed that the army exercised exclusive control over nuclear weapons. Despite the elevated profile of scientists like A. Q. Khan after the nuclear tests, only 8 percent of respondents in Balochistan and Sindh believe that scientists control the country's nuclear program. Even in the Punjab, where most of Pakistan's nuclear facilities are located, only 15 percent thought that scientists controlled nuclear facilities. Therefore, when the army top brass, faced with allegations of nuclear smuggling, zeroed in on Dr. Khan and his associates as the culprits, Pakistanis were largely astonished, having always perceived the army as in control of the nukes.

Although the civilian government of Nawaz Sharif was in the saddle in Islamabad at the time of the nuclear testing, only 6 percent of respondents in the Punjab, 8 percent in the NWFP, 10 percent in Sindh, and no one in Balochistan thought that politicians controlled the nuclear program. All this suggests that the Pakistani public has a fairly good idea as to where the power lies when it comes to Pakistan's nuclear weapons program. Responses to our follow-up question as to who should control Pakistan's nuclear program are summarized in Table 7.5.

As Table 7.5 demonstrates, the three most populous provinces view the Pakistan army as the most reliable force for controlling the country's nuclear program. Only in Balochistan would people rather have civilian politicians in control. This may come as a consolation to nuclear hawks but a cause of worry for those who would like to see civilians at the helm of nuclear affairs. The popular perception of politicians as corrupt and inept may have contributed to the public's lack of support for civilians on this issue. In terms of the impact of these views on the future of Pakistan's nuclear politics, one can safely suggest that the armed forces will continue to employ nuclear custodianship as a legitimizing tool for a nonrepresentative political establishment.

Pakistan's nuclear enterprise assumes that people have the utmost confidence in the country's command and control, and safety, of nuclear installations. This

Table 7.5
Who Should Control Pakistan's Nuclear Program?

	Army	Scientists	Politicians
Punjab	46%	30%	11%
Sindh	49%	18%	12%
NWFP	67%	24%	5%
Balochistan	19%	23%	44%

assertion, however, is belied by the findings of our survey. Seventy-seven percent of respondents in Balochistan, 50 percent in Sindh, and 25 percent in the Punjab expressed dissatisfaction with the command-and-control arrangements in the country. Only in the NWFP were about 85 percent of people "very satisfied" or "satisfied" with the existing arrangements. This high level of dissatisfaction countrywide reflects the peoples' lack of faith in government institutions in general, and in the nuclear establishment in particular. The country's gradual erosion of state institutions and infrastructure has created an overall sense of pessimism about the efficacy of state-run organizations.

Along with the concern of scholars and activists regarding the deliberate use of nuclear weapons as a military tactic, they also worry about nuclear accidents. Even advanced countries like the United States have not been free of nuclear accidents. There is little public education to make people aware of the hazards of nuclear accidents in the country, and the minuscule antinuclear movement has not done much to fill this void.

As shown in Table 7.6, with the exception of the NWFP, most Pakistanis apparently see a real possibility of nuclear accidents in the country. An equally high proportion of Pakistanis are uncertain about this possibility. Clearly the well-informed segments of the population concerned about nuclear safety have a window of opportunity to channel the public's instinctive concerns into a sustained voice demanding more transparency in the workings of nuclear installations.

Another route that can lead to the inadvertent use of nuclear weapons is escalation of a conventional war into a nuclear one. The geographical proximity of India and Pakistan, a history of conventional wars between the two neighbors, and ongoing low-intensity conflict in Kashmir convinced the former U.S. president Bill Clinton to declare the "Line of Control" in Kashmir as "the most dangerous place on the earth"[2] where an India-Pakistan crisis, if not managed properly, could lead to a nuclear exchange. Such alarmist statements notwithstanding, the 1999 Kargil crisis and the 2002 military standoff lasting for months proves the fragile nature of India-Pakistan relations, and the inability of nuclear weapons to prevent adversaries from fighting limited conventional wars.

Table 7.6

Is There a Danger of Nuclear Accidents in Pakistan?

	Yes	No	Don't Know
Punjab	44%	32%	22%
Sindh	46%	28%	25%
NWFP	27%	49%	23%
Balochistan	61%	17%	21%

As Table 7.7 demonstrates, the preponderance of survey respondents believe that crises such as the Kargil conflict and intense military standoffs can escalate into a nuclear conflict. Yet, in light of this overriding public opinion, public pressure for defusion of these crises is not as high as one would expect during these conventional crises.

Conclusion

In light of the survey findings discussed in this essay, I would like to address the question posed by the editor of this volume Itty Abraham in his introductory chapter: "How [did] some South Asian 'atomic publics' [come] to love the bomb, while others grow still further from the meanings, accomplishments, spectacles, and practices of nuclear power[?]"

The overall survey results indicate significant support for the official position on the broad nature and direction of Pakistan's nuclear policy in three of Pakistan's four regions, which should bring reasonable satisfaction to policy makers in Islamabad. The traditional champions of the nuclear program—the army, religious parties, and India-basher strategic analysts—have the most ardent supporters in the NWFP and very few takers in Balochistan. Although Pakistan's strategic enclave does not have a core constituency in Sindh, 61 percent of respondents in that province believe that nuclear weapons have made the country more secure, and 54 percent hold that the nuclear tests have enhanced Pakistan's international stature. The proponents of Pakistan's nuclear program often clamor about the abundance of trust and consensus between ordinary people and those responsible for nuclear policy. That assertion is undermined even in the Punjab, where a quarter of respondents do not believe the government's claims about the nuclear program. The number of disbelievers is even higher in Sindh (45%) and Balochistan (73%). Similarly authorities in Islamabad enthusiastically refer to consensus building and national sentiments as the prime drivers of the country's nuclear policy, but 46 percent of respondents in Sindh, 60 percent in Balochistan, and even 25 percent of those in the Punjab believe they have no say in the country's nuclear policy. Given Islamabad's penchant for political expediency over transparency, this lack of trust is likely to increase in the future.

Table 7.7

**Is the Danger of a Conventional Conflict like Kargil
Escalating into a Nuclear War Nonexistent?**

	Yes	No	Don't Know
Punjab	48%	35%	13%
Sindh	35%	40%	24%
NWFP	49%	38%	13%
Balochistan	50%	40%	10%

The almost diametrically opposed views of the NWFP and Balochistan on the nuclear spectrum is noteworthy for a number of reasons. For one, the staunchest support for nuclear nationalism is in the NWFP and not the Punjab, the region usually considered to be the bastion of nuclear nationalism. Further, the Pashtun subnational movement has been in decline in the NWFP, partly because of that region's greater integration into Pakistan's military and civilian bureaucracy. This has meant less disenchantment with Islamabad in the NWFP regarding the distribution of power in key institutions of the Pakistani state. At the same time political turmoil in neighboring Afghanistan has impacted the NWFP more than any other region of Pakistan. The rise of political Islam has been most palpable in this region. In the Pakistani context, the religious parties, especially Jamaat-e-Islami, has championed the cause of nuclear nationalism and grafted it with Pakistan's Islamic identity. This combination explains why adherence to nuclear nationalism is at its strongest in the NWFP.

Whereas the NWFP has, to some extent, found its voice in running the country's current establishment, Balochistan has long been marginalized economically, politically, and culturally for a number of reasons.[3] The region is the largest producer of natural gas first discovered in the Sui region of Balochistan in 1953. Whereas major cities of the Punjab has received gas connections in the early 1960s, Quetta, the capital of Balochistan, obtained the gas connection in 1986, more a result of Islamabad's decision to station a military garrison in the provincial capital rather than to address the needs of ordinary Baloch people.[4] Of the twenty districts in Pakistan whose infrastructures are most deprived, eighteen are in Balochistan. If Quetta and Ziarat are excluded, all of Balochistan falls into the high deprivation category. Moreover, Quetta's ranking would fall if the cantonment is excluded from the analysis.[5] According to Kaiser Bengali, "the Baloch intelligentsia has seen through Islamabad's colonisation game and the general insurgency is merely a response. The military's operation in Balochistan is a counter response, not to the insurgency per se, but to the challenge posed to Islamabad's colonisation agenda."[6] This apt observation explains why respondents in Balochistan are at odds with the parameters of nuclear nationalism in Pakistan. For them, nuclear weapons are yet another symbol of Islamabad's dominance in which Baloch people and politicians have had little say. The Ras Koh hills, the site of the 1998 explosions, are located in Balochistan, but, at the time of the May 1998 tests, the nationalist Balochistan provincial government was not even informed of the impending decision.

Despite the army's perennial lack of legitimacy in determining public policies regarding nuclear weapons and policy, the army supersedes other actors in terms of public trust. In Sindh, where political alienation during army-led governments is high, 49 percent of respondents still want the army to control the nuclear program. Closer to half the respondents in the Punjab also want the army to be in charge when it comes to nuclear issues. This sentiment, skillfully nurtured by the armed forces, will continue to be used to discredit civilians if they try to exert control or to demand a greater say in the nature and direction of the nuclear program. The eruption of the A. Q. Khan debate narrowed citizens' focus almost exclusively on the personality of the controversial metallurgist. Because the popular wisdom in Pakistan held that the nuclear program was under the effective control of the armed forces, it is highly unlikely that the populace would accept that A. Q. Khan would have acted without tacit endorsement from the military elite. Although the scientist unceremoniously apologized to Musharraf on Pakistani television channels for his alleged wrongdoing, ordinary Pakistanis saw in that spectacle yet another example of military authorities scapegoating Dr. Khan. During and after the A. Q. Khan scandal, military authorities made sure that men in uniform were absolved of any responsibility of alleged wrongdoings in divulging and selling nuclear secrets. Dr. Khan was carefully cultivated as a national hero in the preceding years, and his penchant for personal promotion was known to most Pakistanis. At the same time, ordinary Pakistanis always believed, as evinced in the survey findings, that the control of nuclear weapons lies with the armed forces and that therefore any trade in the nuclear technology could not have been the sole responsibility of the fallen scientist.

Nuclear hawks are comprised mainly of select individuals and institutions in Pakistan, and at their core are certain religious leaders, retired and active military officials, spin doctors, media pundits, as well as scientists. All would be disappointed and dismissive of our survey findings mainly because they run counter to the claims of national consensus on the nuclear issue. With 20 percent of respondents in the Punjab, one-third in Sindh, and a staggering 73 percent in Balochistan, discounting that Pakistan gained international respect or status by becoming overtly nuclear, the findings point to cleavages in what outsiders see as a national consensus.

Nuclear hawks and antinuclear activists see each other involved in a zero-sum game, where the loss of one is considered the other's gain. Our survey findings should enable nuclear dissidents to identify sympathetic ears for their cause in Pakistan's political landscape. The dissent on the nuclear issue mainly has been confined to a select group of analysts who frame their argument mainly in terms of the dangers involved in the deliberate or accidental use of nuclear weapons or the nonproliferation concerns of Western countries, concerns that have not struck a chord with the ordinary populace.

This survey would help antinuclear voices identify the recognizable disenchantment of Pakistan's population with various aspects of the country's existing nuclear policy and program. Creative use of this data may be one way to break the existing isolation of antinuclear activists from the wider public. Only by successfully striking chords with ordinary people can the antinuclear voice lay claim to a legitimate position in the nuclear discourse.

Political realism, which assumes that the state is a unitary actor with objective interests to safeguard, remains the dominant and most prevalent perspective in the field. An increasing number of scholars, including contributors to this volume, are questioning the validity of these assumptions and their explanatory value. A differentiated account of the dynamics of politics of nuclear weapons in Pakistan demonstrates that the myth of consensus on the nuclear issue can only be meaningfully questioned by ascertaining and understanding peoples' views and identifying areas—both in terms of issues and regions—where antinuclear voices are likely to find sympathetic ears. It is my hope that this essay helps us to recognize that different groups conceptualize security and power differently, and that such concepts are always socially situated.

Notes

It is difficult to name all the volunteers who contributed their valuable time to conduct this survey. Rahman Khan, Nasim Qaiyum, Irfan Muzaffar, Asfhaq Ahmad, and Aftab and Hassan Nizamani were the most generous with their time. Aftab Nizamani helped immensely in tabulating the raw data into legible form.

1. The figures are based on the 1998 census. Details of the demographic features of Pakistan are available online at the Web site of the Population Census Organization (Government of Pakistan), which can be accessed at http://www.statpak.gov.pk/depts/pco/statistics/statistics.html.

2. Sumit Ganguly and Devin T. Hagerty, *Fearful Symmetry: India-Pakistan Crises in the Shadow of Nuclear Weapons* (Seattle: University of Washington Press, 2005), p. 13.

3. For a brief overview of the reasons behind Balochistan's disenchantment with Pakistan, see Frederic Grare, *Pakistan: The Resurgence of Baloch Nationalism* (Washington, D.C.: Carnegie Endowment for International Peace, no. 65, January 2006).

4. Ibid., p. 4.

5. Kaiser Bengali, "Wither Balochistan?" *Dawn*, September 14, 2006.

6. Ibid.

8

GODS, BOMBS, AND THE
SOCIAL IMAGINARY

Raminder Kaur

We knew the world could not be the same. A few people laughed, a
few people cried. Most people were silent. I remembered the line from
the Hindu scripture, the Bhagavad Gita: "I am become Death, the
destroyers of worlds." I suppose we all thought that, one way or another.

J. Robert Oppenheimer

A few years after the first nuclear explosion at Alamogordo on July 16, 1945, the "father of the atomic bomb," J. Robert Oppenheimer, cited these lines in recollection of the first time the nuclear genii came out of its lamp.[1] It is well known that Oppenheimer, once an advocate of nuclear power, went on to become a strong opponent of nuclear armament. But most intriguing to me about this quote is the question of silence in the face of something for which the consequences are too awesome and terrifying to behold. Of particular interest is who remains silent or, effectively, which voices are silenced or deemed of little import for a topic as significant as nuclear power.

The scholarly study of nuclear issues has largely been the realm of political scientists, international relations specialists, and nuclear experts. As a result, conventional studies tend to focus on state-orientated policies and programs, along with macropolitical and macro-economic analyses locked in the confines of a modernization narrative about politics. Local or parochial perspectives on the nuclear issue are rarely analyzed. This essay attempts to provide a view grounded in the vernacular cultures of Mumbai, and, in so doing, enable us to appreciate another zone of political engagement not purely concerned with statecraft or the arena of institutions and practices, namely, civil society. Indeed, as Partha Chatterjee proposed: "Most of the inhabitants of India are only tenuously, and even then ambiguously and contextually, rights-bearing citizens in the sense imagined by the constitution."[2]

To pursue this question, Chatterjee developed the idea of "political society occupying a zone between the state on the one hand and civil society as bourgeois society on the other." Such ideas were anticipated in the Subaltern Studies projects that examined the collective actions of subaltern groups, particularly those having to do with peasants who engaged in "politics" in a different way from that of the elites.[3] Here the moral rhetoric of kinship and family loyalty was a premium, as was the significance of cultural and religious understandings of their lives. Classically, political scientists have dismissed such perspectives as somehow premodern, superstitious, irrational, disorderly, and obscurantist, in the mistaken belief that their own viewpoints were neutral and universal. By doing so, important avenues into appreciating various ways of engaging with political worlds were overlooked.

To similar ends, Ashis Nandy discussed the "marginalised categories"— "marginalised by the culture of the Indian state, though not necessarily by the culture of Indian politics"—which configure Indian political life.[4] He elaborated on the supposed "universal language of statecraft" used to describe terrorist activities in the 1980s. By investigating a couple of hijacked airline incidents, he noted the various discourses of hijackers and passengers/airline staff that were distinct from those that emerged from a study of the Indian press, airline bureaucracy, the foreign office, the security machinery, and defense experts. Nandy argued that the recollections of hijacked passengers have the status of a *dialect* which borrowed from vernacular and familial culture. The bureaucracies and media reveled in *language* that characterizes the modern nation-state—a state that emerged out of an objectivist approach on political life and has come to be "a major instrument of modern rationality."[5] To fully understand the vagaries of Indian political life, the focus must not just be on the language and institutions of modernity but also on the "cultures and cognitive orders and interpersonal styles" with which people have to address particular incidents, issues, and problems.

Although there may be difficulties in outlining the boundaries of political and civil society, or differentiating between modern and vernacular approaches to political issues and incidents, both authors certainly have a case with which to consider the question of nuclear power and armament. More often than not, the nuclear issue is addressed in the idioms of statecraft and civil society. It is "the protagonists of rationality"[6] that have had the dominant say in addressing this subject. How we engage nuclear issues within "political society" is little understood; if we even investigate, it is done through the rational logics of surveys, statistics, and opinion polls, not via a perspective developed from a study of vernacular cultures. This is not surprising, for such an approach requires a diverse and complex lens that can accommodate the contingencies and contradictions that characterize everyday lives.

It is such an approach that I hope to develop in this essay by focusing on the effects of the 1998 nuclear tests in Mumbai's popular culture among what Chatterjee may describe as "political society." In particular, I consider the spectacles and audiotaped narratives that accompanied Ganapati Festival displays (Mumbai's major annual festival). I note that discourses evident in many of these sites of popular culture neither follow governmental ideology nor provide a space of outright resistance to state decisions. Rather, they present a space for critique and reflection in culturally inflected and imaginative ways that *draws* upon state/elite and activist discourse but is not hemmed in by them. In so doing, this chapter provides insights into people's reception of the 1998 nuclear tests in India which lie outside the quantitative logic of opinion polls and rationalist predilections of political science.

Nuclear Reactions

How do discourses about nuclear power percolate among the wider populace in India? At least five intersecting discursive elements may be identified. These are embedded in Ganapati Festival *mandap* displays and in other aspects of the public field.[7] In the process, dynamics of science, modernity, ethics, and nationalism quite specific to the nuclear debate are highlighted, as old "truths" are resurrected and new verities created.

The first and most conspicuous discursive element is the intricate entanglement between nuclear power and a religious ethos. Modern technology is sanctified by recourse to a religious discourse, such that it takes on a fetishistic quality. "Fetish" might be invoked both in terms of the "mystical" aura defined by the commodity spectacle and the ritualistic icon, such that the "hyper-modern" meets the "hyper-traditional."[8] That these displays are offered for sanctification by Ganapati is further testament to the need to marry new technology with Indian religious values. Occasionally nuclear weapons are discussed in light of well-known religious stories from the Mahabharata, for example, or gods are shown giving their blessings (*ashirvad dena*) to nuclear power for the national welfare. At the time of the 1998 tests, when shock waves from the nuclear blasts lifted a mound of earth the size of a football field by several meters, one of the scientists is recorded to have said, "I can now believe stories of Lord Krishna lifting a hill."[9] Such narrative strategies enable the updating of an old tale, as well as imparting a moral message to modern innovations. While indigeneity is upheld, modernity and morality become intricately entwined. I refer to this phenomenon as the "sanctification discourse" in my discussions on festival displays below.

Linked to the above, the second discourse is the Gandhian ideal for peace, or *satyagraha* (truth-force or the theory of moral action). *Ahimsa* (nonviolence) is an integral feature of Gandhian notions of *satyagraha*.[10] As is well known, M. K. Gandhi's message was that nonviolence was the means to a higher truth:

> The prerogative of destruction belongs solely to the creator of all that lives.... Non-co-operation is not a passive state, it is an intensely active state—more active than physical resistance or violence. Passive resistance is a misnomer. Non-co-operation in the sense used by me must be non-violent and therefore neither punitive nor vindictive nor based on malice, ill-will or hatred.[11]

However, despite differing perspectives, Gandhi's stress on nonviolent spirituality becomes easily channeled into Hindu nationalism. *Ahimsa* as a resurrected discourse from historical anticolonial struggle facilitates the claims of legitimacy to nuclear armament.[12] India's public profile as a nuclear weapons state (NWS) has allowed the *ahimsa*/nonviolence discourse to be resurrected for a modern purpose, in what critics consider a distortion of Gandhi's ideas. This "new era of *ahimsa*"[13] is about weaponizing but with no intention to use the weapons, accompanied by rhetoric of the need to protect India and promote regional peace.[14] The conjunction of military technology and the rhetoric of peace promotion has arisen out of "the peculiar condition of atomic energy: at one and the same time a potentially peaceful technique as well as being a deliberate means of mass destruction."[15] But it has also to do with earlier tensions between modernity and tradition, where technological developments are most welcome if they are embedded in age-old ideas to do with spirituality and a sense of indigenous ethics, again indicating the harmonization of rationality (science and modernity) and religiosity.

The third discursive element involves the Nehruvian legacy of modernization and national development programs. Since independence, the command of science and technology has represented India's narrative of modernity.[16] The glorification of nuclear weapons follows earlier precedents of celebrating not just the nation's military strengths and achievements but also science, technology, and industrialization, part of which included atomic energy centers. The first of these was the Trombay Atomic Center set up in 1958 and headed by the scientist Homi J. Bhabha. This "civilian" nuclear energy program was potentially transferable into weapons production, where national development merged with issues about national security. The Nehruvian stress on science and large-scale industries as indexes of modern India has been conflated with the argument that nuclear weapons power is also beneficial for India's development.[17]

The legacy of national strength through nuclear development was so persuasive that Prime Minister Atal Behari Vajpayee declared that May 11, 1988, the day of Buddha Purnima, would be known as "Technology Day." The development of nuclear bombs has become deeply entangled with technological progress. Its financial burdens or the environmental damage are not emphasized and, if they are, rest more as cautionary side issues to the main mission of developing the nation. The earlier Nehruvian associations of national development have filtered into most party considerations, whether it is the Congress, the Bharatiya Janata Party (BJP) or more left-wing parties. Along with the new regime of *ahimsa,* the specificities of adjectival references such as Gandhian or Nehruvian are, strictly speaking, rendered redundant.

The fourth discursive articulation is the rhetoric of *swadeshi* (self-reliance), informed as it is by a history of struggle for India's freedom for *swaraj* (self-rule). Nuclear weapons continue this narrative of the self-reliant nation in that the technology grants a degree of autonomy in the global ecumene, and also represents a quest for regional supremacy where India is not vulnerable to neocolonial yokes. *Swaraj* has been a mutable political entity.[18] In the case of nuclear power, the term, replete with its aura of anticolonial struggle, has been adapted to suit more masculinist pretensions to ward off suggestions that India is a "soft state."[19] Notions of nuclear *swadeshi* deploy the metaphor of total autonomy and indigenous control of the premises and outcomes of modernization programs but, in practice, have shown signs of reliance on more powerful countries.[20] The arguments about a "nuclear *swadeshi*" parallel the ambiguity of the BJP's stance on "economic *swadeshi*." However persuasive these claims are, they are not borne out by the actualities of India's international relationships. Nonetheless, as with other drives at indigeneity since the nineteenth century, locating the seeds of scientific innovations in ancient Indian texts has become commonplace.[21] This practice of locating sources that could be seen as coterminous with modern science in ancient Hindu Vedic texts has also arisen over the subject of atomic power.[22] I refer to this bundle of ideas having to do with control and autonomy of the nation-state as the "discourse of independence."

The last interconnected area is the threat of the external Others, specifically China and Pakistan. The nuclear race was accelerated by the fear that neighboring countries would avail themselves of military technology to harm Indian national interests. The mechanism of "threat construction" has underpinned these fears, whether it is China in the 1960s or the later status of Pakistan. Previous wars, border skirmishes, and the threat of invasion and infiltration involving these two countries have provided grist to India's nuclear mill. The notion of the Other sitting right outside the door is a constant reminder of India's precarious geopolitical position, and provides an extra boost to nuclear armament. But the Other is also a changing category that has both internal and external constituents, and where other countries can swiftly become enemies in the vagaries of shifting alliances: "blaming the others (be they Muslims, China, Western hypocrisy, or whatever) has found powerful resonance."[23] Thus this vigilant awareness is supplemented with a penumbra of other nations that are against India's aspirations to go nuclear. The West, or perhaps more to the point, countries already in the nuclear club, have come under repeated attack as Indian politicians appeal for equality in the world of nuclear treaties. But this tension is also complemented with a desire to be like them.[24] So whereas with long-term enemies such as Pakistan the Indian government's desire is to expunge and control, in relation to other nuclear countries its desire is to mimic and attain a comparable international ranking.

We now turn to examine how all these discursive elements are invoked in Ganapati Festival displays and narratives among working- and lower-middle-class residents of Mumbai.[25] Each of the following festival tableaux presents a creative and selective combination of the discourses described above.[26] The tableaux not only reproduce elements of the discourses, they *re-produce* them. The hairline hyphen in re-production alludes to the fact that every practice or display becomes itself a production, not a facsimile copy. *Mandal* members, in their creation of tableaux, select, reject, and recombine elements of these discourses in an interactive and innovative way.[27] Occasionally the re-production leads to some notable ambiguities which we explore below.

Explosive Scenes

The Ganapati festival begins on the fourth day of the bright half of the lunar-solar month of Bhadrapad (around August–September) and hence its other appellation, Ganesh Chaturthi. Months in advance of the festive period, meetings take place among police, district officials, and *mandal* representatives to facilitate a trouble-free festival. Permits must be obtained for setting up public displays, procession routes are verified, and programs overseen. Before the festival begins, frenetic activity, feelings of excitement, anxiety, and anticipation, buzz around the various *mandal* in the city. *Mandal* members and contracted workers prepare the stage and canvas and bamboo construction (the *pandal*), ensuring that it is sufficient protection from the fierce lashings of monsoon rain outbreaks as well as in anticipation of hordes of people in popular precincts throughout the festival period. The whole residence participates in constructing the *pandal* and other related activities such as preparing *prashad,* flower decorations, and so forth. Depending on their authority and skill, some members take on a more leading role in the production, decision making, and construction, and at other times professional artists might be contracted to do the work. The more adept members or professional contract workers mill around the *mandap* stage, organizing the artistic activities to prepare the tableau, usually surrounded by a gaggle of children on their school holidays. Background walls are spray-painted, or canvas is laid down on the ground to be painted before its installation. Two- or three-dimensional models of humans and animals, buildings, and other props are set up, while a space for the Ganapati *murti* is defined and decorated, ready for the installation of the *murti* on the first day of the festival.

The deity, Ganapati, is considered *vighnaharta* (the "remover of obstacles"), *sukhakarta* (one who makes happiness and peace), and *duhkhaharta* (one who removes pain and sadness). The scribe of the Mahabharata embodies wisdom yet mischief. He is considered fearful and warrior-like yet benign and beneficent. Effectively he is an ambivalent god ideally thought of by Hindu devotees as lying on the threshold of the divine and mundane realms[28]—a teller of mythical tales but also a feature of much more earthly legends as shown by the elaborate festive tableaux.

The public (*sarvajanik*) festival was indeed the outcome of an emergent national-ist consciousness. From the 1890s, Bal Gangadhar Tilak and a number of other key community leaders such as the ayurvedic doctor Bhausaheb Rangari were instru-mental in politicizing the Ganapati *utsava*.[29] From the period the British had taken over Peshwas rule in western India in 1818, the festival had primarily been a religious occasion confined to households and *mandir* (Hindu temples). From the 1890s, the celebrations were conducted on a grand public scale over an eleven-day period along with ceremonies, lectures, and debates on current issues. British colonial laws against political gatherings were circumvented with the use of a religious festival to publicly disseminate views against the ills of society including colonialism.

Nowadays the festival displays are examples of collective artworks, the premises of which are also shared by a large number of the *mandal* visitors from the neighborhood. The selected localities are largely working- to lower-middle-class Maratha-dominated areas, what Chatterjee referred to as "political society." The first display considered here was constructed by the Sarvar Vidya Sarvajanik Ganeshotsava Mandal (SGM) located in the northeast Mumbai area of Kurla. It is a representation celebrating India's achievements where technological progress for the betterment of the people as a whole is equated with nuclear weapons. Vignettes represented include electricity pylons, dams, satellite dishes, fighter planes, the Agni missile, an astronaut, computers, and farming technologies.

The translation for the Marathi audiotaped narration is the following:

> For 150 years, the British ruled India. On 15th August 1947, India became indepen-dent due to freedom fighters' self-sacrifice. Love and devotion towards the Mother-land led to her freedom.
>
> The states of India are very powerful—they have their own language, customs, and lifestyles. But all of them were united in the freedom struggle. They all fought for freedom. After that there were several differences and divisions and some people were not loyal to the country. Due to this India has suffered a setback. Now it is the dream of every Indian that in the twenty-first century, India will be such a country: self-sufficient, independent and well-developed.
>
> The progress of the country in the economic field is very important as it makes for employment. The main thing is that unemployment should come to an end. We should concentrate on the agricultural economy. If there is proper farming, India will not need to import food from anywhere.
>
> Secondly, we need to adhere to family planning, because we need to bring down the population of India. We should spread literacy. We should also take care of the environment. India can have cordial relations with our neighbours, but it also needs to be protected if required. Development in science and electronics is important.
>
> India's freedom has been gained through a long struggle. So we should try to keep unity from Kashmir to Kanya Kumari, from Gujarat to Bengal, and maintain

Figure 8.1. Tableau by Sarvar Vidya Sarvajanik Ganeshotsava Mandal in Mumbai, 1998.

its cultural harmony keeping it integrated and alive. India should be a country that is prosperous in science and industry. For this we are prepared to sacrifice everything for the development of the country.

The narrative does not explicitly mention nuclear issues, but as can be seen from the Agni missile replica in the display, it has conflated nuclear weapons with the discourse of national development. The display is presented as if it were a Nehruvian nirvana. Industrialization, literacy, and family planning are invoked to pursue the path of national strength. Notably this is combined with a plea to "take care of the environment." Science along with economic development is held to be in the nation's interests, and for the people's good. This is all enveloped in a sanctification discourse as a prayer to Ganapati. Such tableaux on the benefits of modernization programs to the nation have been prevalent prior to 1998 as well. Displays such as those of dams, pylons, power stations, the Konkan railway linking the state of Maharashtra and Kerala, and the Indian astronaut Rakesh Sharma have become parts of a repertoire of tableau features presenting the best of the nation's achievements. Nuclear weapons have provided an additional technology to add on to the country's credit. The tableau recalls the independence discourse with reminders of "freedom fighters' self-sacrifice" for national autonomy, and the continuing need to be self-reliant and have national integration. It hints at the need to protect India from its neighbors "if required" who, despite "cordial relations," could be potential enemies with their own nuclear development programs. Although *ahimsa* is not articulated in this particular example, the notion is implicit in the idea of nuclear weapons enabling a vigilant force of deterrence, so that "cordial relationships" with neighboring countries can be sustained.

The second tableau was constructed by the Spring Mills SGM. The *mandal* was headed by the president Kalidas Kolambkar, then a Shiv Sena Member of the Legislative Assembly (MLA). Here the members presented a giant mountain (Mount Kailash) with images of Tilak, inside of which was a Shiv *mandir* made to resemble a rock temple.

A Shiv *lingam* is presented inside with a scene of the Pokhran Desert created at the far end. The Pokhran vignette shows Ganapati riding a horse in the desert, nuclear tests are indicated by flashes of light, and deities (Brahma, Vishnu, and Shiva) are represented on a cloud effectively blessing the tests (*ashirvad dena*).

The major nuclear countries—the U.S., Russia, France, Britain, and China—are represented in all their glory with iconic and locational representations of each country to the right of the Pokhran tableau. These include, respectively, scenes of the Statue of Liberty, London's Tower Bridge, a Chinese pagoda with a dragon, Moscow's Red Square, and the Eiffel Tower.

Facing this installation on the other side of the rock temple are tableaux of the Indian parliament building, the Lok Sabha, and freedom fighters. The brief narration runs like a tour guide, providing an overview of the main features of the walk-through display:

Figure 8.2. Main tableau by Spring Mills Sarvajanik Ganeshotsava Mandal in Mumbai, 1998.

Figure 8.3. Side tableau by Spring Mills Sarvajanik Ganeshotsava Mandal in Mumbai, 1998.

> You are about to do darshan of Ganapati. The sceneries around him show the con-
> temporary situation of all the main countries of the world. We have had fifty years
> of independence and are celebrating the progress of our nation.

This tableau relies on a combination of an elaborate sanctification discourse, a recollection of India's independence struggle, alongside an allusion to keep up with other
foreign nuclear powers and not be reined in by them. Not only is the display sanctified
by virtue of being part of a Ganapati Festival display, but there are representations of
other deities giving their blessings to the tests. Pokhran, the site itself, is venerated as
a significant scientific and quasi-sacred site. It is the *karmabhumi,* the proving ground
of destiny. Pokhran's sacred nature has arisen because of the nuclear program's affinity with the nation, already a mythicized entity. With reference to the Shiv *lingam*
in the center of the large area, Itty Abraham's provocative observations seem to be
vindicated:

> Symbolically, the hyper-traditional met the hyper-modern in the shape of the atomic
> reactors, the most modern of objects so similar to the *lingams* found in countless Shiv
> temples across the country.[30]

This *mandal* provides an extravagant display that evokes not only conceptual but also
visual parallels. A few participants also likened the *lingam* to an atomic reactor: "Shiv
lingam is about giving *shakti* (power). So the atomic reactors also provide *shakti*."[31]
The *lingam* is perceived as a prototypical atomic reactor, where the aura of science and
religion converge to each other's mutual benefit: science becomes further ritualized,
whereas religious precedents enable a metonymic historicity to atomic power.

The tableau is defiantly chauvinistic and aspires to present India as a member of
the world nuclear club. As one *mandal* member further explained, "The scene promotes self-dependency. Now we should be able to protect ourselves, otherwise other
nuclear countries will rule over us." There is a recollection of India's freedom struggle
against British colonialism with portraits of Bhagat Singh, Subhas Chandra Bose,
Gandhi, Tilak, and Nehru. The vignettes of contemporary foreign powers recall the
primacy of Indian independence and national strength, but they also represent an ideal
global position for India to aspire toward. However, there is an uncomfortable realization that, despite the *mandal*'s claim for India's greatness, the Nuclear Five—that is,
the legitimate possessors of nuclear weapons as laid down by the Nuclear Nonproliferation Treaty—are reluctant to concede to India's claims for nuclear armament. This
is hinted in the placement of the foreign countries' tableaux on the opposite side of
the Indian displays. The exclusion of Pakistan from the walk-through construction is
also noteworthy.

The next festival organization, the Khetvadi SGM, shows another recombination
of the five main discursive features. The display is narrated in the form of a conversation between a scientist/teacher standing in front of a replica of the Bhabha Atomic
Research Center and a female student.

Figure 8.4. Tableau by Khetvadi Sarvajanik Ganeshotsava Mandal in Mumbai, 1998.

To the other side is a representation of a scene from the Mahabharata involving the characters Arjun, Dronacharya (Arjun's teacher), Krishna, and Ashvatthaman (who was the son of Dronacharya but on the rival side of the Kaurava brothers). The Ganapati deity is situated behind sliding doors and so is not visible at the start of the show. Using slide projections, the model of the scientist discusses various subjects. After an invocation to Ganapati, the narration proceeds as follows:

Man: A person who is powerful should have weapons, but not misuse them. Take a tale from the Mahabharata. Dronacharya, guru of Arjun—whose son was Ashvatthaman—he uses a powerful weapon, the *brahmastra,* to destroy the Pandavas. But if it strikes earth, it'd destroy everyone. Krishna advises him not to use it, otherwise Brahma might have to create another earth. But Ashvatthaman says he only knows how to use it, not to stop it. Krishna changes the direction of it so as it does not destroy the world. It strikes somewhere else.

Krishna cursed Ashvatthaman's third eye. Whereas before it was a source of bright energy, now it'll be a source of pain.

Voice of Krishna: You will never be able to live or die in peace. That's because you tried to use something which is not in your power to use.

Woman to scientist: If it [nuclear power] can be progressive, why is the whole world saying it's bad?

Man: It can be very destructive, but our neighbours can take it upon them to destroy India. We have to be very careful. History itself is a witness that we have never attacked any country, nor turned them into slaves. Our message has always been for peace [slides of Mahatma Gandhi are shown].

We will use nuclear power for positive and peaceful purposes. Only a strong person can talk about peace. A weak person cannot talk about peace. Whatever we have is for our protection. We shall use it positively, such as creating power, developing radioactive isotopes to cure cancer, and innovations to replace farming seeds. We wish that there will be peace all over the world.

[The wall panels slide open to reveal the Ganapati *murti*]

We pray to Ganapati to let there be peace in the world, and let the flag of India fly high.

In this tableau all five of the main features appear in another creative combination. Nuclear power is legitimated with recourse to narratives of religious events from the Mahabharata. The parable from the Mahabharata makes the point that nuclear power is not inherently evil, but its controllers could be selfishly motivated, and therein lies the main problem. The insinuations are that Pakistan, likened to the unscrupulous Kaurava dynasty, is liable to abuse nuclear power because the country does not have a history of nonviolence. India's nationalist history is portrayed as selfless and nonviolent. The narrator claims that the Gandhian discourse of *ahimsa*/nonviolence is inherently Indian—this is overlooking the fact that both countries were carved out of the same landmass. The point is explicated when the scientist comments, "Our message has always been for peace." Nuclear power is justified with recourse to the fact that India is a worthy owner, as it has always pursued a peaceful path.

Nehruvian ideas of progress are hinted at with the development of scientific innovations helpful to the populace. Developmentalist discourses merge with national security issues. It is claimed that India needs to go nuclear, otherwise, in view of the threat posed by its neighbors, it will again become a dependent nation as in colonial times. Reference is also made to the global castigation of India's nuclear weapons program. But the narrator in the form of the scientist reminds the spectator that, because India has never attacked or invaded any other country, it will not deploy weapons as an aggressor force. This reference alludes to the governmental pledge of "No First Use."

This *mandal* does begin to offer an element of doubt as to nuclear weapons and their possible abuse with the parable about Ashvatthaman. But ultimately it is not antinuclear. The story from the Mahabharata represents a cautionary parable for modern times, but its reference point is more toward Pakistan than India. The implications are that Pakistan is not in a position to develop a cohesive nuclear weapons program, nor is it "mature" enough to know what to do with this kind of technology. The *mandal* does not say that India should reject atomic research altogether. It asserts that nuclear power with the legacy of *ahimsa* in political history can be used for the nation's development by not only protecting India but by providing civilian benefits such as energy, agricultural, and medicinal developments.

The fourth *mandal* considered here, the Mazgaon Dakshin Vibhag SGM, again presents a dialogue but this time it goes further in interrogating chauvinistic supporters who have not thought properly about the negative aspects of going nuclear. The

Figure 8.5. Tableau by Dakshin Vibhag Sarvajanik Ganeshotsava Mandal in Mumbai, 1998.

tableau is presented in the form of a conflict between a peace-loving Mother India and her young upstart of a son discussing various aspects of the nation's history, present and future, illustrated by suitable vignettes that are lit up as the narration proceeds. The vignettes include a replica of Bill Clinton behind nuclear arms, skeletons and vultures representing the deaths of the Hiroshima and Nagasaki bombings in 1945, a large green snake—a "bio-political" metaphor for British colonialism—and a creature eating away Kashmir indicative of the conflicts in the region.

The imagery is activated by the following narrative:

Son: Oh Mother, I have made you proud. The whole world recognises you as nuclear. They all know we are very powerful now.

Mother: OK, you have done this, but in my country people have made me proud by crowning me with peace. People like Mahatma Gandhi have been born from my womb. The ultimate truth of life is peace. Only peace can prevent the destruction of this country. So why are you moving to the wrong path?

Son: The century has come to an end. This dream of truth (*sukhasvapna*) has also come to an end. History will say that we have never attacked any other country. But Sikander, Babar, Ala'uddhin Khirji have all destroyed you. The British ruled over India for 150 years, and they took all the wealth from you. To get that freedom it is not that we have only got it by peace, but also by fighting as with Bhagat Singh, Chaphekar and Vasudev Phadke. The British are like a "black snake" (*kalasarpa*). These people did not leave just because of our peaceful conducts, but also due to our blood. Freedom fighters burned the black snake with their blood. Now it has left.

Pakistan is the first poisonous tree (*visha vruksha*) which the British left. From one side Pakistan, from the other, China—they were both attacking causing a storm. Pakistani terrorists have infiltrated your Indian boundaries and started spreading terrorism in India. They converted a heaven like Kashmir into a cemetery.

The message of peace that you were spreading could not save a great leader like Rajiv Gandhi. After we achieved independence, we have always been spreading peace and non-violence. That is why people have taken advantage of us and spoilt us with terrorism. Now we have created so many weapons that we can call all the shots. That is why whatever steps we have taken to become nuclear are right.

Mother: Forget it! Don't even bring such thoughts into your mind. Go back to history and see Japan. America dropped two nuclear bombs in Hiroshima and Nagasaki. Look at the state of them now. Generations and generations have suffered diseases due to the radiation. Even the land has become barren and dangerous. If everyone becomes nuclear, the entire planet will be made barren. I am the mother of a hundred crore children. Even after so many children, if any one of them is destroyed, I will roam around like a mad woman.

Son: OK, I can understand your feelings, but today the world has changed. Non-violence and peace are the words of the weak. Someone comes and hits you on the cheek, and you put the other one forward—this is only part of the story. For if you become so powerful, then no one will dare to touch your cheek at all. That is the whole truth.

Make yourself so powerful that even god will have to come and ask you himself, "Now tell me what is your request?" (*Kudhikor kar boland itna ki khudha khudh apne bande se puche, bol teri razakya hai?*)

So we made Pokhran our proving ground/destiny (*karmabhumi*). We didn't just blast one or two bombs. We blasted five [models of five missiles go up in the air]. But what did the world say when we became nuclear? India is a poor country. A poor country has become nuclear so they imposed more sanctions, because they consider India to have committed a big crime. They say India is not supposed to have done this. It is like telling a newly wedded couple about family planning straight after their marriage ceremony.

The CIA is spending millions of rupees on satellites to detect activities around the world. That satellite could not even detect the nuclear tests in Pokhran. Yet they call themselves a First World country. For that information they had to come to our doors to understand how their satellites did not pick up the tests. We are now self-sufficient in nuclear power so don't even threaten us with your nuclear weapons.

Our hearts are full of patriotism. Let's see how much strength our opponents have. How to live with our neighbours peacefully? There are certain rules and we follow these, but you need to also follow these rules. We are in search of peace. *Ahimsa* is our motive. If you are going to threaten us, we are not going to sit back. Today we are united—*Jai javan, jai kisan*—Victory to the soldier, victory to the farmer. Now it is *jai javan, jai kisan* and *jai vigyan* (victory to the scientist).

Mother: Humanity of mankind has been destroyed. It has been replaced by the devil. Ultimately man only requires 6½ square feet so why do they want the land of someone else? Because man has developed science so much—out of which he developed the nuclear bomb.

O' Ganesh you created the universe and humans, but the same humans are trying to destroy the universe. The human being's wish is that the entire world shall dance under his feet. For that he is sitting around with the remote-control in his hand, and trying to destroy the world. But he doesn't understand he too will be destroyed. Ganesh you are the creator of destiny. If that is the destiny of mankind—self-destruction—then kindly destroy the lines of my forehead [the lines of the forehead are said to decide man's destiny]. You destroy those lines and let mankind be the messenger of peace and let him create an earth which is run by people progressive in nature. It is through man that the creator sees what you want in the world. So show him the right path, because you are the person who creates and can make others work towards creation.

Here the narrative presents an intermingling of discourses involving sanctification, national development, *ahimsa*/nonviolence, independence, and threats of India's enemies with the infiltration of "terrorists" within its borders. The display also mocks the West, specifically the U.S., for its status as superpower and pretensions to be a promoter of world peace. Also interesting about this *mandal* is that its members are predominately Sainiks. The president is Bala Madgaonkar, then a Shiv Sena MLA. Yet the tableau does not present a typical display of unmitigated Hindutva bravado. Instead, the narrative is presented in the form of a debate open to the particular predilections of the spectator. The tableau reflects either the ambivalence of the various *mandal* members or a publicity stunt to appear reasonable and accessible to all. Most likely, it is a combination of both motivations in what appears as a display of diplomacy at a time when the party was in joint power with the BJP at the state level.

The two main characters in the tableau narrative—mother and son—portray a splitting of the pro- and anti-lobbies on nuclear power. The son presents the classic Hindu nationalist view pointing out that India has never invaded another country, unlike, it is argued, the case for Muslims and the British. The mother presents a humanist compassionate view, reminding the spectator of the horrors of Hiroshima and Nagasaki. The son retorts that the world has changed, that there is inequality and aggression everywhere, and that the world is against India's decision to become an NWS: "It is like telling a newly wedded couple about family planning straight after their marriage ceremony." Nevertheless, despite nuclear armament, "*ahimsa* is our motive," he reiterates. The narrative ends with the mother's prayer to Ganapati: the devil is let loose in the world and, as a result, mankind is on a path of destruction: "show him the right path," she requests. Ultimately the preference is to circumvent the nuclear dilemma by offering it as a prayer to Ganapati.

The *ahimsa*/nonviolence discourse is revealed both in its old and new forms. Mother India argues for peace as in the conventional Gandhian sense, while her son proffers the new versions of the *ahimsa* argument, asserting that nuclear power brings peace and stability to the area. Intriguingly, Mother India here is not simply an iconic marker of a masculinist nation but a channel of humanitarian reason that goes beyond mere politics. The double-splitting is also apparent in narratives of India's history: Mother India represents the more peaceful and selfless perspectives on Indian achievements in history, and the son represents the aggressive and masculinist view characteristic of the Hindutva brigade.

Science and technology becomes a playing field for the politics of supremacy. "*Jai jawan, Jai kisan*," "Victory to the soldier, victory to the farmer"—a classic militaristic and developmentalist slogan—is now conjoined with "Victory to the scientist."[32] The narration also parodies the U.S. satellites' inability to detect the nuclear tests, despite the country's status as a superpower. Indeed, the media had reported that military satellites that monitor infra-red radiation could pick up Pakistan's Kahuta plant but not India's dispersed plutonium reprocessing plants.[33]

The last tableau considered here is by the Barvenagar and Akhil Bhatvadi SGM located in northeast Mumbai. The display is split into a presentation of rural and urban issues. Characterizing one side of the display are vignettes of youth dabbling in drinks and drugs, scenes of rioting hordes, water systems, and nuclear missiles with a dove of peace carrying another missile. On the other side is a representation of Buddha sitting under a bodhi tree, tractors and dams, and farmers in the act of committing suicide because there are no annual crop yields. The Ganapati *murti* is not visible at the start of the show, as it has been placed behind sliding doors:

> 11 May, 1998—the time: 3.45 in the afternoon in Rajasthan.
>
> There was a blast in Pokhran and the scientists were very happy. After 1974, this is claimed to be the second success. Lord Buddha is smiling. But what does this mean? Buddha is a god for peace. If he smiles, what does it mean?
>
> Ultimately the blasts are an insult to the god of peace. The major (First World) countries have now put sanctions. This has affected the economy very badly. So the dove of peace is now moving towards the First World country. Now they are preaching peace. Indian peace messengers are trying to go to America and settle it out. But the First World countries are thinking something else about India.
>
> What is the situation in India? There is a lot of religious, caste and economic differences. On top of this, sanctions have been imposed. If India's aim is to be a First World country, how can it achieve such a goal under such circumstances?
>
> The road that India has adopted is self-destructive. When you see the situation of youth in India, Buddha laughs, but now that laugh is frightening, ominous. The youth are important to the development of any country. However our youth are involved in drugs, and our country has become weak.
>
> Now India has become nuclear and this message has been spread all over the world. But there are so many uneducated people in India who don't even know the meaning of nuclear.
>
> Even in this Indian economy which is largely based on agriculture, the farmers are in such vulnerable circumstance that if there is no crop farmers have ended up committing suicide. At moments like this, you can understand why Buddha might be mocking us. These are the harsh facts. Under such circumstances, even though India has become nuclear, is it possible that it can also become a superpower?
>
> To give all people justice, we require alertness and awareness of what is really required. Everyone should be educated, literacy rates should rise, industry should

Figure 8.6. Tableau by Barvenagar and Akhil Bhatvadi Sarvajanik Ganeshotsava Mandal in Mumbai, 1998.

develop, economy should progress. Just by making nuclear explosions and shaking the world, it's not going to solve internal problems. This is not the solution.

[The doors open to reveal Ganapati]

So what is required? Rashtriya nishta—commitment to the nation that will develop the country with the strength of its youth (*yuvashakti*) and not nuclear bombs.

Unity among the people will create a sense of integrity. Just like the seven lights of the rainbow, even though it's one ray of light. Mankind has created such weapons that will destroy mankind itself so what's the use of it? What is required is peace. Ganapati with his hand on the *veena* is giving the message of peace to the world. He makes a promise not to use these nuclear weapons. We're praying to god, to give us the strength to safeguard mankind and to bring peace to the world. We want to be the major country in the world which promotes peace. We want to give the tricolour the status of peace promoter (*vishvashanti*).

Of the five, this narrative is the most critical of India's nuclear policy as it is of the world powers on the nuclear issue. The tableau represents a potent critique of the co-option of *ahimsa* arguments by contemporary political parties; "the blasts are an insult to the god of peace [Buddha]." The code word for the 1974 tests and Vajpayee's use of the phrase after the first three nuclear tests on May 11, 1998, "The Buddha is smiling," is cleverly twisted to show the Buddha is "mocking" as an ironic commentary on India's aspirations for nuclear might.

The narrative points to the economic disparities among the country's populace and the need to promote peace in other ways. It splits the nuclear development issue from economic development by proclaiming that the former is detrimental to the latter. It asserts that more attention and resources need to be channeled toward the latter if "India's aim is to be a First World country." The future development of the country rests largely upon the shoulders of India's youth. Thus the development discourse is more people-centered than technology-centered as in the previous tableaux. The narrative moves the focus from the threat of the external dangers to trenchant problems within the country such as illiteracy, drugs, and sectarianism. It points out that internal injustices and inequality need to be rectified before India can claim to be a superpower: "there are so many uneducated people in India who don't even know the meaning of nuclear."

Even though this *mandal* is critical of nuclear armament, there is still a reluctance to advocate the total dismantling of India's nuclear capacity. By the end, the narrative relapses into an argument about how "Ganapati makes a promise not to use these nuclear weapons." The message appears to be that now that nuclear weapons are declared, there is nothing that can be done to reverse the trend, but the country can set an example by never using nuclear weapons. As one *mandal* member said, "We want to explain to the West that they are now here to promote peace." Whereas India's claims to peace reside more on its history of non-invasions and *ahimsa,* the claims to peace of the U.S. rest on its superior military technology and international diplomatic status.[34] Peace promotion also becomes a means of disputing the claims for other nations to equip themselves with nuclear arms. To the skeptical, having weapons and yet also promoting peace is a case of having your *barfi* and eating it, too.

The Destroyer of Worlds

Clearly Oppenheimer's prescient remarks about the destruction of the world have now been brought home to the land of their inspiration in the spirit of national duty and "peaceful aggression." Whereas the scientist turned toward the parable of Krishna to emphasize his point, festival participants in Mumbai show recourse to a plethora of narratives about religion, history, the nation, and international politics through localized filters. Even though the Ganapati Festival organizations and their displays are distinct, they partake of similar discursive agendas, and position themselves within it with variations upon a theme. Each had a different inflection on the nuclear debate current in August 1998, some more oppositional than others. However, the narratives highlighted above are less antinuclear to the point of advocating their total dismantlement and more pronuclear so long as the weapons are considered for the promotion of peace.

The reluctance of *Mandal* members to disparage nuclear power altogether arises out of the twin discourses of sacralization and normalization of aspects to do with

science and technological progress being for the national good.[35] The festival participants largely support the view that "science may not quite be ready to go out of the
business of making weapons."[36] The momentum science has attained is unstoppable, so
much so that scientists have fast become the feted heroes of a projected future India.
The display narratives reflect this celebratory tenor, and demonstrate a tenuous hold
on the intricacies of nuclear debates, policies, and treaties. Instead, nuclear issues are
embedded in cultural and religious narratives, along with the resurrection of Gandhian
notions involving nonviolence, Nehruvian ideas of state-led development, and the
rhetoric of self-reliance and independence. The viewpoints mainly arise out of the need
to keep vigilant yet peaceful relations between neighboring countries, and a love-hate
relationship with the Nuclear Five countries.

With such an investigation of vernacular cultures, we can begin to appreciate the
engagement of a marginalized sector with an issue that has massive implications for the
whole of humanity. But, for various reasons, viewpoints running throughout political
society have been overlooked or silenced, the nuclear subject being authorized by only
a particular sector of society, variously defined as civil society, the educated intelligentsia, protagonists of rationality, and so forth. Other perspectives on the nuclear issue
offered here are not entirely divorced from governmental or activist ideologies, or the
discourse of scholars and scientists, but they are filtered with the varying dialects of
vernacular cultures which differ from area to area. They constitute Nandy's cultures,
cognitive orders, and interpersonal styles with which people have to address particular
incidents, issues, and problems. This is a "messy" arena requiring in-depth, qualitative
studies that are not always suited to the dictates of academic articles such as this[37]—
nonetheless, the attempt is useful in the quest for a fuller appreciation of how views
about nuclear power and armament are articulated at various levels of society, and not
just in the corridors of rationality and power.

Notes

1. For an excellent analysis of the use of this quote, see M. V. Ramana, "The Bomb of the
Blue God," *South Asian Magazine for Action and Reflection* (winter/spring 2001). Available at:
http://www.samarmagazine.org/archive/article.php?id=36 (accessed 16 April 2008).

2. Partha Chatterjee, "Democracy and the Violence of the State: A Political Negotiation
of Death," *Inter Asia Cultural Studies* 2, no. 1 (April 2001): 7–21.

3. The Subaltern Studies group (if it can be called that) encompassed those who developed
Gramscian perspectives on subaltern histories to those who adopted more post-structuralist
perspectives.

4. Ashis Nandy, *The Savage Freud and Other Essays on Possible and Retrievable Selves*
(Princeton, N.J.: Princeton University Press 1995), ix.

5. Ibid., 24

6. Chatterjee, "Democracy and the Violence of the State," 18.

7. *Mandap* refers to a shrine inside a pavilion. Ganapati—literally "Lord of the hordes"—is
the more frequently cited name for Ganesh in western India.

8. Itty Abraham, *The Making of the Indian Atomic Bomb: Science, Secrecy, and the Postcolonial State* (London: Zed Books 1998), 10.

9. *India Today,* June 22, 1998.

10. Indeed, the only weapons Gandhi would have advocated would have been yarn balls and spinning wheels (*charka*). As he once said of the *satygrahis:* "Yarn balls were their lead and the spinning was their gun" (cited in B. G. Kunte, ed., *Source Material for a History of the Freedom Movement in India: Non-Co-Operation Movement, Bombay City, 1920–1925,* vol. 6 (collected from the Maharashtra State Archives) (Bombay: Gazetteers Department, Government of Maharashtra, 1978).

11. Gandhi's article of August 25, 1920, "Religious Authority for Non-co-operation" (cited in Kunte, *Source Material for a History of the Freedom Movement in India,* 45). In his autobiography, Gandhi asserts: "The principle called satyagraha came into being before that name was invented" in Mohandas Karamchand Gandhi, *An Autobiography or the Story of my Experiments with Truth,* trans. Mahadev Desai (Harmondsworth, UK: Penguin Books, 1982). This was largely during his time spent in South Africa. Interestingly, he noted that "passive resistance" could be misconstrued. Europeans thought of it as a "weapon of the weak" that could possibly result in hatred and violence. Through the *Indian Opinion,* Gandhi offered a nominal prize to the reader who made the best suggestion. The selected term was *sadagraha* (truth and firmness), which was later modified to the term we know today.

12. The process has its parallels elsewhere in the overlap between Gandhian and Hindu nationalist ideology of "integral humanism." See Thomas Blom Hansen, "The Ethics of Hindutva and the Spirit of Capitalism," in *The BJP and the Compulsion of Politics in India,* ed. Thomas Hansen and Christophe Jaffrelot, 291–314 (New Delhi: Oxford University Press, 1998). The latter uses concepts such as *Swadeshi* and *Sarvodhya* (welfare for all) and also advocates decentralization and small-scale industries, where

> the more radical dimensions of Gandhian thought were subsumed within a framework which assigned undisputed subservience of individuals and groups to the nation as a corporate whole. Richard Fox has aptly characterized this entire operation as an "ideological hijacking" and an "ideological transplant" designed to appropriate the legitimacy of the Gandhian idiom in Indian politics. (Hansen, "The Ethics of Hindutva," 295)

13. Rustom Bharucha, "Politicians' Grin, Not the Buddha's Smile," *Economic and Political Weekly,* May 30, 1998, 1295–1298.

14. There appears to be another twist to the *ahimsa* argument. Gandhi once stated in a letter of March 2, 1930, to Lord Irwin: "Many think that non-violence is not an active force. My experience, limited though it is, shows that non-violence can be an intensely active force. It is my purpose to set in motion that force as well as against the organized violent force of the British rule [against] the unorganized violent force of the growing party of violence" (K. K. Chaudhari, ed., *Source Material for a History of the Freedom Movement: Civil Disobedience Movement, April–September 1930,* Vol. 11 [Bombay: Gazetteers Department, Government of Maharashtra, 1990], 9; brackets in original). Today the implications of Gandhian rhetoric are that the "organised violent force" is that of the NWS. The "unorganised violent force" is that of the newer states with claims to holding nuclear weapons, particularly with reference to Pakistan. The history of nonviolence has acted as a kind of guarantor for India to make ethical claims to the nuclear bomb as principally a "weapon for peace."

15. Itty Abraham, "Science and Secrecy in the Making of Postcolonial State," *Economic and Political Weekly,* August 16–23, 1997, 2136–2146, quote at 2145.

16. Abraham, *The Making of the Indian Atomic Bomb.*

17. Abraham notes that this is despite the fact that Nehru proposed steps toward nuclear disarmament. Vanaik's observations on Nehru's involvement in India's nuclear program point out the discrepancy between official "abstinence" and individual interest in nuclear potential. The disjunction between Abraham's and Vanaik's views might be taken as another instance of India's "dual character" with regard to its nuclear program.

18. Bal Gangadhar Tilak, on the other hand, preferred to think of it as more rights and powers invested in Indian people without necessarily implying, initially at least, total autonomy from British rule. See *Bal Gangadhar Tilak: His Writings and Speeches,* with an appreciation by Babu Aurobindo Ghose (Madras: Ganesh, 1922), 343–345. Gandhi's use of the term at a later point in anticolonial struggle was to advocate national autonomy where self-reliance could be developed by nurturing India's cottage industries.

19. The suggestion of a "strong state" has been there since independence. This strength was perceived largely in terms of nation building, federalism, anti-communalism, and opposition in possible wars with neighboring countries. The difference now is that, according to Hindutva opinion, Congress governance, particularly its purported "secularism" has led to the "feminization" of the state. The strength discussed now comes in the form of masculinist chauvinism and Hindu representation trumped up by ambitions to be a regional superpower.

20. Abraham, "Science and Secrecy in Making of Postcolonial State," 2136–2146.

21. Gyan Prakash, *Another Reason: Science and the Imagination of Modern India* (Princeton, N.J.: Princeton University Press, 1999).

22. Abraham, *The Making of the Indian Atomic Bomb,* 26–27.

23. Praful Bidwai and Achin Vanaik, *South Asia on a Short Fuse: Nuclear Politics and the Future of Global Disarmament* (New Delhi: Oxford University Press, 1999), 93.

24. This appears as another vindication of the dialectic of desire-disdain noted in the literature taken from such notables as Hegel, Freud, Fanon, and Lacan. See Homi Bhabha, *The Location of Culture* (London: Routledge, 1994) for its articulation in the colonial Indian case.

25. See also Anand Patwardhan's documentary film, *Jang aur Aman (War and Peace)* for examples of multimedia displays of nuclear weapons in the Ganapati Festival of Mumbai.

26. The five discursive elements are all replete with metaphors of gender, such that making gender into a separate heuristic category becomes implausible. Instead, issues to do with gender will be commented upon as invoked by particular combinations of these elements in the tableaux below.

27. *Mandal* refers to an organization or a committee. There are several thousands of these in a city like Mumbai dedicated to the preparation and activities around the Ganapati Festival.

28. Paul B. Courtright, "The Ganesh Festival in Maharashtra: Some Observations," in *The Experience of Hinduism: Essays on Religion in Maharashtra,* ed. Eleanor Zelliot and Maxine Bernstein, 76–94 (Albany: State University of New York, 1988), 84–85.

29. Raminder Kaur, *Performance Politics and the Cultures of Hinduism: Public Uses of Religion in Western India* (New Delhi: Permanent Black, 2003; London: Anthem Press, 2005).

30. Abraham, *The Making of the Indian Atomic Bomb,* 10.

31. Additionally, the 1998 tests were code-named "Shakti."

32. The earlier slogan emerged with Lal Bahadur Shastri in reference to the 1965 and 1971 wars with Pakistan. See Christopher Pinney, "Moral Topophilia: The Signification of Landscape in Indian Oleographs," in *The Anthropology of Landscape: Between Space and Place,* ed. E. Hirsch and M. O'Hanlon (Oxford: Oxford University Press, 1995), 78–113. In fact, Vajpayee used the term *Jai vigyan* (Victory to the Scientist) after the nuclear tests.

33. *Frontline,* September 11, 1998.

34. On the U.S. program of "Atoms for Peace" underwriting the promotion of nuclear reactors across the world from 1953 to 1961, see Richard G. Hewlett and Jack M. Holl, *Atoms for Peace and War, 1953–1961: Eisenhower and the Atomic Energy Commission* (Berkeley: University of California Press, 1989).

35. Praful Bidwai and Achin Vanaik locate the insidious power of nuclear weapons in their simultaneous sacralization and gradual normalization where "the transcendental is connected to the everyday and the ordinary" (*South Asia on a Short Fuse*, 4).

36. *India Today,* August 31, 1998.

37. For a fuller enquiry into the context and reception of such festival displays, see Kaur, *Performance Politics and the Cultures of Hinduism.*

9

NUCLEARIZATION AND PAKISTANI POPULAR CULTURE SINCE 1998

Iftikhar Dadi

Figure 9.1. Lapel pins, the top three bear the text "CRUSH INDIA," the middle top lapel also bears the text "GORI MEZILE [*sic*]." ca. 1998.

Figure 9.2. Nationalist medals. The bottom two medals show Altaf Hussain, leader of the MQM party (left), and Jinnah paired with a missile (right). ca. 1998.

Figure 9.3. Buttons. The top left button shows Nawaz Sharif, Dr. A. Q. Khan, the "father" of the Pakistani bomb, and a mushroom cloud with the Pakistani flag emerging. ca. 1998.

Figure 9.4. Paper hat. Text includes "Atomic Blasts *mubarak*," "Independence Day *mubarak*," with a mushroom cloud decorated with the Pakistani flag, framed by the Ghauri and the Shaheen missiles. ca. 1998.

Figure 9.5. Button. Shows Dr. A. Q. Khan, the "father" of the Pakistani bomb, with Jinnah, Iqbal, and Liaquat Ali, framed by the Ghauri and the Shaheen missiles. ca. 1998.

Figure 9.6a–c. "Samsonite" bag with camouflage design. The patterns on this remarkable bag are not composed of organic shapes but of military images and texts including "FAUJIMAN," "ISLAMIC BOMB," "WINNER-65 WAR," "MOST WANTED." 24 × 16 × 18 inches, nylon. ca. 1998.

Figure 9.6b.

Figure 9.6c.

Figure 9.7. Missile-shaped lapel pins. ca. 1998.

Figure 9.8. Missile-shaped lapel pin, "Ghauri missile." ca. 1998.

Figure 9.9. Poster, General Zia-ul-Haq with other nationalist leaders, Jinnah, Iqbal, Liaquat Ali, Ayub Khan, framed with heroic images of the Pakistan Army. ca. 1988–90, 19 × 13 inches.

Figure 9.10. Poster, Benazir Bhutto with her father, Zulfiqar Ali Bhutto, with the words "Kashmir is ours" and "We will fight for a thousand years for Kashmir." ca. early 1990s, 12 × 18 inches.

Figure 9.11. Billboard, Benazir Bhutto framed by portraits of war heroes, Karachi. ca. mid-1990s.

Figure 9.12. Anonymous inset in the "Social Roundup" pages of *Akhbar-i Jahan*, June 29–July 4, 1998, p. 59. Titled "Atomic Capabilities—We ought to humbly prostrate ourselves in thanks to the Almighty," the inset critiques the Pasban's glorification of belligerent nuclearization.

Figure 9.13. Chagai Hills monument in a public park, Islamabad, 2006 [?]. Photographer unknown.

Introduction

This essay discusses how nuclearization in Pakistani public space was manifested by discursive constructs and material artifacts, and argues for a structural and thematic continuity between the pre- and post-nuclear eras by looking at nationalist and military representations produced in Pakistan before and after the 1998 atomic tests. The emphasis, however, is on the enactment of a new nuclear popular public in Pakistan, which the state attempts to appropriate by creating grandiose monuments celebrating nuclearization. Practices both by the state and non-state actors in visualizing nuclearization have created an important popular and political arena for a paradoxical, spectral debate on nuclearization. This essay briefly examines this period and its aftermath through the lens of popular culture, arguing that developments in the wake of the 1998 tests also rendered the question of nuclearization in Pakistan to discursive and popular visibility, and to unfolding effects in the public sphere that cannot be predicted. To convey the character of this debate firsthand, I rely on extensive quotations from commentators and actors, as well as on reproductions of the rich range of material artifacts produced since 1998.

Economic and Political Context in 1998

Pakistan conducted its nuclear tests at a time when the Nawaz Sharif–led government was facing persistent crises—allegations of corruption and nepotism, ethnic violence in Karachi, and difficulties meeting outside financial commitments. The Indian nuclear tests of May 11 and 13, 1998, were widely perceived in Pakistan to have forced the Pakistani government to conduct reciprocal tests as early as possible, and these were carried out on May 28 and 30 after a suspenseful seventeen days.

Although the Pakistani government's intention to conduct the tests enjoyed widespread public support after May 11, this sentiment was not universal, even within the government itself.[1] Samina Ahmed has argued that the pressure the unanticipated Indian tests exerted upon the Pakistani public produced "one positive development," which was to open up public debate regarding the wisdom of proceeding with reciprocal tests—even though this debate had little immediate effect on official policies. According to Ahmed, the debate circled around three groups: hawks, including Islamic parties, senior retired bureaucrats, and the other usual suspects as described in the introduction to this volume; doves, encompassing numerous regional political parties, progressive activists, and even establishment figures; and those who were ambiguous about the nuclear issue, including respected figures such as the former chairman of the Pakistan Atomic Energy Commission and influential members of major political parties. Among those who were ambiguous, surprisingly, was Prime Minister Sharif himself, as he "appeared hesitant to opt for a nuclear test, conscious of the threats of international military and economic sanctions."[2] Thus, although Pakistan's nuclear program dates back to the 1970s, it was the urgent atmosphere of these seventeen days in May 1998 that brought the nuclear issue to the attention of non-elites.

In the immediate aftermath of the Pakistani tests, both the press and the public celebrated the successful crossing of the nuclear threshold. This sense of triumph, however, must be viewed in the context of ongoing crises, which the Urdu and the English press continued to highlight before and after May 28. The need for the tests and the anticipated political and economic fallout, which was extensively debated in the press and in popular circles even before May 28, remained topics of debate even as the uncritical celebratory mood rapidly vanished. Indeed, the speed with which "normalcy" resumed is striking. Diplomatic and fiscal implications of "going nuclear" manifested themselves quickly, exacerbating and intensifying the general sense of crisis, which resurfaced even more acutely after May 28. The press, for example, continued to report allegations of corruption against the ruling party, killing and terrorism in Karachi, and a general sense that little was going right.

Further anguish was created when Sharif's government, in an emergency move, froze all private U.S. dollar accounts, an act coinciding with the atomic tests. Substantial foreign currency reserves in private accounts, totaling U.S.$11 billion, were formerly exempt from many regulatory and taxation mechanisms. Now the government, facing immanent default on its international financial obligations, audaciously appropriated this reserve by allowing the withdrawal of funds but at a low, officially controlled rate in rupees. This move not only stunned the elite, but also the middle classes and the petty bourgeoisie.[3] For example, a report by Aamer Ahmed Khan in *The Herald* of July 1998 states:

> Today, there is increasing bitterness amongst a class that feels it wasn't "taken into confidence" about the exact implications of going nuclear. . . . The biggest shock for the trading community has undoubtedly been the freeze on foreign currency accounts, a move which might have been anticipated in higher business circles but came as a bolt from the blue for the bulk of the trading class. For a cash-oriented and wholly uncounted market, dollar accounts immune from official scrutiny have become as much a basic necessity as food and water. It is hard, for example, to find a single trader worth his name in Lahore's electronic market who does not hold at least one dollar account.[4]

The freezing of dollar accounts became even more scandalous when persistent rumors surfaced that figures close to the government had been tipped off in advance, and had thus managed to transfer their dollar accounts into safe offshore accounts before the freeze took effect. These allegations were reported extensively in the English-language press but also in vernacular venues such as the *Akhbar-i Jahan,* a widely circulated weekly published in Urdu.[5] In a full-page column devoted to economics that appeared regularly, Najam al-Hasan Ata, in the June 8–14, 1998, issue, deemed the government-imposed emergency measures were unconstitutional, echoing the observations of a senior general, who stated that the real danger to Pakistan's security was posed by its own poor economic condition rather than any hostile external power.[6] In a subsequent article, the columnist criticized the national budget unveiled for the next fiscal year, suggesting it failed to advance any favorable program for the public good.[7]

Representing Nuclearization in 1998

While nuclearization meant the crossing of a conceptual and psychological threshold in public perception, the tests were also assimilated into an imaginary predating the 1998 events. Bear in mind that Pakistan celebrated its fiftieth anniversary only recently, in 1997, which brought about an amplified and lingering presence in the popular and public sphere of nationalist imagery such as the flag, the image of Jinnah, portrayals of army heroes, and so on.[8] *Akhbar-i Jahan* had also generally followed a pro-establishment view in its cover stories from May and June 1998,[9] and in its regular features that continued during the May and June developments, including reports of Lollywood models in middle-class fashion spreads and serialized stories such as the Phoolan Devi saga.

The nuclear tests closely followed another symbolic confrontation between India and Pakistan earlier in 1998: the testing of ballistic missiles. Pakistan tested its *Ghauri* missile on April 6, 1998, to counter the Indian development of the Prithvi missile, already in the Indian arsenal for several years. The name of the Pakistani missile, *Ghauri*, is freighted with historical connotations when set against India's name for its missile, the *Prithvi*. Writing in the monthly *Herald*, Aamer Ahmed Khan analyzes the symbolism of the missiles' names, seeing them as a consequence of managing crises largely internal to 1990s Pakistan:

> Unfortunately for the region, especially since the early 1990s, relations between India and Pakistan have suffered more from frivolous rhetoric that has flown between the two foreign offices than from the actual physical proxy war that is being fought in Kashmir and Siachin.

When the Pakistan army began its largest ever overland exercise in 1989, it chose to call it *Zarb-e-Momin* (blow of the believer). Similarly, Ghauri was developed under the name of *Hatf* (meaning target in Urdu). But when it came to test-firing the missile, it was rechristened *Ghauri*, in memory of the Afghan Muslim invader who overran the subcontinent during the rule of Prithvi-raj in the 12th century.

What may not be clear to India is that the nomenclature, as well as the war cries that followed *Ghauri*'s testing, are better explained by placing them in the context of Pakistan's internal politics rather that external security concerns.[10]

However, Srinivas Aravamudan has insightfully argued that this symbolic enactment of myth is not limited to Pakistan.[11] Rather, developments within India also participate in this economy of "speculation and specularization," which are a consequence of the continuing trauma of Partition in 1947.[12]

The issue of representing nuclear tests in Pakistan was inflected in at least two ways. On the one hand, the imagery of the nuclear tests synthesized and re-territorialized existing nationalist imagery and the icon of the *Ghauri* missile to create a visual culture of nuclearization that had been absent before May 1998. The buttons, hats, bags, and other materials being sold in the informal sector to mark the Pakistan Independence Day celebration on August 14, 1998, items that were acquired by the author from street sellers in Karachi, clearly express this complex assimilation (Figures 9.1–9.8). The new images draw upon existing imagery of national leaders and heroes of the Pakistani army, pictured in earlier political posters (Figures 9.9, 9.10, and 9.11),to recode the new developments of 1998 within preexisting matrices of meaning such that Jinnah himself becomes incongruously associated not only with Dr. A. Q. Khan but with the *Ghauri* missile itself. This tactic, however, is not without its own equivocations. The lengthy, unpopular military regimes in Pakistan, especially Zia's regime, aroused ambivalent views of the army among the public. So if the tests are indeed assimilated into preexisting images of the army, would the public understand them only as transcendent national events or would their association with the army open the tests to controversy and political jockeying?

On the other hand, the tests clearly reveal a new set of concerns in the popular arena, as evidenced by the imagery of the mushroom cloud, which was not present beforehand in the popular realm. Indeed, the *Ghauri* missile and the mushroom cloud icons indicate a struggle to resolve the paradox of depicting the "nuclear" itself, as underground tests are invisible and difficult to denote with a compelling visual sign. Although photographs of the Chagai mountain range test site were printed in *Akhbar-i Jahan*,[13] the very passivity and banality of the images of the mountain range meant that the photos reappeared in none of the popular images shown here, though they were adopted later as icons for official commemoration. The nuclear test was thus depicted and indexed as an icon during the initial weeks following May 28 by the missile and the imaginary mushroom cloud, over which the Pakistani flag is placed in a somewhat macabre gesture (Figures 9.3, 9.4).

The informal sector artifacts produced in 1998 are striking because of their miniature size. Apart from the economic and technical constraints necessary to hastily produce inexpensive souvenirs, the scale and colorful everyday appeal of the artifacts render the "nuclear" as bounded and capable of assimilation into the popular imagination rather than as the terrifying and unrepresentable, which is how the bomb has been understood in the Western imagination since the Cold War.[14] The artist Saira Wasim, drawing on the rich allegorical vocabulary of seventeenth-century Mughal paintings, has also produced a number of potent allegorical miniature paintings to address nuclearization of Pakistan and the symbolic contest between India and Pakistan.[15] In works such as *Cricket Match* (2000) she depicts the Pakistani and Indian cricket teams armed with missiles and other modern weapons, facing each other, each straddling a gigantic accusing finger. *Weapons & Stars 2* (2000) shows the celebrated hero Maula Jat, played by the actor Sultan Rahi in the hyper-violent Punjabi film *Maula Jat* (1979). This genre of Punjabi film depicted an outlaw response to rural exploitation, but, according to the film historian Mushtaq Gazdar's important argument, it also enacted an allegory of the repression instigated by General Zia ul-Haq's martial law regime.[16] Here Maula Jat, posing with his signature axe and framed by Pakistani missiles, is surrounded by cherubs and *putti* in the heavens, offering an allegory of Pakistani militarized masculinity rendered in miniature format.

Dissent from establishment consensus was expressed in *Akhbar-i Jahan,* albeit in an oblique and qualified fashion, even before the Pakistani tests were conducted, and there are several cases where photographs and images carry connotations that are at cross-purposes to the text. For example, a three-page essay from the June 8–14 issue, giving an eyewitness account of the test at the site, also showed a photograph of a poor rural family displaced from the village because of the tests, hinting at the human costs the residents of the area had silently borne (37). The issue of June 15–21, 1998, included a photograph of Indian women protesting the Indian nuclear tests, perhaps implying that Pakistanis might find this act of resistance worthy of emulation (8). And in his column titled "India's Atomic Hysteria Will Lead to Financial Instability in the Region" (the word "hysteria" was transliterated from English) from the May 25–31 issue, Najam al-Hasan Ata decried the financial and strategic costs of developing nuclear technology by poor countries in general, pointing out that millions of Indians continue to suffer from poverty and misery, and underscoring his thesis by illustrating the essay with multiple photographs of poverty-stricken Indians (14). In these representations, even when the subject is ostensibly Indian, the costs and implications of reshaping Pakistan's economic and social landscape, necessitated by nuclearization, are implicitly challenged as well.

Dissent was also conveyed in *Akhbar-i Jahan* at one of the first public monuments to nuclearization by referring to a makeshift missile erected in Karachi by the Pasban, a youth group associated with the Jamaat-e-Islami.[17] In an anonymous inset in the "Social Roundup" pages in its issue of June 29–July 4, 1998, Pasban's glorification of belligerent nuclearization is criticized by echoing the failure of an earlier spectacle related to the Cricket World Cup (59):

Atomic Capability—Let Us Prostrate Ourselves in Thanks to the Almighty
Hasan Square, located in Gulshan-i Iqbal, Karachi, has become a permanent site for colorful spectacles, and by now bears a proud tradition in adding splendor to the city. The Pasban have virtually taken an oath to continually make this area lively and interesting. During the 1996 Cricket World Cup, the Pasban created a 50-foot long cricket bat and initiated a rally through the city from this very site. The impression was thus created that Pakistan will definitely win this World Cup. But perhaps nature [*qudrat*] felt that our manner of celebration was arrogant and was meant to belittle the other [team]. That is why it [nature] granted victory to the Sri Lanka's apparently weaker team, in order to teach us the lesson, "the arrogant are to be humbled [*ghurur ka sar necha*]." Now that Pakistan has attained nuclear capability and we have finally become able to humiliate the enemy [blacken the enemy's face] by mounting the atomic bomb on the Ghauri missile, the nation's fervor has again reached a climax. We have successfully created the bomb and strengthened our defense capabilities; therefore we ought to humbly prostrate ourselves in thanks to the Almighty. But it seems we are again boasting in pride. Pasban has apparently not derived any object lesson from the 50-foot bat [experience], and by now making a 50–foot bomb, has repeated an act that does not behoove a nation such as ours. This bomb [mockup] was again made at the same location, the Hasan Square roundabout, and its makers even turned its direction towards Delhi. The question however remains: we are a fruit-laden tree, why are we not bent down? We are not an empty vessel, then why do [hollow] sounds emerge from us? If India explodes its bomb and indulges in degraded rhetoric [*choti baat*], let it do so, why should we demean our language/ tongue [*zaban*] in turn? Pasban's enthusiasm is enviable, but should this not have been expressed in another fashion?

The image accompanying the text shows the missile mockup on the back of a flatbed truck, labeled "PASBAN ISLAMIC ATOM BOMB and decorated with flags of various Muslim countries (Figure 9.12).[18] The anonymous text above, from *Akhbar-i Jahan,* deploys the trope of religious piety to criticize the Pasban, demonstrating the possibilities but also some limits of this nationalist and religiously inflected critique of nuclearization.

Monumentalizing the Nuclear Since 1998

The hastily constructed Pasban monument, and the lapels and buttons were quickly adopted as paradigms for official commemoration of nuclearization. By the first anniversary of the tests, ephemeral materials were handed out, such as "little badges with mushroom clouds free . . . to children,"[19] but the government was also promoting "a competition of ten best songs, seminars, fairs, festive public gatherings, candle processions, sports competitions, bicycle races, flag-hoisting ceremonies, etc."[20] Here, the formalized official commemorations clearly seem to appropriate the initiatives originally undertaken by the informal sector and non-state actors at a small, human scale.

Possibly inspired by the Pasban, the state also initiated a series of large-scale public and official monuments in numerous locations in Pakistan, which typically assumed the form of the *Ghauri* missile or a scaled-down reproduction of the Chagai mountain range. But unlike most civic public monuments in Pakistan that are fairly bland and generally ignored by the public, the monuments to nuclearization have become significant objects of contestation. Four press reports from recent years are discussed here to give a sense of how official public monuments, perhaps for the first time in Pakistan's history, have become active sites of controversy.

The following press report, dated December 12, 2003, provides some clues to the bizarre anxieties the government faced when hosting a regional cooperation summit, as it had already constructed prominent and grandiose nuclear monuments in Islamabad:

Pak Peace symbol to Greet Saarc Summit
ISLAMABAD: Peace monuments are getting a touch of polish and symbols of aggression being demolished in this Pakistani capital as the city gears up to host the South Asian association for Regional Cooperation (Saarc) summit next month. To make Islamabad Saarc-friendly, the government here has planned to build a "peace monument" in place of a missile replica at the main square of posh residential area in F-10 sector. The missile structure, which is 15.2 metres long and 1.2 metres in diameter, which had been installed at the F-10 Square in September 1998, was said to be a life size replica of the surface-to-surface missile Ghauri. But when residents of the area woke up on Wednesday, they found the Ghauri replica missing. Instead they found huge machines used for construction work parked in middle of the square that is a busy spot during office hours. "We have removed it and instead a peace monument

will be built there," Malik Aulia, a director at the Capital Development Authority (CDA), told IANS.... Besides the missiles, the replicas of Chagai Hills—where Pakistan tested its nuclear devices—were also set up in major cities including Islamabad. The first thing that visitors to Islamabad notice is the bright-shining 20-metre-high and 45-metre- wide replica of the Chagai Hills at the main entrance of the city. The replica is made of fibre and tin that resembles the Chagai Hills that were said to have been glowing seconds after the nuclear tests Pakistan conducted in a tit-for-tat gesture to Indian tests. When asked if the replica of the hills too would be dismantled before the Saarc summit, Aulia said: "We don't have any such instructions.".... A senior member of the ruling Pakistan Muslim League-Quaid-e-Azam (PML-QA) said removing the hills replica was being considered. "We are yet to take a final decision ... We are a bit worried about the public reaction," he told IANS.... However, there is a strong feeling that the replica could be removed "any night" before the summit.[21]

The monuments were constructed by the top-down decisions of a state intent on redirecting the apparent visibility of nuclearization in the informal sphere toward its own ends, but without any public democratic debate. Aware of the difficulty of now removing them without facing controversy, the state is, ironically, forced to resort to shadowy and secretive maneuvers to undo its own monumentalizing in its attempts to redefine these public sites to render them less embarrassing internationally.

A staff report in *The Pakistan Times,* February 10, 2004, briefly reports on the arson of the Chagai monument in Karachi. Although Pakistani public monuments are commonly subject to graffiti and vandalism, this apparently well-planned act of arson may well signify an antiestablishment protest against a state apparatus from which many Karachiites have become alienated since at least the mid 1980s:

Chaghi Monument Burnt in Karachi

KARACHI: A monument of Chaghi Mountain was burnt to ashes at Bagh-e-Jinnah (old polo ground) here on Monday morning by some unknown persons. Two firetenders extinguished the fire after one-hour struggle. Police Station, just in front of the monument situated at a few hundred metres distance had neither arrested any person nor registered a case of the loss of this precious asset. The monument located next to the wall of Governor's House in the west was built in 1999 on the occasion of the first anniversary of the nuclear explosions at Chagai Mountains in the Balochistan province by the government of ex-Prime Minister Mian Muhammad Nawaz Sharif. The then Governor of Sindh, Lt General (Retd) Moinuddin Hyder had unveiled the plaque of this national monument on May 28 in 1999. It was built with the cost of Rs.50 million approximately.[22]

One certainly wonders how a kitschy monument to nuclearization, albeit built with considerable public funds, acquires the status of a "precious asset." Nevertheless, by lamenting its loss, the report certainly hints that the official response goes well beyond the usual bureaucratic bungling and indifference, perhaps toward a degree of apathetic complicity in its destruction, possibly suggesting divided views on these monuments within governmental institutions.

The following excerpt is from the column of journalist Kamran Shafi in the *Daily Times*, December 29, 2005:

> Let me now thank the good person who has had the missile at the F-9 park and E-8 crossing removed. This missile, if you will recall, was "inaugurated" by a big noise in our nuclear set-up and came fitted with a red light in its bottom that flashed whenever a high personage passed along the road.
>
> Thank you, whoever you are, and while you are at it will you please also remove the model of the Chagai mountain that glowed white when our bums [*sic*] were detonated in its bosom; or when it "rumbled," according to a gushing scribe? The model makes us look like idiotic children, showing off for no reason at all and needs to be removed immediately. If the government/CDA doesn't do anything about it, could a kindly soul who has the good name of the country close to his heart just go and burn the damned thing down? Just like somebody did in Karachi? It is highly embarrassing trying to explain the thing to visitors.[23]

Shafi's comments, especially how the presence of the nuclear monuments make Pakistanis out to be "idiotic children," parallels the observations made earlier by the vernacular *Akhbar-i Jahan* on the Pasban's activities.

This press report from May 29, 2006, shows how the removal of these monuments was no longer a normal civic matter but was subject to heated political contestation:

Pakistan Nuclear Tests Anniversary Turns Political
Islamabad, May 29—The anniversary of the 1998 nuclear tests took a political colour when activists of the Pakistan Muslim League (Nawaz) protested the removal of the Chagai monument and laid the foundation for a fresh one in Lahore, only to be removed by the police.[24]

Here, strangely enough, the position of civilians and the military regarding the celebration of nuclearization is reversed, as the Pakistan Muslim League (Nawaz group), a civilian political party not in power at the time, struggles to claim the mantle of promoting popular nuclearization against a military dictatorship that would usually be accused of promoting militarism.

Conclusion

The recently contested visibility of official monuments indexes the emergence of the imaginary of the "nuclear" in the vernacular, informal, and popular visual spheres, and suggests that the debate regarding nuclearization is no longer confined to official and elite discourses alone. The 1998 tests, therefore, also produced significant interventions in popular culture, as they combined three factors in popular imagery: existing nationalist imagery deployed by politicians and augmented earlier by the fiftieth anniversary celebration in 1997; the testing of the Ghauri missile in April 1998; and the response to India's test by Pakistan's own explosions in May 1998. The tests did create a widely shared (but by no means universal) sense of national purpose for a short period, but this brief sense of national unity emerged against and was undermined by other news in the media that worked at cross-purposes by continuing to highlight various crises in the Pakistani body politic. In attempting to appropriate popular perceptions of nuclearization, the state itself borrowed and monumentalized numerous initiatives from the informal sector, but these appropriations have been riven with conflict. These actions by both non-state and state actors created paradoxical new opportunities to contest and debate Pakistan's nuclearization program, which includes discursive critiques as well as spectral play between secrecy and visibility.

Notes

I am grateful to Itty Abraham for his helpful suggestions and advice. All translations from *Akhbar-i Jahan* are mine. All Web sites were accessed on May 6, 2008, unless otherwise noted.

1. Itty Abraham, "Introduction: National Security and Atomic Publics," chapter 1 in this volume; Dr. Mehtab S. Karim, "Figuring It Out: Going by numbers, Pakistan's majority gives nuclear detonation an overwhelming thumbs up. A *Newsline* survey," *Newsline*, July 1998, pp. 34A–37.

2. Samina Ahmed, "The Nuclear Debate: The very existence of the three distinct nuke camps—the hawks, doves, and proponents of nuclear ambiguity—testifies to the dawning of a nuclear debate," *Newsline*, July 1998, pp. 30–31.

3. The July 1998 issue of *The Herald* covered this extensively, with a prominent cover story by Azhar Abbas titled "The Great $11,000,000,000 Bank Robbery."

4. "The Big Chill," *The Herald,* July 1998, pp. 36–37.

5. Aurangzeb, "Who was allowed to withdraw foreign currency past banking hours?" Lahorenama, *Akhbar-i Jahan,* June 15–21, 1998, p. 12.

6. Najam al-Hasan Ata, "The freezing of dollar accounts in the absence of a financial emergency," June 8–14, 1998, p. 14.

7. Najam al-Hasan Ata, *Akhbar-i Jahan,* June 22–28, 1998, p. 16.

8. This nationalist imagery however, was itself subject to political reinterpretation since the late 1980s. See Iftikhar Dadi, "Political Posters in Karachi, 1988–1999," *South Asian Popular Culture* 5, no. 1 (April 2007): 11–30.

9. For example, *Akhbar-i Jahan,* June 8–14, 1998, pp. 11, 35–37.

10. "Testing Times," *The Herald,* May 1998, p. 40.

11. Srinivas Aravamudan, "Chapter Four; The Hindu Sublime or Nuclearism Rendered Cultural," in idem, *Guru English: South Asian Religion in a Cosmopolitan Language* (Princeton, N.J.: Princeton University Press, 2006).

12. Ibid., p.182.

13. *Akhbar-i Jahan,* June 8–14, 1998, p. 35.

14. For example, the popular humanist photographic exhibition, *The Family of Man*, at the Museum of Modern Art in New York, in 1955, was organized around and against a large central image of a mushroom cloud. See Mary Anne Staniszewski, *The Power of Display: A History of Exhibition Installations at the Museum of Modern Art* (Cambridge, Mass.: MIT Press, 1998), pp. 235–259. I am grateful to Natalie Melas for alerting me to the miniature quality of

the Pakistani artifacts produced in the informal sector. The aesthetic and political ramifications of this difference in imagining the nuclear as beautiful rather than sublime cannot be pursued further here.

15. Her work can be viewed on her Web site: www.sairawasim.com.

16. Mushtaq Gazdar, *Pakistan Cinema 1947–1997* (Karachi: Oxford University Press, 1997), pp. 133–134.

17. Additional information on the Pasban is available on their Web site, http://www.pasban.org.

18. A photograph by Aamir Qureshi, published in the December 2001 issue of *Scientific American* (pp. 72–73) to illustrate the article "India, Pakistan, and the Bomb" by M. V. Ramana and A. H. Nayyar, shows a similar (possibly the same) *Ghauri* mockup being paraded in Karachi by the Pasban in February 1999.

19. Pervez Hoodbhoy, "Pokhran-Chaghi Audit: Winners and Losers." http://www.chowk.com/articles/4568.

20. Zia Mian, "The Thousand-Year War with Ourselves," *Outlook India,* July 23, 2001. http://www.outlookindia.com/author.asp?name=Zia+Mian

21. Available at http://www.southasianmedia.net/index_story.cfm?id=72475&category=Frontend&Country=MAIN. Accessed December 12, 2006.

22. Available at http://pakistantimes.net/2004/02/10/top9.htm.

23. Available at http://www.dailytimes.com.pk/default.asp?page=2005%5C12%5C29%5C-story_29-12-2005_pg3_3.

24. Available at http://www.nerve.in/news:2535002966.

10

GUARDIANS OF THE NUCLEAR MYTH: POLITICS, IDEOLOGY, AND INDIA'S STRATEGIC COMMUNITY

Karsten Frey

In 1977 the then foreign minister Atal Behari Vajpayee stated that India "would never manufacture atomic weapons nor proliferate the technology of weapon development. It is our solemn resolve that whatever the rest of the world may do, we will never use the atomic energy for military purpose."[1] Two decades later, immediately after becoming India's new prime minister, Vajpayee authorized the testing of nuclear devices and subsequently declared India a nuclear weapons power. Most major parties and segments of India's society effectively welcomed the tests as a national achievement and a major source of national pride. What had happened in the country over the two decades after Vajpayee's "solemn resolve"?

The fundamental change of heart on the nuclear question cannot be convincingly explained through security analyses. India's security-related incentives to nuclearize, in any case, had been reduced by the end of the Cold War, the reduction of global stockpiles of nuclear weapons, and the ongoing process of Sino-Indian rapprochement. Instead of assessing changes in the external threat environment, this chapter focuses on the fundamental change that took place in India's domestic discourse on the nuclear question. Within India's democratic setup, the interaction between the elected leaders and the public on nuclear issues is not direct, but occurs through the mediation of a small number of strategic thinkers. This strategic community has managed to monopolize the nuclear discourse and create a social reality of its own in which nuclear weapons have become the chosen symbols of what India stands for in the world.

The strategic community sets the parameters of the nuclear discourse by exercising opinion leadership through extensive media presence and newspaper publishing. The main forums for the debate on the nuclear issue were India's major English-language daily newspapers and weekly journals. To assess the dynamics behind India's nuclear (dis-)course, this chapter summarizes the findings of a textual analysis of 705 nuclear-related editorials and opinion articles published in five of India's major dailies: the *Hindu,* the *Hindustan Times,* the *Indian Express,* the *Times of India,* and the *Statesman.*[2] The analysis shows that the strategic community's success in linking the nuclear question to ideology was decisive in paving the way for India's nuclearization.

Reflections on Nuclear Myths

In most countries today the development of nuclear weapons is considered morally prohibitive, incompatible with the country's international outlook. In some states, however, these negative norms are overridden by other norms that lead to the glorification of nuclear weapons as either symbols of invulnerability, perceived threats, or the regalia of major power status. This phenomenon is termed the "nuclear myth."

The concept of nuclear myth is closely related to the idea of international prestige. States seeking this prestige have generally "lost the last major-power war and/ or have increased their power after the international order was established and the benefits were allocated."[3] Within the international nuclear order, established in 1968 through the Nonproliferation Treaty (NPT), an antiquated balance of power has been preserved in that five states are granted superior status. Those states that think of their status and power as having increased since then tend to oppose the regime. This opposition is, in most cases, limited to diplomatic gestures, but in other cases it may cause the state to seek system change by building up nuclear arms.

The motives of nuclear arming behavior are thus bound to the socially constructed values attached to such weapons. According to Scott D. Sagan, "from this sociological perspective, military organizations and their weapons can therefore be envisioned as serving functions similar to those of flags, airlines, and Olympic teams; they are part of what modern states believe they have to possess to be legitimate, modern states."[4] The identity of a modern state translates into norms that determine behavioral patterns. Norms are defined as "a prescription or proscription for behaviour 'for a given identity.'"[5] In the process of norms creation, emotions such as pride and fear are attached to these symbols.

The overall number of states that consider the acquisition of nuclear weapons a prerequisite for being a modern state is rather low, as most states develop diametrically opposed norms. This process of glorification also is limited to nuclear weapons and excludes other, comparably destructive weapons systems. For instance, most states possessing or developing nuclear weapons (except for Israel and North Korea) signed the Chemical Weapons Convention even while explicitly applying moral, normative-driven arguments. Thus the nuclear myth stems from the widely accepted understanding that nuclear weapons are different—incomparable to any other weapons system.

Two factors are crucial for actors to enthusiastically pursue the acquisition of nuclear weapons. First, the actors define themselves in nationalistic terms, and they perceive that the nation's status equals or tops the status of a real or imagined antagonist. Second, the nation's identity is defined in oppositional terms, in contrast to what Jacques E. C. Hymans terms the "sportsmanlike identity conception."[6] Whereas the oppositional identity denotes a dichotomized us-against-them pattern, the sportsmanlike identity concept places that pattern "within a broader, transcendent identity conception."[7] Through this multilevel identity, sportsmanlike actors do not define their relationship to antagonists in purely oppositional terms, but they develop a sense of commonality by maintaining a certain we're-all-in-the-same-boat attitude. The stronger the actors' sense of commonality, the more likely they are to develop a sense of abhorrence and opprobrium regarding weapons symbolizing the other's potential total annihilation. In contrast, actors who define their relationship to antagonists exclusively in oppositional terms tend to be attracted by the sense of omnipotence symbolized by nuclear weapons.

Thus, those who define their national identity in both nationalist and oppositional terms are most likely to attach a positive set of norms to nuclear weapons. As E. C. Hymans concludes,

> Oppositional nationalists see their nation as both naturally at odds with an external enemy, and as naturally its equal if not its superior. Such a conception tends to generate the emotions of fear and pride—an explosive psychological cocktail. Driven by fear and pride, oppositional nationalists develop a desire for nuclear weapons that goes beyond calculation, to self-expression. Thus, in spite of the tremendous complexity of the nuclear choice, leaders who decide for the bomb tend not to back into it. For them, unlike the bulk of their peers, the choice for nuclear weapons is neither a close call nor a possible last resort but an absolute necessity.[8]

Pride, or, for that matter, the desire for status, is the second crucial factor determining the relationship between the self-defined "us" and the real or imagined antagonist. In contrast to what many scholars suggest, pride is not necessarily a lesser motivator than fear. History is rich in examples of states that were actually willing to sacrifice some of their perceived security if this was considered the price for increased status. As Randall L. Schweller reminds us, these states "must gain relative to others; and throughout history states striving for greater relative power, often driven by prestige demands for their rightful 'place at the table' or 'place in the sun,' have routinely sacrificed their security in such a quest."[9] Within the identity conception of states, the nuclear myth turns the bomb into a particularly prestigious device and, as such, provides the perfect trajectory for increasing international status.

With 180 odd countries in the world abstaining from the acquisition of nuclear weapons and 8 countries in possession of them (with two other countries assumed to pursue their acquisition), one might consider the dominance of the nuclear taboo, that is, the negative norm of nuclear abhorrence, over the nuclear myth to be the rule. The core question is thus why and how this relationship is reversed in the case of defectors. In other words, from the viewpoint of the defector, which dynamics within the norms composition made nuclear weapons symbols of international prestige and immunity, rather than abhorrence? The Indian experience appears to be particularly relevant in answering this question.

India's Strategic Community

Generally it is assumed that the nuclear taboo trickles up from an increasingly sensitive civic society to the policy elite, frequently in opposition to the defense community. In countries where the nuclear myth prevails, on the other hand, this normative predis- position appears to have followed a trickle-down dynamic in which the policy-making elite attached a positive set of norms to nuclear weapons that was adopted, in turn, by larger segments of society.

In India, the interplay between the policy making elite and society is affected by certain conditions. First of all, during most of India's nuclear course, decisions were traditionally made by India's prime minister in a personalized, rather ad hoc manner, detached from clear institutional procedures. Second, India's polity is gener- ally inward-looking, and foreign policy issues (with the exception of Indo-Pakistan antagonism) receive only sporadic attention. As a result, public opinion on issues of foreign policy, particularly in the nuclear field, has proved highly volatile and emo- tional. Third, the organizational position holders among India's policy-making elite have traditionally taken a passive stance on the nuclear issue, usually delaying decisions until outside pressures restricted their ability to maneuver.

These three basic conditions—the lack of institutionalized decision-making structures, the volatility and mood of public opinion, and the passivity of decision makers—created the space necessary for the country's strategic community to set the direction of India's nuclear course. This well-defined community of strategic thinkers and opinion leaders comprises three broad groups: strategists with military backgrounds, members of the nuclear-scientific community, and a heterogeneous group of politico-strategists including journalists, political scientists, political activ- ists, independent intellectuals, members of nongovernmental organizations (NGOs) and various associations, as well as active and retired politicians and diplomats. This strategic community is able to monopolize the security discourse and thus hold an element of power which, according to a Habermasian definition, comprises both *communicative power,* arising from the successful process of deliberation within the public sphere, as well as *administrative power,* associated with the functions and institutions of the state.[10] Correspondingly, the strategic community was able to determine India's nuclear course by directly and personally advising India's policy makers, and by guiding public opinion and generating public pressures on the government.

The traditional exclusion of active service members from the political sphere has created the space for a large community of retired military personnel entering the think tank community. Several think tanks staffed by retired officers have emerged, most prominently the Delhi-based Institute for Defense Studies and Analyses (IDSA). Created in the 1960s in reaction to the debacle that was the 1962 war, the IDSA soon emerged as India's most important strategic think tank, and it immediately took a position between the military-strategic and politico-strategic sections. The IDSA and its longtime leading figure, K. Subrahmanyam, were quite successful in setting the ideological foundation of India's strategic debate.

Throughout the history of India's nuclear program, the leaders of its nuclear establishment did not, as with many of their foreign counterparts, hide behind professional discretion but actively sought to obtain communicative power through publicity. Most of the heads of India's Atomic Energy Commission, from Homi Bhabha to A. P. J. Abdul Kalam, were quite successful in generating public praise and surrounding themselves with an aura of genius. The exhibitionist positioning of nuclear scientists in India's society and its consequences on the nation's nuclear program strongly affected the general public perception of what the nuclear competition was really about.

Since the beginning of the nuclear program, India's scientists were aware that neither the (rather marginal) role of nuclear power production for India's development[11] nor the controversial role of nuclear weapons for the country's security could, in themselves, justify the enormous budget allocations to the nuclear program in the long term. As such, the projection of various symbolic meanings for nuclear technology was considered an intrinsic part of the scientists' work. The scientists enjoyed enough confidence among the public and the policy makers not only to develop nuclear devices but also to contribute to the broader nuclear policy of the country. This, again, is a unique feature of India's nuclear course.

The politico-strategists' opinions reflected the zeitgeist to a greater extent than those with military or scientific backgrounds. They also tended to support the respective government's policy decisions. Nevertheless, the politico-strategists' support was based on the condition that the government left untouched the fundamental ideological pillars of their concept of the nation. Right from its creation, the politico-strategists linked the nuclear program inseparably to the idea of India as a proud and sovereign state. Stephen P. Cohen elucidated this phenomenon:

Most Indians, especially those in the Delhi-centered strategic and political community, strongly believe that their country is once again destined to become a great state, one that matches the historical and civilizational accomplishments of the Indian people. This view is encountered at nearly all points along the Indian political spectrum. Over the years, there developed a complex linkage between the greatness of India and the nuclear question.[12]

The Strategists, the Public, and the Press

The crucial factor behind the strategists' communicative power is the democratic framework in which it functions. In no other country has the nuclear question been so openly, intensely, and emotionally debated among the public than in India. Public opinion on the nuclear question reacted to the inequalities of the existing global nuclear order by reasoning in simplified moralistic terms of absolute good and absolute evil. The conditions under which India's political elite tried to obtain public support strongly favored the pursuit of status and prestige through nuclear policy. In other words, India's approach to nuclear weapons was driven by the endeavor for prestige and international standing as a result, to a certain extent, of the impact of emotionalized public opinion on the nuclear policy-making process.

The strategists act as agents in the creation of public opinion on the nuclear question. Their appreciation of the role of public opinion became apparent in their frequent calls for a national consensus on nuclear matters, which were substantiated with a Lockeian idea of public opinion: government performance could be measured within the social contract between the state's citizens. However, the fact that the general public's opinion was mainly invoked by those strategists taking a pro-bomb position based on affective arguments might suggest that the implicit reason for these calls was rather Machiavellian, defining the role of public opinion as a means to achieve power either by accommodating or manipulating it.

In a study on the role these agents play, Haider K. Nizamani uses the expression "nukespeakers" to describe the group of opinion leaders on the nuclear question in both India and Pakistan.[13] "Nukespeak," in his definition, is introduced by the strategists not only to provide an appropriate medium for expression but also to create a social reality of its own, thus rendering dissenting modes of thought difficult, if not impossible. The preferred means of the strategic community to establish this reality is by extensive publishing in India's print media, primarily in English-written dailies and journals.

The reason why the strategists choose these newspapers and journals as preferred forums to express their views on the subject is that, in contrast to indigenous-language newspapers, which generally have a rather local or regional outlook, the English-written newspapers focus on national and international issues. Their readership is mainly concentrated in the country's metropolitan areas, and the readership profiles largely coincide with the profiles of those sections of the Indian public where the discourse on India's nuclear path is taking place, as it has a widespread appeal among India's upper and middle classes.

The aforementioned analysis of nuclear-related editorials and opinion articles from five of India's major English-language daily newspapers shows how the strategists established their views on the bomb in the minds of the interested public, and how their discourse strategies changed over time. First of all, this random sample gives some indication of the intensity of the nuclear debate in India: Although nuclear-related analyses were rare before the Brasstacks Crisis of 1986/87, the debate gradually intensified thereafter, reaching its peak during the Geneva negotiations on the indefinite extension of the Nuclear Nonproliferation Treaty in mid-1995 and the Comprehensive Test Ban Treaty (CTBT) in mid-1996. It then remained on a high level until the nuclear tests in May 1998. Although the tests triggered a wave of editorials and analyses, public interest in the nuclear question began to decline soon thereafter. In the new millennium, this trend was only sporadically interrupted by specific events, such as the Indo-Pakistan crisis of 2001/2002 and the Indo-U.S. nuclear deal of 2005/2006. As expressed within the analyses since the Brasstacks Crisis, the strategic community had been strongly in favor of acquiring the bomb.

Only 2.27 percent of all nuclear-related articles dealt with the threat posed by China. In most analyses, China was displayed only as a nuclear supplier to Pakistan, not as an independent international actor in its own right. The marginal role of the China factor raises a big question: If, as most academic accounts claim, India's nuclear buildup was mainly motivated by the Chinese nuclear threat, why was this issue largely ignored in the Indian nuclear debate?

Within the analyzed sample, those articles dealing with the role of nuclear weapons in India's domestic polity, primarily articles relating the nuclear issue to the party competition, form the single most addressed issue, indicating the inward-looking nature of India's nuclear debate. Furthermore, Pakistan figured prominently as a factor in India's nuclear calculus during the Brasstacks Crisis of 1986 and 1987, the Kashmir crisis of 1990, and the tensions in Kashmir in 2001 and 2002, when President Musharraf asserted Pakistan's nuclear first-use option. However, in the critical period from the mid-1990s up to the tests in 1998, as well as in the immediate aftermath of the tests, threats from Pakistan played a minor role within India's nuclear discourse.

In the view of India's strategic community, the United States—the second most addressed country behind Pakistan—was not viewed as an immediate threat to India's security but as the ringleader of those Western countries attempting to maintain their supremacy through the discriminatory international nuclear order. Issues relating to the international nuclear order dominated the debate during the crucial years: between 1996 and 1998, two-thirds of all nuclear-related articles addressed the unfairness of the international nuclear regime. In this period the Indian debate about the regime gained a momentum unprecedented in other countries in which the tangible security aspects of the treaty were largely replaced by emotional arguments related to dignity, national pride, anticolonialism, and collective defiance. Within the logic of this emerging debate, opposition to the international nonproliferation regime was largely accepted by India's opinion leaders as the legitimate raison d'être for India's nuclear program as a whole.

Significantly, the heated debate on the international nonproliferation regime overshadowed the debate on the rise to power of the Bharatiya Janata Party (BJP), which occurred during the same period. Between 1996 and 1998 only 14.71 percent of all nuclear-related articles were concerned with the BJP's rise and its impact on India's nuclear course. This empirical evidence weakens the popular perception that it was mainly the paradigm shift on the nuclear issue after the BJP's emergence in the government that accounted for India's nuclear breakthrough in 1998. More plausible than the BJP argument are those explanations that view the developments in Geneva in 1995 (NPT extension) and 1996 (CTBT) as crucial for the events in May 1998. The analysis of the nuclear debate in India in the years before May 1998 suggests that the overall decision to go nuclear was made by the strategic community, thereby paving the way for the BJP's shrill pro-bomb rhetoric of the 1990s, and not, as many suggest, the other way around.

After the May 1998 nuclear tests the share of articles commenting on India's stance toward the nuclear nonproliferation regime dropped from two-thirds to 10 percent. More remarkable than this drop was the change in writing style, from emotionally overblown to nearly prosaic. Further, the stance of India's strategic community shifted from a categorical rejection of the status quo of the international nuclear order to its cautious support. Before 1998 the dominant argument in the nuclear debate in India, which was to reject the nuclear order, was based on the perceived discrimination of the so-called nuclear club, which admitted some countries while closing the door to others, namely, India. Now that India had broken down the club's door, an increasingly important objective of India's opinion leaders appeared to be fixing the damage and closing the door behind them.

The Ideological Pillars of the Nuclear Myth in India

"The West" as the Antagonist Other

The normative disposition of a country toward nuclear weapons is rooted in the ideas a society has about what its country stands for in the world compared to other states. This concept of comparative identity determines whether a country views its position as competitive or accommodative, reclusive or inclusive, or of high or low status in the perceived international ranking. The concept of identity translates into norms as behavioral patterns determining foreign and nuclear policy choices. The way such intersubjectively established norms, stemming from a collective identity, manifest themselves in nuclear policy is through an us-against-them pattern that contrasts the

self-defined "us" to a real or imagined antagonist. During the Cold War this antagonism was defined through ideological antinomies; in postcolonial states—which most
of the proliferating powers in the post-Cold War era are—the role of the "other" is
almost inevitably assigned to the former colonial power or its perceived successor. This
pattern is most visible in the case of India, where the nuclear narrative carries a strong
anticolonialist undertone. This discourse displayed emotional patterns in which the
opposition against the "global regime of nuclear apartheid" resembled the struggle
for independence.[14]

Postcolonial identities tend to add strong feelings of humiliation and pride to the
definition of the us-against-them antagonism and to strongly impact the collective
sense of sovereignty. This mind-set clashes with an international nuclear order maintained by former colonial powers or their perceived successors that claim supremacy
through an inequitable treaty imposed by a safeguard regime often perceived to violate
the sense of sovereignty and national dignity defined by postcolonial states. The strong
sense of sovereignty that postcolonial states display, and their search for the "right place
at the table" in the international arena, often translates into a strong sense of national
prestige and status, both crucial for the emergence of the nuclear myth.

In the coded language of the strategic community's nuclear discourse, India's
antagonists were referred to either as the "nuclear club"—denoting the exclusivity
of the states owning nuclear weapons—or "the West."[15] The term "nuclear club" is a
metaphorical reference to the British social clubs in pre-independence India, where
admission was restricted to white people, and thus the term is a powerful reminder of
India's humiliation under colonial rule. The parallels between India's struggle against
the nuclear order and India's struggle for freedom prior to 1947 appeared as a recurring
theme in the emotional nuclear debate of the mid-1990s.[16]

Although formally defined as the five states officially recognized by the Nuclear
Nonproliferation Treaty, the symbolic meaning of the term "nuclear club" did not apply to all its members equally. Russia was frequently exempted from the club's negative
attributes—discrimination, colonialism, and, more generally, immorality—and France
hardly played a role at all. China's position was carefully distinguished from that of
other members of the club; in the strategists' nuanced language, China was thought
to have adopted a somewhat passive membership: though it had gained admittance, it
was unable to make decisions over new membership or change the rules. Great Britain
was largely perceived as a junior partner of the U.S. Prior to 1998 America epitomized
club leadership and was thus the main suppressor of Indian aspirations. This role helps
explain the tremendous attention American nonproliferation policy received among
India's strategic elite during the 1990s.

The frequent use of the term "the West"—more a metaphoric reference than
geographic—denoted the states heralding the discriminatory order—a perceived
monolith with America at the top.[17] This perception was further aggravated by America's explicit nonproliferation rhetoric. Between 1995 and 1998 the escalating nuclear

debate in India was dominated by the expressed desire to "teach the West a lesson," which was increasingly perceived as an end in itself and, as such, enough to justify India's nuclear breakthrough.[18]

Paradoxically, most articles published by the strategic community not only morally condemned the members of the nuclear club in increasingly rigorous terms but at the same time expressed an eager desire to become one of them. Similarly paradoxical was the strong drive to emulate the West (read: the U.S.) asserted in many articles, particularly during the heated debate of the mid-1990s. This was rooted in the Indian elite's strong emotional affinity for America, as America's self-image as the leader of the free world resembled what India's elite since Nehru's time had envisaged for its own country as the world's largest democracy and leader of the underprivileged world. The myth of moral exceptionality and its corresponding sense of mission play a prominent role in the self-perception of both countries. These underlying similarities explain the undercurrent of admiration in many commentaries on America's foreign and nuclear policy, as well as the high emotional value of these accounts.

Moral Exceptionalism

India's self-image as the leader of the underprivileged world, evident in its foreign policy discourse since 1947, was guided by its quest for social recognition as a morally superior international actor. Deeply rooted in India's independence struggle and closely connected to Mahatma Gandhi and Jawaharlal Nehru, this norm translated into the idea of equity, which emerged as the cornerstone of Nehru's foreign policy and its main source of legitimization. In the nuclear field, the idea of equity played a particularly prominent role as a result of the nuclear order's explicit inequality, as laid down in the Nuclear Nonproliferation Treaty of 1968. Since that date, virtually every account of the international nuclear order published by India's strategic community noted the discriminatory character of this order, which divided the world into 5 "nuclear haves" and some 140 "nuclear have-nots."[19] The Indian government at the time thought its moral duty was to force the nuclear weapons states to abolish, or at least significantly reduce, their arsenals as the only way to overcome this "global regime of nuclear apartheid." This principled call for total global nuclear disarmament became a recurring demand by India in all international forums, regardless of how unrealistic the demand was.

India's self-image as the leader of the underprivileged nuclear have-nots suffered its first setback in 1974, when most Third World countries did not, as India's strategic community had expected, greet India's nuclear test with the same warmth as they had welcomed the Chinese tests in 1964, but instead reacted with indifference, even criticism.[20] Despite this setback, the idea that India made its nuclear policy in the name of all nuclear have-nots remained a popular element in the nuclear debate. In the 1980s, the formally recognized nuclear weapons states sharply increased their arsenals, thereby violating their commitment to nuclear disarmament as laid down in NPT Article VI. This caused many Indian strategists to conclude that India had to acquire nuclear capabilities in order to force the nuclear weapons states to take global nuclear disarmament seriously, a logic that was little understood internationally.[21] The international audience increasingly viewed India's continued calls for total nuclear disarmament as an empty phrase applied only to legitimize India's quest for the bomb.

In late 1985 India became isolated internationally for the first time, when it voted against a Pakistani initiative to create a nuclear-weapons-free zone (NWFZ) in South Asia. In a similarly defiant action, India voted against the indefinite extension of the NPT in 1995 and the creation of the CTBT in 1996. Although India's isolation was of concern to some strategists, many Indian pundits maintained that India had developed its nuclear option in the name of all nuclear have-nots, thereby creating the myth of India as the "lonely moralist" standing firm against pressure from the nuclear haves.[22]

This attitude of defiance partly explains the emotionally escalating debate on the international nonproliferation regime in 1995 and 1996, during which the regime was fiercely condemned in a substantial number of exceedingly emotional accounts that strengthened India's resolve to declare itself a nuclear weapons state. In this period a negative feedback process emerged between India's strategic community and the international audience in which the increasingly acrimonious debate in India heightened international fears about nuclearization in South Asia, which in turn increased the bitterness of the Indian debate.

Yet another immediate effect of the idea of moral exceptionalism was a strong sense of victimization. This feeling bolstered the perception of suffering discrimination that dominated India's discourse on the international nonproliferation regime and its relations to Western countries. Until the present day, the persisting sense of victimization has largely prevented India's strategic community from discerning any active role India might have played in the development of its nuclear arsenal. Thus survives the continuing claim that India was forced to develop that arsenal by the unavoidable circumstances of Western discrimination, Chinese blackmail, and Pakistani aggression.

After the 1998 nuclear tests the idea of equity gradually reversed as more and more strategists suggested that India's main objective should be to keep the door of the nuclear club closed. India's moral exceptionalism was no longer expressed by projecting itself as the leader of the underprivileged nuclear have-nots. Instead, India's nuclear opinion leaders, following the nukespeak of their Western counterparts, expressed their country's exceptional position by referring to it as a responsible nuclear power. A cornerstone of responsible nuclear power was the idea that India's democratic structure was an important factor legitimizing the acquisition of nuclear weapons. Implicit here is that democracies might be more prone to the nuclear myth regarding the acquisition of nuclear weapons, but in contrast to their autocratic counterparts they insist on a moral taboo with respect to their use. Indeed, among the eight countries with proven nuclear weapons capabilities, six are democratic (including Russia as a defective democracy) and only India's two neighbor states, China and Pakistan, are largely non-democratic. However, the evidence in support of the assumption that autocratic states are more likely to use nuclear weapons is weak, better yet nonexistent. Despite this flaw, democratic India's self-perception as a responsible nuclear weapons state reflects a normative axiom of the international discourse on nuclear weapons that is dominated by democratic nuclear weapons states.

The Nuclear Option

A crucial factor behind the dynamics of India's nuclear course, and discourse, was the friction between the quest for moral exceptionalism (based on the negation of power as a means of foreign policy) and the quest for social recognition as a military power. In an attempt to maintain both norms, the strategic community developed the concept of the nuclear option. This concept was technically meaningless, since a nation can claim to have a nuclear option only once it has developed nuclear capabilities. Nevertheless, for maintaining the two underlying norms, it was essential.

When the nuclear option became a popular idea in the 1970s, it proved to be highly successful in accommodating various divergent views among strategic thinkers and India's various parties. It appeased anti-bomb moralists and pro-bomb nationalists alike, while allowing the nuclear scientists simply to ignore the political debate and continue their work. During the 1970s and 1980s it permitted India's governments to officially pursue the policy of "keeping the nuclear option open," thereby successfully obscuring the fact that an active, clear-cut nuclear policy actually did not exist. According to the widely accepted definition, the option meant the technical ability to convert the peaceful nuclear program into a military program should external pressures force India's hand. Until the late 1980s the program's peaceful nature was emphatically defended by the strategic community, despite the fact that India had already produced rudimentary nuclear devices.

In the years after the Brasstacks Crisis, the option concept was no longer about whether India should "keep the nuclear option open" but rather whether India should exercise it. India had a choice, according to the emerging mainstream opinion, not between "peaceful" and "military" but between "military in principle" and "weaponized." When the nuclear debate began to intensify during the 1990s, this semantic distinction was further marginalized. Analysis of the strategists' published opinions provides ample evidence that, by the mid-1990s, the notion of a nuclear option had already been reduced to a rhetorical device. From that point on, it had not presented political decision makers with a real choice, if indeed it ever had. From 1996 to May 1998 many of the strategic opinion leaders derived India's moral superiority from the mere fact that, although having acquired nuclear weapons capabilities, so far India had restrained itself from openly declaring them. Even though a consensus had emerged that India should unveil its nuclear program, until 1998 many strategists still preferred the nuclear option to openly claiming the status of a nuclear weapons power. In the dialectic of its strategic community, India "exercised its nuclear option" in May 1998.

Nationalism

The scientists involved in India's nuclear program perceived their work as part of a competition with Western countries for scientific excellence. Within this framework, the most important quality of the work was its indigenous nature, which explained the scientists' strong emphasis on self-reliance. The scientists' rejection of the international nonproliferation regime was not guided by moral principles but by their perception of the NPT as a discriminatory instrument in the international competition for status and prestige.[23] Soon after India's self-declaration as a nuclear weapons state, the pragmatists in India's strategic community adopted the scientists' view and began to throw their moral postures overboard and appreciate the benefits of the existing international nuclear regime. In their modified view, India's nuclearization "completed," in a positive manner, "the architecture of the global non-proliferation regime by accommodating India into it."[24]

An increasing number of strategists considered this international nuclear order useful for preserving the exclusivity of India's status. Implicit in this change of attitude after the tests was the general understanding that India had a natural right to the superior status of possessing nuclear weapons because of its size, cultural heritage, democratic achievements (of particular relevance for distinguishing India from China and Pakistan), and, more generally, its grandeur. This intrinsically nationalistic element had been promoted by scientists since the beginning of the nuclear program but had remained largely hidden behind the morally defined postures in the nuclear debate prior to 1998.

Securitizing the Nuclear Discourse

Although many of India's opinion leaders in the 1990s shaped the nuclear discourse around emotional and moral arguments, some strategists acknowledged the pitfalls of the emotional debate and insisted on security-related motives behind India's nuclearization. Similar to their counterparts in other nuclear weapons states, these strategic thinkers refer to security seeking as the most relevant motive of nuclear arming behavior. Indeed, all states owning nuclear weapons or actively pursuing them can reasonably claim to be threatened by other states. Thus security-centered theories, such as Neorealism, developed by scholars in Western nuclear weapons states to explain, rationalize, and legitimize their nuclear arms, gained popularity in India's strategic community as well.

Using this line of reasoning, "a country without nuclear allies will want nuclear weapons all the more if some of its adversaries have them," or, alternatively, a country "may want nuclear weapons because it lives in fear of its adversaries' present or future conventional strength."[25] These arguments may appear to reasonably justify India's nuclear weapons program as a response to the threats posed by China or Pakistan, but they also reveal a major flaw common to most security-centered approaches: similar threats to national security are seen in similar security environments where states have abstained from developing the bomb.

In most nuclear weapons–related articles written in the 1990s, the perceived threats posed by Pakistan and China, and the resulting need for India to build up a nuclear arsenal, was taken as axiomatic and unworthy of additional scrutiny. One rarely saw further analyses of how nuclear weapons could be effective deterrents and increase India's security.

Most authors, moreover, not only maintained that Pakistan and China threatened India's security, but they placed the role of these countries in the larger context of the ideological superstructure. A striking example is K. Subrahmanyam's authoritative account of India's nuclear course after the May 1998 tests.[26] Subrahmanyam begins by emphasizing that Pakistan had assembled its nuclear device in 1987, one year earlier than India. This chronology is crucial for displaying India's nuclear development as a reaction to external circumstances.[27] However, the security-centered nature of this argument becomes increasingly blurred as the article progresses. First, similar to most accounts by India's strategic community, Subrahmanyam negates any active role on India's part: "India, which had observed unparalleled restraint from 1974 to 1988, . . . was compelled to develop its nuclear deterrent in the light of Sino-Pak collaboration and US indulgence of proliferation." He then emphasizes the stability of the Indo-Pakistan nuclear competition: "If one were to compare the eight years of Indo-Pakistan nuclear coexistence with the first eight years of US-USSR, US-China and Sino-USSR nuclear relationship, the former has been much more stable. . . . Developments on the ground have totally disproved western predictions about this region being the world's nuclear flashpoint." Finally, Subrahmanyam denies any nuclear competition with Pakistan, as Pakistan is incapable of engaging in such a race: "It is totally unrealistic to talk of Pakistan starting a nuclear arms race against India since it is not an independent self-sufficient producer of arms."[28] Despite contradicting the security-centered argument, his emphasis on Pakistan's imported (and therefore inferior) nuclear arsenal compared to India's indigenously built nuclear program was considered essential to indicate India's elevated status.

The alternating references to security- and status-related arguments become even more pronounced in the strategists' assessment of the China factor. Many considered the Chinese nuclear threat as the only strategic incentive that could credibly legitimize India's nuclear bomb program. Although the overall China issue was rarely addressed, such commentaries almost inevitably came out in favor of the bomb. One general inconsistency in pre-1998 accounts that addressed the role of China was the authors' suggestion that India should respond to the Chinese threat by "going nuclear," that is, declaring itself a nuclear weapons state. The mere symbolism of this act, without the prior development of deployment strategies and delivery systems necessary for creating a credible nuclear deterrence, would have been disadvantageous for India's security vis-à-vis China. Implicit in these calls was the perception of China as India's competitor for status, for China was a member of the "nuclear club" with a veto power in the UN Security Council, and thus had already achieved the international standing to which India aspired. The obvious success with which China had used its nuclear capabilities for status gains since the mid-1960s proved to be a compelling argument for the proponents of India's nuclear program. Chinese diplomacy, while becoming increasingly accommodative toward India's security needs after 1988, carefully distinguished between the two countries' international status, leaving little doubt about Chinese superiority. This attitude helps to account for the persistently negative image of China within India's foreign and strategic community, despite improvements in the countries' security and economic ties.

Conclusion

The U-turn that occurred in India's nuclear discourse regarding the nuclear question was neither caused by changes in India's external threat environment nor by the rise of the BJP. The way toward India's full-fledged nuclearization was actually paved by the strategic opinion leaders who successfully attached symbolic values to the possession of nuclear weapons appealing to their concept of India as a proud, modern, and powerful nation. The BJP did not create the pro-bomb mood among India's public but rather used its existence for partisan purposes.[29]

The analysis of nuclear reporting in India shows that, prior to 1998, a negative correlation existed between security concerns, on one side, and, on the other, the intensity of the nuclear debate and the determination to build up nuclear weapons. In the critical phases of India's nuclear program, security was clearly not the dominating motive, if it was even a motive at all, in India's nuclear discourse, a discourse monopolized by the strategic community that created a social reality in which perceived external threats did not overly influence India's national identity. Instead, this identity was formed by portraying the nuclear buildup in the context of a global competition defined by the social values that determine prestige and status.

Seeking international status through the acquisition of nuclear weapons is by no means a strategy confined to India. But because various socially constructed values that drove this strategy, particularly in the moral realm, were deeply rooted in India's postcolonial, multiethnic society, the emergence of the corresponding norms was genuinely Indian. Once the publicity that followed India's self-declaration as a nuclear weapons state had abated, several of the norms that had defined India's quest for status either ceased to exist, like the equity norm, or fundamentally changed in outlook, such as moral exceptionalism and nationalism.

What lessons might we learn from the Indian case? For one, it demonstrates that supply-side control mechanisms might affect the nuclearization of states contrary to their intentions by promoting the nuclear myth and, accordingly, boosting some states' ambitions to "master the atoms." Further, they might increase the "oppositional" attitudes of the aspiring nuclear weapons power. The cornerstone of the international nonproliferation regime's role in promoting the nuclear taboo is its clear distinction between the peaceful and military applications of nuclear technology. But by creating a two-class system of states, the existing nonproliferation regime elevated nuclear weapons to be the symbolic currency by which an exclusive and privileged "nuclear club" came to be defined. Instead of emphasizing the supply side of the nuclear problem, any effective nonproliferation policy would first have to tackle the demand side—a nation's motive for seeking the bomb. A precondition to this is a clear understanding of how the demand side functions.

The creation of international regulatory institutions, such as the NPT and the safeguard regime of the International Atomic Energy Agency (IAEA), is assumed to influence the norms of individual states by strengthening the nuclear taboo. This assumption was invalidated recently in the case of Iran, where the processes supporting the nuclear taboo reversed, and the international nuclear regime wound up buttressing the nuclear myth. Similar to the Indian case before the 1998 nuclear tests, the nuclear discourse in Iran carried strong anti-Western (and, in its self-definition, anti-imperialist)[30] undertones. Similar to the Indian debate, Iranian opinion leaders created a social reality in which "teaching the West a lesson" became the most popular slogan. In both cases, an imagined nuclear-armed "West," epitomized by the United States, became the antagonist.

That those nuclear-armed Western states dominate the nonproliferation discourse with Iran greatly increases Iran's determination to build up nuclear technology, just as with India before 1998. The structures of the international nonproliferation institutions, in fact, actually increased the determination of both Iran and India to oppose the regime at all costs. Both countries saw the IAEA as a mere vehicle for their perceived antagonist to push through its discriminatory objectives. Next to the supply bias of their policies, that the international nonproliferation institutions are led by nuclear powers is surely the biggest obstacle to their effective functioning. Incentives for establishing independent and equitable structures will hardly come from the nuclear weapons states themselves, even if they informally recognize that such structures are necessary. The reason for this is their dual interest, which is the prevention of the spread of nuclear weapons and their ambition to explore their own nuclear capabilities to enhance their status.

Notes

1. Atal Behari Vajpayee, quoted in *The Indian Express,* 2 October 1977.

2. For an extensive textual analysis of India's nuclear discourse, see Karsten Frey, *India's Nuclear Bomb and National Security* (London: Routledge, 2006).

3. Randall L. Schweller, "Brother, Can You Spare a Paradigm?" *International Security* 25, no. 1 (summer 2000): 177.

4. Scott D. Sagan, "Why Do States Build Nuclear Weapons? Three Models in Search of a Bomb," *International Security* 21, no. 3 (1996/97): 74.

5. Nina Tannenwald, "Stigmatizing the Bomb: Origins of the Nuclear Taboo," *International Security* 29, no. 4 (2005): 8.

6. Jacques E. C. Hymans, *The Psychology of Nuclear Proliferation: Identity, Emotions, and Foreign Policy* (Cambridge: Cambridge University Press, 2006), 13.

7. Ibid., 23.

8. Ibid., 2.

9. Randall L. Schweller, *Deadly Imbalances: Tripolarity and Hitler's Strategy of World Conquest* (New York: Columbia University Press, 1998), 21.

10. Jürgen Habermas, *Between Facts and Norms: Contribution to a Discourse Theory of Law and Democracy* (Cambridge: Cambridge University Press, 1996).

11. In 2001 only 3.7 percent of India's total power production was generated by nuclear power plants (IAEA Data Center, 2004).

12. Stephen P. Cohen, *India: Emerging Power* (Washington, D.C.: Brookings Institution Press, 2000), 17.

13. Haider K. Nizamani, *The Roots of Rhetoric: Politics of Nuclear Weapons in India and Pakistan* (Westport, Conn.: Praeger, 2000).

14. See Jaswant Singh, "Against Nuclear Apartheid," *Foreign Affairs,* September/October 1998.

15. The expression "nuclear club" was most frequently used before the nuclear tests of 1998, but it almost completely disappeared from the debate thereafter.

16. See Nikhil Chakravartty, "The Nuclear Hegemony," *The Hindu,* 22 September 1994.

17. K. Sundarji, "Where Third World Differs from the West," *The Hindu,* 11 January 1991.

18. Correspondingly, many opinion leaders express their gratification in this vein after the tests. As K. P. S. Menon described it, the "nuclear weapon powers see their cosy little world of nuclear supremacy dissolving before their eyes. They react with the petulance of a spoilt child deprived of its toys" ("Why Are Nuclear Powers So Upset? Petulance and Opportunism," *The Indian Express,* 29 June 1998).

19. "A monopoly club appears to have been set up which patently divides the world community into the nuclear haves which have the authority to dictate, and the vast number of the nuclear have-nots, who are sought to be bound down to an inferior status of subservience to the nuclear bosses . . . It is for India to raise its voice against this grotesque discrimination in the field of nuclear threat" (Chakravartty, "The Nuclear Hegemony").

20. N. N., "Nuclear Fall-out," *The Hindu,* 22 May 1974; N. N., "Strange Logic," *The Times of India,* 31 May 1974; Sitashu Das, "India and N-weapon Dissemination," *The Indian Express,* 14 July 1974; V. M. Nair, "India Isolated from Nuclear Club," *The Statesman,* 4 September 1974; N. N., "Constraints on A-Power," *The Statesman,* 27 December 1974.

21. As K. Subrahmanyam authoritatively stated: "India can play an effective role in multilateral nuclear disarmament at the global level only when the world comes to believe that India is a nuclear weapon power and therefore it is not an ignorable factor in respect of disarmament negotiations" ("N-arms and Unilateralism," *The Hindu,* 23 May 1989).

22. J. N. Dixit aptly expressed this attitude by quoting Winston Churchill: "It is better to be alone in deciding what is right and relevant than being part of a crowd going downhill in every sense of the term" ("Post-Pokhran Pressures on India: Stoicism it'll have to be," *The Indian Express,* 23 July 1998).

23. Expressing the view of India's nuclear scientific community, O. P. Sabherwal states: "It would be puerile to expect the Indian nation and its scientific community to succumb to the unacceptable stand which places a premium on weaponization and belittles Indian nuclear attainments so as to deny this country its rightful status" ("India's Right to a Nuclear Status," *The Indian Express,* 25 August 1995).

24. C. Raja Mohan, "The Art of the Nuclear Deal," *The Hindu,* 9 July 1998.

25. Kenneth Waltz, "The Spread of Nuclear Weapons: More May Be Better," *Adelphi Papers,* Number 171 (London: International Institute for Strategic Studies, 1981), 7–8.

26. K. Subrahmanyam, "Arms Race Myth," *The Times of India,* 30 May 1998.

27. This chronology is being questioned by many experts who claim that India's first nuclear devices were assembled in 1985 or 1986, and Pakistan's in 1988 (e.g., Rodney W. Jones and Mark G. MacDonough, eds., *Tracking Nuclear Proliferation: A Guide in Maps and Charts* [Washington, D.C.: Carnegie Endowment for International Peace, 1998]).

28. Subrahmanyam, "Arms Race Myth."

29. This view is challenged by some authors who believe that the BJP's rise to power was the crucial factor for India's nuclearization (e.g., Jacques, *The Psychology of Nuclear Proliferation;* and Prawful Bidwai and Achin Vanaik, *New Nukes: India, Pakistan, and Global Nuclear Disarmament* [New York: Olive Branch Press, 2000]).

30. Often states seeking to increase their status vis-à-vis their antagonist refer to anti-imperialism as moral legitimization and ideological proof that the current system of status distribution deserves to be overthrown in the name of higher principles.

CONTRIBUTORS

Itty Abraham is Associate Professor and Director of the South Asia Institute at The University of Texas, Austin. He is author of *The Making of the Indian Atomic Bomb* and editor (with Willem van Schendel) of *Illicit Flows and Criminal Things: States, Borders, and the Other Side of Globalization* (Indiana University Press, 2006).

Iftikhar Dadi is Assistant Professor in the Department of History of Art and Visual Studies at Cornell University. He is editor (with Salah Hassan) of *Unpacking Europe: Towards a Critical Reading.* His work has been exhibited in the United States, the United Kingdom, Europe, Asia, Australia, and South America.

Ammara Durrani is Development Outreach and Communications Specialist of the U.S. Agency for International Development (USAID) Mission in Pakistan. She was trained in history at the University of Karachi, Pakistan, and in international relations at Cambridge University, England.

Karsten Frey is a research fellow at the Institut Barcelona d'Estudis Internacionals, Spain. He is author of *India's Nuclear Bomb and National Security.*

Raminder Kaur is Senior Lecturer in Anthropology at the University of Sussex. She is author of *Performative Politics and Cultures of Hinduism;* co-editor of *Travel Worlds: Journeys in Contemporary Cultural Politics* and *Bollyworld: Popular Indian Cinema through a Transnational Lens;* and co-author of *Diaspora and Hybridity.*

Sankaran Krishna is Professor of Political Science at the University of Hawai'i at Manoa. He is author of *Postcolonial Insecurities: India, Sri Lanka, and the Question of Nationhood.*

Zia Mian was trained in physics and directs the Project on Peace and Security in South Asia at the Woodrow Wilson School, Princeton University. He has written extensively on Pakistan and India's nuclear programs.

Haider Nizamani is Lecturer at the School of International Studies, Simon Fraser University, Canada. He is author of *The Roots of Rhetoric: The Politics of Nuclear Weapons in India and Pakistan.*

M. V. Ramana, a physicist, is a senior fellow at the Centre for Interdisciplinary Studies in Environment and Development, Bangalore. He has written extensively on the Indian nuclear program, is the recipient of a Guggenheim Award for his writings on science, and is co-editor of *Prisoners of the Nuclear Dream.*

Srirupa Roy is Associate Professor of Political Science at the University of Massachusetts, Amherst. She is author of *Beyond Belief: Culture, Politics and Nation-State Formation in India.*

INDEX

Khan controversy and, 91, 95

middle class, 15, 79–84; alienation from masses, 82–84; mass politics, distaste of, 81–82; merit, emphasis on, 80–81, 81–82; prominence of, 79–80

nuclear debate, 152–155, 201–209; *ahimsa/* nonviolence discourse, 153; China and, 201; independence, 154; international nonproliferation regime, opposition to, 201–202; international prestige, 15; modernity discourse, 153–154; moral exceptionalism, 204–206; nationalism, 207; nuclear option, 206–207; oppositional discourses, 115–117; Other, threat of external, 154–155; Pakistan, 201; postcolonial identity, 203–204; public debates, 60–61; public sphere, 14–15; sanctification discourse, 152; security-centered argument, 207–209 (*See also* Ganapati festival tableaux; India, strategic community)

nuclear disarmament, advocacy of, 204–205

nuclear myth phenomenon, 202–207

nuclear program: criticism, intolerance of, 49; energy production costs, 56–57; health and environmental concerns, 48–49, 53–56, 83; intent of, 51–52; media support of, 50; opacity strategy, 42, 43–44; security breakdowns and lapses, 58–60; weapons production costs, 57–58 (*See also* DAE)

nuclear question reversal, 4–5, 195–196

nuclear weapons testing, 1; international criticism of, 204; national pride in, 71–72, 116; public awareness of, 14; state legitimacy and, 78–79

Pakistani relations, 25, 92–93, 142–143, 145, 187

science: nationalism and, 76–77; social development and material progress, alienation from, 77–78; state legitimacy and, 75; unrealistic expectations of, 77; Western colonialism, impact of, 74–76

state legitimacy, 4–5, 75, 78–79

strategic community, 11, 196, 198–200, 202; administrative and communicative

powers, 199, 200–201; composition of, 198–199; monopolization of nuclear debate, 196, 199; nuclear club, condemnation of, 203–204 (*See also* India, nuclear debate)

Supreme Court, 9, 54

See also mass death narratives, India; nuclear South Asia

Indian Industrial Policy Resolution (1948), 2, 4

Indian Institute of Public Opinion, 49

industrial accidents, 126–127, 132n46

Institute for Defense Studies and Analyses (IDSA), 10, 199

International Atomic Energy Agency (IAEA), 210

Iqbal, Allama, *178, 181*

Iran, 1

Islamabad, Pakistan, 134

Israel, 1, 42, 51, 197

Iya, Vasudev, 52

Iyengar, M. A. R., 49

Iyengar, P. K., 67n80

Jamaat-e-Islami, 133, 137, 147

James, Morris, 25

Jang aur Aman (documentary), 43

Jang (newspaper), 96

Khan controversy and, 11, *97,* 98, 99, 100–101, 102–103

Japalpur riot (1961), 125

Japan, 52

Jinnah, Mohammad Ali, 24, 25, 29 depictions of, *175, 178, 181*

Joan B. Kroc Institute, 19n21, 136

John D. and Catherine T. MacArthur Foundation, 10

Joshi, Sanjay, 79–80

Kahuta Research Laboratory, 94

Kakodkar, Anil, 44, 56

Kakrapar reactor, 55–56, 61, 67n80

Kalpakkam reactor, 59, 67n77

Karachi, Pakistan, 135

Kashmir, 25, 145

Kaur, Raminder, 14

Kaviraj, Sudipto, 81

Kennedy, John F., 20

CPSIA information can be obtained
at www.ICGtesting.com
Printed in the USA
LVOW05s1401150116
470833LV00027B/887/P